D1174937

ENTREPRENEURISM

ENTREPRENEURISM

The Mythical,
The True and The New

THOMAS F. JONES

with

T. P. Elsaesser

DONALD I. FINE, INC.   *New York*

Contents

Foreword

It is a relief to find a book dealing with entrepreneurs that is as free of cant and nonsense as this one. I have to assume that there is a market out there for all the magic formulas and guarantees, the weird slogans, the hortatory language, the hysteria that sounds like fundamentalist preachers on Sunday night cable TV. If the word "entrepreneur" still turns you on after all that, you are a person whose resilience and persistence deserves a reward. And you are finally about to get it. In this book, Thomas F. Jones guarantees nothing, but he delivers a lot.

Jones has written a useful book for anybody who is hooked on the idea of going into business for himself. At the same time, he has produced a work that is interesting, even fun for people who just like to read about business. That is to say he is a good business reporter. He pays attention to what his subjects tell him. He never seems to try to get them to say something just so he can shoehorn it into a chapter heading or a magical equation. Don't look for a PMLA or an HPD or any of those trick formulas that can't miss if you follow the instructions.

There aren't any instructions in this book. But there is lots of smart talk. That is because Jones really seems to know what he is talking about all the time. Every time you think he is going to fall into one of those formulas, he fools you and falls into reality instead. That is where the book is grounded, and that, I think, is why it works so well. It may be such unspectacular observations about his subjects as

1

this that do the job best: ". . . it was by performing key activities better than the competition on a routine basis that they prevailed." No formula, no magic; just do it good and smart.

Jones doesn't spend too much time dealing with the psychological profile of the classic entrepreneur. It's there all right. It has to be. After all, people who want or need to go into business for themselves don't want to or can't work for others. If nothing else, that says that they are different from postal clerks and General Motors middle managers. More than that, it suggests that there is something fundamental about their nature that makes them act the way they do. A lot of observers think that has something to do with their upbringing, especially their relations with their fathers. But Jones doesn't get caught up in that, though he doesn't deny that entrepreneurs aren't great at working for others.

Essentially, Jones's approach has been to read just about everything written on the subject and then get to know some effective entrepreneurs who have confronted the basic problems of creating and building a business. What he finds is interesting, even compelling, and much of it can work even for postal clerks who want to be postmasters and GM middle managers who care whether their monstrous organization survives (though at this point, with the bouncing of entrepreneur Ross Perot from the corporation's board, it is hard to imagine that anything innovative and entrepreneurial has a chance at GM).

He minimizes none of the problems. His dealing with planning is most instructive and even amusing. He and his subjects recognize that *trying* even to know what's going to happen next month may be impossible. (The CEO of one of the most successful conglomerates of the 1960s once told me that when he appointed an executive to the job of long-range planning, he had retired him.) The fact that many start-up businesses must look to venture capitalists these days for capital, means, as he notes somewhat ruefully, that there will have to be more focus on "serious" plans and numbers even when they are meaningless. But that's part of the game, because venture capital firms have often become as rigid and unimaginative as major corporate enterprises.

Jones tells us that "informed doing is the best plan." And he headlines a section "two open ears can be visionary." That is typical of his approach, because it is what he has found that works for the effective people who are his principal sources. "The most important aspects of planning for the prospective or newly initiated entrepreneurship," he writes, "start with questions of what and how, not how much or how many."

Unquestionably the biggest problem confronting the small start-up enterprise, once it is reasonably safely alive, is getting bigger. The classic entrepreneur of the psychological profiles can't do much because he is paranoid, doesn't trust anybody, can't delegate, has to do it all himself, and so nothing much can happen beyond his physical reach and the range of his voice. That doesn't mean he won't build a good solid business. I was once at a banquet given by an association of regional distributors of architectural glass in Houston. They had come to honor an ancient member of the group. Practically everybody in the dining room got up and told how he had once worked for the honoree, who lent him money to go into business for himself. What that said was that the old man couldn't allow the people who worked for him to open plants and warehouses around the rest of the state for his company. He didn't think he could encompass those activities in his head, so he let them leave to start up their own companies in Dallas and Midland and San Antonio and other growing markets, all of which could have been part of his organization if he had understood himself a little better.

This book deals with that fundamental problem of delegation (or the big D, as Jones calls it) admirably in its entire attitude and approach. But it doesn't guarantee a solution, because if you can't let go, you can't let go. At least it confronts the type and the problem.

What occasionally may seem mildly contradictory is intentional. When your business gets bigger, it and you have to act differently. Here's a typical example of the way Jones cuts through the baloney: "It isn't entrepreneurship versus bureaucracy. You need to move beyond the one-dimensional myth of the typical owner-founder without succumbing to an across-the-board campaign of formalization that could destabilize the organization." When he deals with personnel problems, he confronts issues like marrying your accountant. And he concedes readily that employees who were perfect for an unstructured start-up operation may not work at all in an organization that has to become more structured. But Jones suggests that certain kinds of focussed individualists, notably scientists, may have to be given special treatment even when you get on the New York Stock Exchange. I think he may be just a bit condescending about scientists here, but he is drawing on the actual experiences of some solid entrepreneurs. So maybe he's right about that too. In any case, if you worry about dealing with quirky people, ask yourself if those who seem content working in rigid slots in huge outfits are any less quirky in their ways.

You can read this book almost at random, because the realities are scattered through the text like raisins in rice pudding. And there is virtually nothing left out. Every time I thought Jones had fallen into the typical traps of the anti-organization nonsense that characterizes practically all the inspirational literature on the subject, he surprised me by being knowing and realistic. His coverage of titles is cautionary: you've got to have them whether you hate them or not. But, he says, "the point is to use titles to indicate who knows and does what, not who has the highest walls and the deepest moat and the most retainers."

Job descriptions get the same kind of treatment if misused. Consider the case of Atari, a classic entrepreneurial creation that went bad (but may be in the process of salvage). When it was in deeper trouble than, it seemed, anyone suspected in 1983, the CEO of Warner Communications, Inc., decided Atari needed a new top man who could reverse its fortunes. So he went to the top man at a top headhunting firm, Gerard Roche of Heidrich & Struggles, and asked him to find the top marketing man at the top marketing company. Roche found James Morgan, a nearly top man at Philip Morris, who for reasons that had nothing to do with competence in marketing, was about to be passed over for his company's top job. Nobody said, "Hey, wait a minute. This guy may have been terrific at selling Marlboros, but that's a product that's been using the same campaign for more than twenty years. Maybe we need somebody who is used to a different track." But Morgan fitted the job description, and Atari was sold less than a year after he arrived. That's the kind of trouble you can get into if you live by job descriptions. I am sure that Jones won't mind me adding this bit of my own research to prove his point.

The best summation I can make is that the book is accurately titled—*Entrepreneurism: The Mythical, The True and The New.*

—Stanley H. Brown
New York, December, 1986

Acknowledgment

The gathering of material for this book was guided by Executive Dean Paul A. Albrecht and Professors Peter F. Drucker, Allan W. Wicker and Harvey H. Wichman at the Claremont Graduate School.

I would also like to offer my gratitude to President Marvin L. Goldberger of the California Institute of Technology, and to Dean J. Clayburn La Force and Associate Dean Alfred E. Osborne, Jr. of the UCLA Graduate School of Management for their introductions to a number of the owner-founders whose stories follow.

And of course, special thanks to my fellow entrepreneurs themselves for their time and candor in sharing just what it means and takes to start and run your own business in America.

Introduction

This book is the result of conversations with more than two dozen owner-founder entrepreneurs who have defied the odds—who have not only gone into business for themselves and *stayed* in business for themselves, but have also managed the businesses they created through significant growth.

After a final reading of the hundreds of pages of transcripts I have compiled, detailing the stories told by these owner-founder entrepreneurs, I have come to the conclusion that no one free of the reptilian lubricant is going to be able to offer up a recipe for sure-fire entrepreneur. In this book you will find a number of distilled observations about things you can do to enhance your chances of survival as a small businessman—for that matter enhance your chances of survival as a manager in any setting. But it is important, however presumably self-evident, to remember that each business and individual entrepreneur is unique. As a group, entrepreneurships may have common developmental stages and problems, and I'll detail and illustrate, but each also has its own set of fingerprints and quirks; each has its own family photo album.

Leo Imperiali was driving a cab. He had been in business for himself several times. His most successful start-up had been a produce business, but Leo had to work seven long days a week and in the end the business never quite left the dock. So Leo went to work for Douglas Aircraft for a while, where he was one of twenty people picked out of thousands to work on the X-15 project. Just about the time he got his first paycheck Leo was off, as was his custom, trying to start something up on his own. At this point Leo was back driving a cab. On the way home one day he stopped at a Goodwill store. The family needed a new coffee table, the kids had made short work of the old one. If only there was something he could do to child-proof one of the things. . . .

Which was when the notion struck . . . why not put some of that hard stuff on it, tile, the stuff they put in kitchens and bathrooms. But where to get it? It was 1955 and home improvement centers were yet to come. Leo had to go to a factory. He met a tile installer there who complained about his own difficulty in getting a full line. Which was when Leo had a second idea. Within a month he had managed to borrow $300 from a bank and had opened a storefront, the precursor of what was to become the first of a chain of Tile World stores, "the largest tile store in the world." Now Leo personally imports tile from a number of nations and continents, and he'll be telling us later in this book what he believes are the core strengths of his company.

Warren Dennis, a self-described "perennial student," twenty-six years old, had left yet another campus and had finished a stint designing and building modified production racing cars. "I was a part-time machinist who had spent a good deal of time studying history, a guy who liked to tinker with fine machinery but hadn't really settled down to his first serious job."

Warren was watching the television one night when he saw a local feature on a fellow machinist named—truly—Burton Burton. Burton Burton liked to fiddle with fine machinery too. Both men realized you had to go back to antiques if you wanted to get inside a machine that still held enough human quality to meet their fancy. Warren contacted Burton. They restored some slot machines together. Then they came on this ceiling fan. It had been designed in 1895 and hadn't been produced since 1905. You've all seen one by now, the richly grained wooden paddle blades, the shining brass and the delicate, opaque, flowerlike glass lamps—that slow, rhythmic swirling above that seems to keep the talk muted, the air moving, the ambience civilized.

The first few years Warren and Burton congratulated themselves on their ability to build and sell enough fans to restaurant designers to support a rather eccentric hobby and a commitment to making the highest quality product of their choice on the market. Then a dry hostile wind blew out of the Middle Eastern deserts in the early 1970s, parching the impatient tongues of Americans as they waited in line to buy gas. The energy crisis hit and soon the rest of the country was sipping cool drinks under Casablanca Fans: $65 million in sales in eight years. But Warren is the first to say demand is a wonderful thing, as long as you are organized well enough to supply it before the competition does. Competition is no respecter of who got there first. Be prepared, like the Boy Scouts say, or be damned.

Then there is Gordon Moore. Gordon was perfectly content to be working as a top manager in a company owned by an eastern parent, Fairchild Camera. Gordon and his fellow scientists, by then managers, had built Fairchild Semiconductor from the ground up after stepping out of the Palo Alto lab of William Schockley with the technology that would bring computers to the fore in the seventies. Gordon Moore says he can quite easily imagine himself still working for Fairchild Semi—that is, if the parent corporation hadn't started taking them to the barn every morning, not only milking them but inserting outside management. Gordon Moore and Robert Noyce figured there was nothing to do for it but put up their own shingle, investing the quarter-million they each had earned while building Fairchild Semi to start Intel. Gordon, we shall see, has some cogent points to make about the type of participative, team-oriented environment that has kept Intel in the thick of the white-hot competition within his industry.

Joseph Solomon was working as stockboy in one of Vidal Sassoon's hair salons in New York City. Vidal had two of them at the time, a growing reputation and a prestigious list of clients. He was doing nicely within his field, attracting international notice. But he wasn't doing well enough in the eyes of Joseph Solomon, a young man from Brooklyn with an A.A. degree and some evening law school classes under his belt. Joseph got the idea that Vidal could put his name on a bottle of shampoo and sell it to other salons—eventually directly to the public—and that millions of people who couldn't afford or manage to come to one of the salons for servicing could still be touched by Vidal's name and his system of hair care. The all-knowing marketing consultants —usually self-styled "experts"—said nay. They performed some tests. Modest sales at best, said they. These seers didn't understand what was going to become of designer names over the next decade, didn't foresee the impact of the consumerism of the two-income family and career women. Joseph took Vidal Sassoon Hair Products from an orange crate in a garage in Canoga Park, California to $400 million in domestic and international sales in eleven years. There are some obvious and inherent lessons here, and preeminent among them is to withhold excessive respect for people who say no, won't work, can't do. They have a vested interest—most of them have never *done*.

James Collins was working as an architect in Pasadena assisting in the design of churches when his father-in-law offered him a vacant warehouse in front of his trailer park in West Los Angeles. Said father: "Why don't you try turning it into a cafe or something? Service the people in the trailer park?" A man from the electric company, out to hook up the power, told Jim about a couple of brothers flipping burgers out in San Bernadino. Craziest thing this guy had ever seen. It was like, well, a food factory the way they went at it. Jim drove out to see the brothers McDonald in action just about the time Ray Kroc was moving around town with his milkshake machines. Jim didn't run into Ray, but he did meet another fellow who was similarly intrigued by the McDonalds' tight operation, and Jim went to work for this man in his Long Beach stand for a month until he felt he understood the business. Jim then opened up his own stand in Los Angeles.

Jim started out with beef patties, building a string of hamburger stands during the fifties. But he ended up frying chickens. An awful lot of chickens—and steaks, and seafood, and salads, and pizzas, and he's not exactly sure what next, all at different chains, of course . . . Collins Foods International, NYSE. It's not as if there's only one opportunity associated with every good idea. Opportunity usually stands there, right in front of you. Opportunity doesn't blink. You do. Either you turn and walk away or you step up to the window and accept the order. Opportunity is written all over the board up there, often right in your own back yard —in your own industry.

John Anderson was a graduate of the Harvard Business School, with a law degree from Loyola Marymount and a C.P.A. All right, whoever said the modern-day entrepreneur has to come from a log cabin? He started with a partner before coming across a small beer distributorship that was going belly up. John bought it in 1956. During the early days he would ride the routes with his drivers in downtown Los Angeles. He worked out the numbers. The problem was the load factors on the trucks. It was fairly simple: They needed more product. John couldn't get the brand he most wanted but did manage to line up a new and struggling entrant in the local market: Budweiser. Now he owns a private holding company with diversified and integrated public and private holdings in insurance, financial institutions, beverage production and distribution and health care, and teaches graduate management courses in acquisition theory.

Fifty years ago R. Stanton Avery found himself in a predicament many men and women born during the Baby Boom can relate to. Stan was the son of a Congregational minister with a degree in the humanities from Pomona College. Stan says he was not highly qualified for entrance into the job market during the tough economic times of the depression. He had little choice but to pack flowers for the San Lorenzo Nursery from four to eleven each morning and tinker with the machine and sticky mixture he had devised to make self-adhesive price stickers the rest of his waking hours. Once he got it working, he installed the machine and an office desk on top of a large commercial refrigerator in the San Lorenzo Nursery in the Los Angeles Flower Market. Stan's wife began mailing advertisements for "Kum Kleen Self-Adhesive (Removable) Price Stickers" to all the gift shops listed in the Los Angeles telephone book. "I had to say 'Removable' because nobody knew what self-adhesive meant," Stan says. Today there are few of us who haven't peeled or touched a product from Avery International.

Throughout the following chapters I will tell considerably more about these entrepreneurs and others as well. I will cover entrepreneurs who had planned to go into business for themselves from the time they were children, entrepreneurs who all but stumbled into business for themselves and some like Gordon Moore who claimed to have been forced to go into business for themselves. We will lay out a good many *hows,* and try, at the same time, to uncover some of the more elusive *whys* regarding the start-ups and after-experiences that contributed to these entrepreneurs' successes.

There is one large problem with so-called how-to books, whether about starting companies or knitting sweaters. Most never get to the "how" stage, never get past the "why." It's almost axiomatic that we resist *doing* anything, correctly or incorrectly, until moved to do it. When we are talking about starting a company we are talking about laws of motion and resistance. In some cases we are talking about theorems concerning coaxings in the posterior. In many instances the very reasons that moved an entrepreneur to start a business turn out to be crucial to the unique development and success of his or her venture. So I hope you will also find this something of a "why-to" book.

CHAPTER ONE

Why You Might Soon Be Leaving Your Job

I begin, but not for long, with myself. Almost twenty-five years ago I was sitting at a desk in the accounting department of a Fortune 500 communications corporation. I had an M.B.A. (before they had become quick-order calling cards). I was in my mid-twenties. So I had credentials, opportunity, time. But I also had a budding dissatisfaction with the predictability of the career that appeared to lie ahead. I could look up a couple of levels and see myself in five, ten, fifteen and twenty years down the pike. On my way down the hall I could peek in the offices that might one day be mine. They were a little bigger and had a better view than mine; I'm sure they would have been quite comfortable. In a way I even looked forward to the feeling that would come the day I closed one of those doors from the inside. Now, I'm not simply looking back and thumbing my nose. I had and still have respect for the men and women who continue to fill those offices. In fact, if I hadn't been in part curious about what had happened to my fellow trainees throughout corporate America I would never have pursued the research that led to this book, once my own corporation was running smoothly enough for me to do so.

Still, hospitable and comfortable as those offices appeared at the time, one day they simply weren't enough, just as I'd suspected might be the case.

I am not just talking about rewards. True, I had sat down and calculated the promotions and raises that seemed available to a person of my talents, as well as a person of my

15

limitations—I recommend the exercise—and decided there would be some who would rise faster, some who would rise slower. I wasn't kidding myself that I had any inside track to the top office. But just as important, I did not stay around the corporation because I just wasn't sure I had what it would take to do the kinds of things I would have to do to make it there. If I am allowed to thumb my nose just a little, I would say I simply wasn't mean enough. Coming from a successful entrepreneur, this may sound a little odd to readers accustomed to thinking of entrepreneurs as basically not the kind of people you would want to share a provision sack with on a survival hike. As you'll discover here, this popular misconception of the entrepreneur doesn't hold for those who succeed in the long run.

Back to that day, sitting at my desk. As I sat there staring down at the future I had calculated out on a pad in front of me, my whole life appeared frighteningly set. There would be money enough for some dreams, in their time, not enough for others seemingly at any time. I suspect it was especially the thought that there was only going to be so much I would be able to do to determine what my rewards would be, high or low, that led to the sinking feeling in my stomach. I'm not saying the deck was stacked against me. Let's just say I didn't like the way some of the guys had begun winking at each other. It just didn't feel like the right table. Those of you who know the feeling as a fairly constant companion are likely prospects for doing something about it, as I did and others have done, whether you know now what it will be or when.

That night I began to think more seriously and concretely about going into business for myself. I had given it thought, just like we all probably have given it thought, from time to time in passing daydreams. I had talked about starting a real estate investment and management business with two workmates, as many workmates sometimes do. In this case the talk did not turn out to be only idle chatter. Within a few months a workmate turned out to be my first partner. Within a year I had talked twenty fellow management-trainees into investing with us and had taken on a second partner from the outside. Both partners are now financially independent but continue to work anyway.

What decisively made the difference, led me to go into business for myself? I'm not sure. I was fortunate and continue to be fortunate to have the example of my father, who in his time was an entrepreneur as well, a butcher who eventually came to own a string of independent markets, a man who could sit at the head of the dinner table and immediately state whether he had had a good day or not—usually measured by the size of the roll I saw him take home from the registers. As you read on you will see just how important such an example appears to be for many who go into business for themselves. If you are accustomed to seeing someone untied from a regular paycheck and dealing with the roller coaster you will be much better equipped to treat the pressures that come with having to pull your own weight.

But with or without the experience of a role model, nobody entirely circumvents the pressures. As the duke who wore a six-gun once said: Courage is being scared silly and still climbing into the saddle. Which is what it is to be an entrepreneur, to control your own destiny for better or worse. You really have to want it. Successful entrepreneurs learn to thrive under the pressure. Some even seem to seek it out.

I consider myself fortunate for another reason. In the mid-1960s "entrepreneurship" had yet to blossom into the much-ballyhooed cult it now increasingly represents in the public mind. We have good reason not to want the owner-founder entrepreneur to go the way of the Hula Hoop and Pet Rock. During the 1970s there were pronunciamentos that the day of the owner-founder and his built-from-scratch business had passed. Sure, people would still start businesses but their impact on the national economy had been reduced or replaced by that of the multinationals and conglomerates. Dewey wins! As Peter Drucker recently pointed out, businesses less than ten years old accounted for three-quarters of a million new jobs between 1980 and 1984, while during the same period the Fortune 500 companies were *losing* three million. In the face of all the talk about "entrepreneurial management" in large corporations, the men and women I choose to call entrepreneurs, those starting businesses from relative scratch, are quietly and persistently going about *their* business, even if, heaven forfend, some of them are in the process of building conglomerates and multinationals themselves.

When I went into business for myself entrepreneurs were still mistrusted outsiders—people, it was assumed, who couldn't make a go of it as organization folks. Knowing studies of the day concluded that they were typically "socially marginal" individuals who were mostly intent on bucking the status quo. "Entrepreneur" was not a polite word. Large corporations were having a field day. There was plenty of opportunity and "Made in Japan" was still the punchline for TV comedians' jokes.

Ask Harold Haytin about some of those "Made in Japan" jokes. In 1960, veteran of failed electronics ventures, Harold Haytin read articles and concluded consumer electronics was to be a booming field. He contacted Japanese companies he had heard were making strides in the area and secured importing and distribution rights. He had to listen to carloads of guff from prospective customers of his "inferior" Japanese products in the early days before he built Telecor, Inc., into the $140 million NYSE corporation he would sell to Panasonic in 1980.

I was hardly a born entrepreneur. At the time I went into business for myself, though I had been to management school, all I really knew was that you either worked for yourself, which I was to learn meant working for others but only in an indirect sense, or you worked for others, which I had begun to realize meant working *under* others in a most direct sense. If I was twenty-five years old again and sitting at a desk within a Fortune 500 corporation I'm not so sure I would be able to see my way through the tapioca of rhetoric covering the word "entrepreneur" to step out and start a business.

Entrepreneurs are popularly viewed as, essentially, risk-takers and innovators. It's true, as some of my examples will attest. But something I suspected, and have since verified through my talks with the entrepreneurs I will tell you about, is that the actuality of succeeding in business is often far more dependent on less spectacular matters of management and attitude than modish talk suggests. I don't intend to put you to sleep with prosaic replications of other "business" books; I just want you to understand that I will be writing about the entrepreneurs I've spoken with for one purpose only—to highlight some of the important aspects of attitude, approach and management practice that have contributed to their success. True, some of these aspects may not send off rockets. But after digesting them, you will, I hope, be better able at least to consider doing some of the same things yourself. You may even realize that you *already* possess and in some instances are practicing the approaches and skills that are vital to traveling up this entrepreneurial avenue. And *that* can lead to a life with some rockets going off that would never happen as a conventional employee.

I also hope to bring you to the realization that opportunity still exists, that the risk-takers and innovators who inspired today's broad-brush application of the term "entrepreneurial management" are not dinosaurs. We are alive and well and thriving and looking for more good men and women. For some time down the road we will continue to supply the lion's share of new jobs, the lion's share of new growth and therefore opportunity for any of you who might now be sitting at a desk, peeking down the hall, with dreams of creating the self-determined life that really built this country and is central to its ethos.

The degree of myth surrounding the nature of the owner-founder entrepreneur had a good deal to do with my decision to write this book, after returning to graduate school in management to learn more about the state of the art in management thinking. During my studies I found a good deal was *apparently* known about the "typical" entrepreneur, whose egocentricity and demanding personality are much celebrated in both the academic and popular media. I also learned that this so-called typical entrepreneur almost always fails. And this is when I decided to try to learn more about the atypical entrepreneur—the entrepreneur who doesn't conform to myth and who *succeeds*—the focus of this book.

I also hope corporate entrepreneurs, "intrapreneurs," those learning how to manage their bosses, how to build their parachutes and how to do whatever they are going to have to do next—that they all learn well. If you are not scared enough yet, sitting at your desk, still willing to gamble as you see the fat being trimmed from management levels above and all about you in our nation's largest organizations, consider this: By the turn of the century, as a result of the Baby Boom, there will be something like twenty highly qualified candidates for every single upper-level position in corporate America. We're talking sharp bayonets. I believe there is another way. The rate of newly initiated ventures has more than doubled over the last ten years. More people are going into business for themselves than ever before—dramatically more people—hundreds of thousands more people are going into business for themselves. And beyond numbers reflecting this current within our nation's economy, there is reason to suspect that even more good God-fearing people who neither grow body hair under full moons nor dedicate themselves to finding new ways to pour rain out of a rain barrel will in fact go into business for themselves in the coming years—there's compelling reason, indeed, to suspect we haven't even begun, sorry about the mixed metaphors, to see the tip of the iceberg.

Before launching into the stories I've had the pleasure of tracking down, and along the way beginning to deflate some of the myth (making you, I hope, a little more familiar with the reality of running your own business), let's take a look under the surface.

Consider some of the Baby Boom's continuing echoes:

The post-war Boomers demonstrated a marked early, though more recently moderated, distrust of big organizations. We all need to be reminded to be careful about what we choose to rebel against—more often than not we end up growing the hair of the dog we bite. Useful rebellion is a means of taking over, not walking away. The Boomers went from an aggressive distaste to an aggressive appetite for running this country and economy in about the time it took to end a war and experience triple-digit inflation—about a decade. Actually more than a few of them got quite a taste of independence, or at least unstructured life, along the way. Their parents were trained and conditioned to function in large organizations. The Boomers were exposed to a period of mild to extreme chaos—a state not so different from the early days of a new business.

The Boomers were a generation made aware of many of the dynamics of business and economics as they watched the evening news or read below the headlines. They are also a highly competitive generation. They haven't been kept busy enough just going to school and holding down jobs; they've had to start organizations in an attempt to match their numbers and ambitions. They've headed out into the entrepreneurial frontier.

I spoke with a young biologist, an academic researcher, who told me he was successful in his field because he ran his operation like a business: "I realize I can't afford to be confused. I make the tough decisions first and let the easy ones take care of themselves. I establish a goal and do what I have to do to achieve it. I don't muse about what I *should* be doing anymore."

Yes, the Boomers are coming of age, and coming to grips with middle-management efficiency cuts in the larger organizations, *decreasing* the number of traditional outlets for talent, skills and achievement. Look out, Small Business Administration—(and not just for the Reagan administration cuts in budget)—you conceivably might replace Social Security as the only real means of support in the early years of the next century.

Consider some of the other social dynamics that have accompanied the Boomers coming of age. This is a generation accustomed to the material benefits of two incomes, having fewer children (and fewer having children), in large numbers skilled and relatively secure financially, coming into nest eggs as their parents pass on, for whom striking out on their own might involve considerably less financial risk and social pressure than existed for their parents during the post-World War II corporate and organizational boom.

But let's not only be focused on the new kids on Wall and other streets. Consider how much older our populace is also becoming. It once was a rule of thumb that entrepreneurs tend to start off on their own in their early thirties. There are going to be a lot of age-related rules of thumb going by the boards in the coming decades.

And what about right now? What about the wave of restless middle-aged middle managers and early retirees being displaced? What about the wave of venture capital organizations meeting weekly across the nation, with growing memberships of men and women possessing skills, industry knowledge, financial resources, significant contacts and time to start second, more independent, careers? These people know what a team is and how to put one together, and with each day there are an increasing number of ways to circumvent absolute personal financial risk.

Consider also the recent immigrants from less stable and developed sectors of the world. Such individuals with grit, talent and desire have always struck out on their own. I believe they will continue to do so.

Consider too the advantages of the high-technology sector. Knowledge-intensive technology and knowledge-intensive individuals, as Peter Drucker has pointed out, are a present future. A microcomputer can be a business in itself, can serve as the heart of a cottage industry such as a mail-order business or as the nucleus of the control-and-productive apparatus of a growth-minded corporation and all for about the cost of one employee. From advisory stints with the California Institute of Technology and the Claremont Graduate School I've at least learned that such opportunities will only multiply, that we have really only begun to see the first ripples of some of the fundamental scientific and technological breakthroughs which will continue to come from this generation. A new technology company can indeed go from a proposal to hundreds of millions of dollars in sales in five years. Those involved in such a venture as a founder or employee will surely benefit from the experience of the individuals I've spoken with for this volume, some of whom have already survived the roller coaster with stomachs intact.

Consider too the increased availability of creative means of venture funding, institutional and private. Anyone who came of economic age in or simply passed through the inflation of the seventies knows about them: venture capitalists, going public, leveraged buy-outs, grandad's will, limited partnerships. Economic trends and opportunities have for many become the batting averages, hot cars and movie idols of our day.

Also, one shouldn't overlook the importance of heroes. I've mentioned my own experience and the importance of my father as an entrepreneurial role model. Previous studies indicate that most entrepreneurs came from small business or farming families in which as an example there was a parent in business for himself.

And so it goes . . . two-thirds of the entrepreneurs I spoke with had the example of a mother or father going into business before they themselves set out on their own. Ralph Crump, president and chairman of Frigitronics, Inc., about whom you will hear much more, prominently displays a photographic portrait of his father behind his desk in his office. After he left home Ralph remembers getting letters with surprising new postmarks from his father, a man he fondly describes as an "itinerant nomadic baker and miscellaneous entrepreneur." They each carried the same basic message: "Son, your mother and I have greatly enjoyed our fine neighbors and customers here the last few years, including their abundant good will and ample patronage. However, after thinking long and hard we've decided to try the waters in the state of Alaska, a state rumored to provide significant opportunity for a man of my inclinations. We now have a store on the main street and expect great success." Ralph's grandfather had also been an entrepreneur, coming from Scotland to start a shipyard on the Ohio and Mississippi rivers.

Howard Morrow, founder of a chain of Morrow's Nut and Candy stores, described a succession of generations within his family who had always made money selling nuts, whether in the front window of a general store or from a booth at a county fair. Howard followed suit after experiencing a partner-influenced failure in an electronics business.

The father of another entrepreneur I interviewed was a self-employed barber. A mother of still another had a small grocery store. Dr. Si Ramo of TRW grew up the son of an independent pharmacist. Many others described their fathers or mothers as having been small-time mom-and-pop-type entrepreneurs. A significant number had a parent who had been in the same business, working for himself, though on a smaller scale.

On the other hand—yes, the ubiquitous other hand—many with whom I spoke, especially those who went on to manage the largest fastest growing enterprises, had no such familial role model. For example, Eugene Rosenfeld, president of the Anden Group, national builders and marketers of homes, with annual sales in excess of $250 million within less than ten years of their founding, learned his trade working his way up to the presidency of a NYSE corporation before striking out on his own—and had *no* family members who went into business for themselves. He founded his company in 1976, and may be more representative of a new wave of entrepreneurs that I predict will swell within the U.S. economy.

It had been the prevailing wisdom that anyone with access to a corporate career wouldn't waste time gritting it out by striking out on his own. Prior to the eighties it was not "in" to go into business for oneself. Right after World War II large organizations flourished both in product and status. The latter sixties and early seventies favored protest against the "establishment." Even within the generation of Boomers there appears to be a bias toward the professions, though this seems to be changing as a good many lawyers now find themselves forced by a glut to ply their trade in less than purely legalistic avenues. There is even talk that we are beginning to produce too many doctors.

Still, the vogue increasingly has been to glorify another rags-to-riches overnight miracle. Entrepreneurs are on magazine covers. Indeed, we have our own magazines—started, by the way, by other entrepreneurs. It is now not only acceptable that our daughters marry entrepreneurs, but that they too be entrepreneurs. Strategies and mechanisms for initiating new ventures are taught in business schools. It's a mainstream shift in attitude and scale of values, and it's not going to go away.

Actually, of course, this is all in key with the American ethos. This is still the place where a migrant farm worker can buck the admittedly tremendous odds against self-improvement. Listen to Baldemar Rodriguez, an entrepreneur I've had the good fortune to do business with. Rod was born in Mission, Texas. He was five when his father, a man who had emigrated from Mexico and spent his life at menial jobs, died and left a wife with five children, the oldest nine and the youngest ten days. Rod himself spent his childhood working as an itinerant crop-picker.

"It was the usual story of a Mexican-American family in Texas. We spoke Spanish at home. We were aliens in every sense of the word. It was different in the early fifties in Texas, though it's not all that great now. You could tell who you were and were not just by the way they looked at you. But even when I was young, even after my father's death when there was sometimes not enough to eat, I *knew* all I had to do was get a little older and grow a little bigger and that I would, somehow, make it. All I needed was to be old enough and big enough to work in this country."

Between his tenth and fifteenth birthdays Baldemar Rodriguez picked cotton in Texas, Arizona and California, onions in Indiana, pickle cucumbers in Michigan, sugar beets in Colorado and hops and cherries in Washington. His family was never on government assistance but he remembers once accepting stale corn chips from a factory in Lubbock, Texas, when they were between crops and without income.

At age sixteen Rod entered what he then thought was the mainstream, taking a job delivering prescriptions for a drugstore in San Diego—by car! "You don't know what a relief that was to start driving a machine and stop being one."

The next year his family moved to East Los Angeles, where he went to work as a helper in a Jewish bakery. For the next five years he worked as a journeyman baker for the Union Maid Bakery. At the same time Rod fought to become educated, completing his high school education at age twenty because of the work and other interruptions of his childhood. He managed to continue his education while he worked, attending Los Angeles Trade Technical College and earning a certificate of proficiency in electrical and mechanical drafting. With this in hand Rod landed a job as a draftsman at an engineering firm in Los Angeles.

He could have stopped there, having already achieved a long shot. But he didn't. He continued to go to school, taking English and math classes at East Los Angeles College, making it through the California State Polytechnic University at Pomona, earning a B.S. in electrical engineering in the early sixties, and all long before the Civil Rights Movement had made its way to the *barrio*—for that matter, long before most Americans had heard the word *barrio*. He then went to work for General Telephone and Electronics, but within a few months had started his own business on the side— purchasing, improving and managing apartment buildings.

What does Rod attribute his success to? Well, he surely doesn't deny the opportunity of America and the hard lessons of a less-than-privileged start. But he zeros in on something surprisingly prosaic.

"My success has resulted from our organization's management techniques."

Later I'll tell more about some of Rod's techniques and how they helped him engineer leaving a hard-earned corporate job after only two years to find himself at age forty-seven completing a ten-million-dollar private residence after less than twenty years of expansion.

If I were a gambler I would not hesitate to wager that this decade-long trend reflecting a dramatic rise in the rate of new venture initiations will continue upward throughout the rest of this and the early part of the next century.

But it's not all wine and roses. A closely related trend is that the failure rate for new ventures is staggering. There are statistics that say only a fifth or a quarter ever see the light of their fifth year. Whatever: Most new businesses do fail. But keep it in perspective. My mother and Einstein were right: Everything is relative. Some entrepreneurs fail despite their managerial prowess and best intentions. Some gain tremendous success despite fundamental managerial weaknesses, having dynamic products, markets and ideas. And, as in sports, it's still said that it's better to be lucky than good.

I've found from my research that there are qualities among owner-founder entrepreneurs common to success and failure. In the following pages I'll try to develop these.

But before we get to them, a little myth-mashing is in order.

Chapter **TWO**

In Search of the Typical Entrepreneur

The Myth of the Alley Cat

Why do entrepreneurs start businesses? What is it that leads them to act on a dream we all share—a dream so close to the heart of the American experience? Many, attempting to explain this, have set owner-founder entrepreneurs off as a peculiar sort of animal. But during the course of my hunt I failed to find one successful entrepreneur who neatly fit into the suit of clothes our preconceptions have tailored.

Some twenty years ago a respected Harvard researcher, David C. McClelland, likened the entrepreneurial personality to the mythological Greek god, Hermes—"a cunning, ruthless, self-interested merchant . . . an outrageous liar and thief; an aggressive, socially mobile entrepreneur who threatened the established and wealthy." Another prominent research team concluded that on the whole owner-founder entrepreneurs "do not have the qualities of patience, understanding and charity many of us admire and wish for in our fellows."

Ask about the species entrepreneur and you're likely to hear tales about odd spoons hellbent on individuality, self-assertion and proving themselves in a world yet to grant them their due. Some who've done business with an entrepreneur, still viewing the individual through myth-tinted glasses, may tell tales of an overly determined, often whimsical, sometimes vengeful character, with an exaggerated sense of self-importance. The myth is so pervasive one won-

ders whether as a nation we perhaps don't have a primal
stake in continuing it, now that our cowboys have ridden off
into the sunset on imported three-wheel motorcycles.

"How did your meeting go?" a salesman is asked when he
returns in the afternoon.

"With Simpson?"

"Right, with Simpson."

"Oh, all right, I guess. You know. He's an entrepreneur . . ."

Enough said.

I once had reason to deal with a printer. After introducing
myself as an entrepreneur he cringed. He said the last entrepreneur they did a job for, an owner of a company that
manufactured Mexican food products, turned a one-hour
press run into a twelve-hour job, getting the green-and-
yellow shadings on his chilies *just* right—half a day with
the graphic artist and master printer going cross-eyed and
colorblind. A story that reinforces the notion that the entrepreneur is an individual who, above all, even at the risk of
having things the wrong way, must have things *his* way.

So the typical entrepreneur is often described as a renegade, a maverick, a misfit, an outsider—at the very least
off-center. He is said to be driven to achieve just by virtue
of his *being* an outsider—if they won't let me in the club I'll
start my own and make my own rules. . . . We see only one
side of such as Donald Trump and other entrepreneurs captured through editing on television. We view heads of companies steamrolling humanity through films and novels.
Ask how an entrepreneur makes it to the top, and most will
say: usually at the expense of others.

It's no myth to say that entrepreneurs do tend to be scrap-
pers—people who have had personally to inch over obstacles or *through* them. Few spend much time in conscious-
ness-raising or at the sociable games of poker and bridge.
Most who have made it work their tails off, keep long hours
and *love* it. They are not, especially in the formative stage,
the easiest folks to keep company with. But they are not
wild-hair alley cats either. They build successful entre-

preneurships not by kicking, scratching and biting—though they do depend on an abundance of determination and will. Please don't stop reading here if you don't consider yourself driven to eat your competition for breakfast and, what's more, willing and anxious to brag about it. Let me tell you a few stories about what it really took for some successful entrepreneurs to crack the nut.

I DID THINGS WHOSE WAY?

At first flush Ed Stevens' story appears to satisfy many of the preconceptions that have grown to form the image of an owner-founder. Ed was the son of a hard-working Polish immigrant. One of the conclusions of a well-known study made in the early 1960s, a study that continues to influence the way most think about entrepreneurs, was that a majority of those who go into business for themselves are foreign-born or first-generation Americans. Foreign-born or first-generation Americans don't have immediate or easy access to mainstream avenues in which to channel their ambition. Entrepreneurship is seen as the one way they can prove their personal worth. Another conclusion of the study was that the majority of entrepreneurs don't come from families in which the breadwinner worked for a large corporation or inside a profession. I've mentioned I think this might be inaccurate, particularly with regard to a new and coming breed of owner-founder entrepreneurs, but in Ed's case it held true.

Ed Stevens' father opened a restaurant with his two brothers in downtown Cleveland at the time of the First World War. Toward the end of the roaring twenties Ed's father moved the family to Los Angeles and opened a restaurant in Glendale to be nearer Hollywood, where his four-year-old future entrepreneur son worked as a child actor with the Meglin Kiddies. But times got tougher. Customers had increasingly less to spend as the depression hit, broadened and deepened. The family was forced to move back to

Cleveland, Ed's father went back to work with his brothers, and Ed went into business for himself for the first time, producing and distributing a neighborhood newspaper on a small press out of the family basement.

Ed then went to work as a copy boy at the Cleveland *Plain Dealer,* where he ran the halls with the writer Herbert Gold. But he also continued to act. Sitting in front of Ed one can easily see him on the screen, his full head of silver-gray hair topping smooth, expressive features. Ed is a patient man, he listens with relaxed concentration. He waits. He doesn't seem easily surprised. It's the sort of patience one might be expected to earn with the varied sort of career Ed has known.

Early on, most of Ed's energy and efforts still were dedicated to acting. He was at the Cleveland Playhouse with Joel Gray just before World War II broke out. He spent time in New York's Greenwich Village and in summer stock in the Northeast. Clearly Ed manifested early on a desire to make something of himself, an above-average need to achieve.

How come? Owner-founder entrepreneurs have traditionally been characterized as individuals driven to prove their worth in a world that turned a cold shoulder. Some researchers who don't buy social or cultural influences in plumbing the entrepreneurial drive turn to psychological explanations. The entrepreneurial act is a form of rebellion, nurtured by mother during early childhood, against father, whom the boy entrepreneur wants to succeed, replace—all very Oedipal and, if I may say so, at odds with my findings and the facts. Some have even suggested a desire to make up for a physical "shortcoming" is at the root of the drive —pointing out that corporate managers are *taller* as a group than entrepreneurial types.

The sort of drives that lead one to start a business aren't usefully laid to a negative start of one sort or another. The logical consequence of that approach would be to say that a healthy, sane, socially adjusted human being would go to work for the government or some highly bureaucratized structure. And said individual wouldn't be so disturbed as to want or try to get ahead. He or she would have a drive toward stasis—toward wearing out one's couch and television set. From talking not only to a number of entrepreneurs but others with similar drives, I've concluded that the desire to make something out of oneself is not only entirely normal but seemingly pervasive. The better question might be how do so many come to suppress their entrepreneurial urges.

Back to Ed Stevens and some others who didn't manage to suppress their *normal* entrepreneurial urges. After the Japanese attack on Pearl Harbor Ed volunteered. He started out in the army driving trucks, until his training as an actor was discovered and he was assigned to the USO and traveled throughout the Pacific entertaining troups. At the end of the war he was in Japan. Back to Cleveland, where he went to work first as a disc jockey, then as a station manager for WERE. Sandwiched in was a stint as "Uncle Ed," the host of one of the country's first children's television programs. "You should have a look at some of the footage from that one if you want to learn the meaning of the word 'blooper,' " Ed told me.

As a station manager Ed foresaw the future of radio in building chains of stations. He tried to convince others but the owners of WERE did not want to commit to growth. Ed decided to buy a station. So contrary to a popular perception of the entrepreneur as someone who has a great idea out of the void, Ed, like most of the successful entrepreneurs I spoke with, pursued a deliberate strategy within an industry he was intimately familiar with.

Now, though, Ed needed investors. He talked with the sponsors of the children's show he had done. He talked with a friend, at the time one of the nation's most popular disc jockeys, a young fellow with spare income. *Both* chipped in. Then Ed searched for an affordable station.

His first was in the desert town of Banning, California. In the mid-1950s Banning was a main street and gas station where people stopped on the drive between Beverly Hills and Palm Springs. There was also an Indian reservation bordering the town, plus tumbleweeds and an occasional stray burro. Ed did trade-offs with local merchants to make ends meet. His wife conducted an interview show, talking with the local dogcatcher and such. Social life was getting together with anyone who had lived at some time out of the county. It was what Ed doesn't hesitate to label "a cheap station in a very, very limited market." But it was *his* station. Like the typical entrepreneur, he was willing to sacrifice for a goal and relative self-determination.

Ed went on to buy another station in Colorado Springs, Colorado, a bit of a step up, but neither station took off. Ed was never able to expand and build the chain with the sort of economies he'd envisioned. Television, of course, wasn't helping. Finally Ed went back to being a manager, first at the station he had left in Cleveland, then as general manager of KFAC in Los Angeles.

Here too Ed was running rather true to form. Many studies suggest that the typical successful entrepreneur does *not* succeed with his first toss. It can work out that through failing an entrepreneur learns lessons that later will bring success—there are matters of "basic dealing," the noted research team at Collins and Moore pointed out, that need to be learned and can only be learned by being in business for oneself, and the price of learning is often an initial failure or even two. (It is worth pointing out, however, that among the successful entrepreneurs I interviewed, two-thirds did make the grade their first time out).

In Ed Stevens' case, having been once bitten he was far from cured. The old feeling lurked beneath the long-sleeved white shirt in the company car as he made the rounds for one of the largest stations in the biggest broadcast markets in the country. And here especially is where Ed begins to go cross-grained to some of our preconceptions about the so-called typical entrepreneur. Certainly it was not that Ed couldn't cut it in the corporate world. He remained general manager of KFAC for most of a decade. Ed served as board chairman of the Southern California Broadcasters. He was well-known within the local and national broadcast communities.

The typical owner-founder is supposed to be unable to work for others, is said to be just too ornery and contrary to take orders. Well, to a limited extent this may be true. But a related preconception is that entrepreneurs are people not able to *achieve* in more organized settings. Some have suggested this is the key mix that makes for the fermentation of an entrepreneurial spirit: people with a high need to achieve, stuck in a frustrating organizational situation in which they're unable to express their true worth.

For the majority of those I spoke with this was not the case. Many, as we'll see later, were doing very well indeed by conventional standards, but just not well enough by *their* standards—which included an overriding desire for independence and more self-determination of ultimate financial rewards.

In addition to his own desire for independence Ed Stevens had always liked to tinker with gadgets. He also liked to read. In fact in those days he was a voracious reader. He'd put in only one year at a university before the war, but it was long enough for him to fall in love with learning. So here too Ed's background at least in part reflected another dearly held notion about the entrepreneur—that the animal is neither as broadly or highly educated as the professional manager. The daring scrapping innovator succeeds *in spite of* not being an expert, not being traditionally trained or educated in a discipline. But as I will continue to illustrate, many of today's successful entrepreneurs are finding ways to put traditional qualifications, skills and education to work in their quest for independence. Of those I spoke with the great majority were college graduates and several had advanced degrees. So there's no reason to count yourself out if you don't fit the more sensational profile of the offbeat counterculturalist who comes out of nowhere to catch the brass ring. You might even have gone to the Harvard Business School.

Ed the reader described himself as somewhat "anti-computer" when he ran across an article about a program IBM had started in an effort to market time-sharing on their large computers to smaller customers. After all, in the 1960s only giant corporations and government agencies could afford computers. Time-sharing appeared the wave of the future and IBM was offering free computer time to anyone interested in experimenting with custom applications in new industries.

Ed gave them a call. He had an idea for organizing the process of dealing with the flexible advertising rates for radio spots. Different time slots had different prices. Further, there was a standard practice of dividing up unsold slots and distributing them free to sponsors on the basis of the amount of ads they bought. Up to then all this had to be managed by hand. They had experimented with some customized calculators but Ed knew there was strong, industry-wide need for something more. Now with the free time IBM provided he began teaching himself to program at nights and on weekends. His eventual program not only handled the immediate problem but also automated the government-required air-time log system. Salesmen were immediately able to offer pricing packages as well as the latest information on complimentary spots that were incentives to customers. They could offer such data on-line, tying directly into the system through a mobile terminal and modem. Entrepreneurs are impatient? Well, it took two years from the time Ed sensed the need until he had demonstrated it could work at KFAC.

Coincidentally at that time KFAC was put up for sale. Ed's old dream returned. He tried to get together a group of investors to buy the station as he watched other station owners beginning to practice the strategy he had envisioned in the late 1940s. It didn't work out, but during the unsuccessful effort he developed contacts with the Bank of America's Wilshire branch, and over a postmortem lunch one day he told about what he was doing with his free time on a computer, about ideas he had for computerizing the whole broadcast industry.

"There were something like 5,000 radio stations out there at the time, all of them in need of the system I had proved could work. The competition at the time was next to nothing. It was a wide-open field. If I could get enough customers to accept the system, enough to support the purchase of a computer, then I wouldn't even have to pay retail for time-sharing. I realized it could become a very profitable operation."

The bankers bit into more than ham and cheese at that lunch. Purely on the basis of Ed's pitch, with no written proposal, they agreed to enter into a joint-venture, the bank putting up the seed money in exchange for 40 percent.

"It would never happen today," Ed lamented, "now that venture capitalists want everything but your horoscope written down."

Compunet, the company Ed Stevens eventually sold to the Control Data Corporation, pioneered data processing within the broadcast industry, and Ed has gone on to build another company, EMDA, Inc., which among other things has computerized one of the nation's leading auto-rental firms. At this writing he is forming a joint-venture involving a number of researchers affiliated with the California Institute of Technology, and he spends a good deal of his time consulting with a public library system trying to steward a non-profit institution into the twenty-first century.

Something is missing, right? I haven't said a word about how Ed manhandled the broadcast industry into accepting his innovation. I haven't said a word about how he muscled his ideas into reality, scattering bodies and the plans of others to make his come true. You were perhaps waiting for me to get to the gory part, complete with the casualties of Ed's triumphant march. All of this would be in synch with the myth surrounding the successful entrepreneur. I have, of course, left this part out for a very good reason: Except for the level of determination and energy Ed Stevens did put into the creation of Compunet, in his case the myth stops here. Ask Ed what he does to remember what it was like to get over the hump, what it was like to be an entrepreneur

during the early days of his company. You'll get an answer
defying most of the popular image surrounding the entrepreneur. When Ed Stevens wants to get nostalgic he pulls
a few tape recordings of early phone conversations out of a
bottom drawer. The calls usually came from station managers or owners, but in the background one hears pronounced
sobbing. Ed flips the switch.

"That's a traffic director in the background. A woman.
Most of the traffic directors were women. You could tell if
it was a man. He would be screaming and cursing in the
background. You see, computers cost $7 million or $8 million dollars in the early seventies and were rarely backed
up in time-sharing situations. You just couldn't talk the
large computer companies into dedicating a back-up,
though it would have definitely hastened the public's acceptance of data processing if the first buzz words they
learned hadn't been 'I'm sorry, the computer is down.' The
big ones, as everybody knows, tended to go down quite a bit
back then. Compared to what we now have they were like
tube radios. Sometimes they went down almost daily. It was
before minis and the routine networking of cpu's . . . I could
play you one of my tapes with a male traffic director in the
background, if you have the time."

There wasn't any need. The station manager in the fore-
ground is now doing a pretty good job of demonstrating his
gender's version of frustration directly into the phone.

"What you are listening to right now is a good deal of the
reality of what it is to be an entrepreneur. To establish your
credibility, to get yourself firmly into business you have to
go out of your way to satisfy clients and customers. You
have to give, give and then give some more. Some people
think entrepreneurs spend their days sitting around issuing
orders and making other people hop around their private
kingdoms. Sure, that's part of it, you are the boss and you
do have to keep things moving in the right direction, but it
doesn't begin to capture the full experience of owning your
own business. If you go into business for yourself you are
going to put in a number of years bending to the rest of the

world, including some of your employees, before you begin
to forget the early days and tell yourself you did things your
way. Sure, I did things my way, but nobody talked to me like
that when I was working in broadcasting, even when I was
working under others at my first job at a radio station. Or
when I was driving trucks in the army. And yet I listened
to it, and I responded. I offered sympathy and I offered
results. It was the only way we could make it."

So along with Doing It My Way there's a lot of Doing It
Their Way.

IT'S NO OPEN FIELD FOR AN EGO

Ralph Crump is another example of an entrepreneur who,
in spite of a pretty good growl, didn't in the end fill the
"typical" entrepreneur's bill. Ralph started Frigitronics in
1962 after having worked for twelve years for Electrofilm,
a firm Ralph characterizes as a mom-and-pop manufacturer
making aircraft and missile de-icers. Ralph has an engineering degree and did much of the initial engineering himself. Ralph continues to exude the determination, curiosity
and love of inquiry of a researcher. He still has a chalkboard
in his office in Shelton, Connecticut, and during our interview drew and paced, at one point jumping up to grab his
chalk and draw an x and y axis to demonstrate his thoughts
about the early growth of entrepreneurships and the influence of luck.

"De-icers work by passing current through radiating con-
ductors, wires or some other filament material," he ex-
plained. "In many ways they work like an electric blanket.
Not much to them."

In twelve years Ralph had risen to co-chief executive at
Electrofilm, but the family that owned the company didn't
want to share ownership. They had, though, been good to
Ralph and he didn't want to go into direct competition.
Though he was contractually free to do otherwise Ralph set
a personal restriction on the research he was doing in the

laboratory he had set up in his garage. (Yes, Ralph was one of the ones who literally did start in a garage.) He decided he would develop a product to reverse the process in heat conducting semi-conductors—devise a semi-conductor frequency device exchanging energy in the opposite direction, thereby creating a refrigerant. These weren't to be just any old refrigerators; they were to be microcontrollable refrigerant devices—head-of-the-pin type engineering.

Ralph does at times begin to project near-mythical proportions. Seating his tall athletic middle-aged frame back down in his chair only begins to temper his considerable dynamism. No scarcity of confidence or self-esteem here. Indeed, at the start of the day I thought I might be hot on the trail of the mythic entrepreneur. I asked him how he motivated his first few employees.

"I was a despot. During my good moments a benevolent despot. I have always been too bossy to be tentative. And I've always said exactly what I meant and exactly what I wanted. I captained a ship in the navy. I wasn't afraid to go ashore and drag a sailor out of a bar when we had orders to sail. When I started my company I wasn't afraid to do the same if I had orders to ship."

Yes, Ralph Crump might well lead one to shout eureka, the typical entrepreneur has been unearthed—a man to match mythology. Later I will give reasons to the contrary. Ralph, for example, lets one know that no rampant ego could have put up with the egos of his customers. To Ralph's mind, the ego of an entrepreneur isn't even in the ballpark with, say, the average doctor's. Never mind his inclination, he couldn't afford it.

Ralph had hoped to find industrial applications for his microrefrigerant devices and he did, but the avenue opening widest was in medical instrumentation. So Ralph devised a small, pin-point refrigerator on the tip of a pen-sized instrument that could be used in eye surgery. His medical device allowed ophthalmologists to do things they had only dreamed of doing. It made, for example, cataract surgery a much safer, more precise, more doable procedure. Nonetheless, Ralph relates that more than a few doctors treated him like a sewing-machine repairman or mechanic who manufactured the brushes they performed their *art* with.

"You just have to live with it," he says. "I practiced a lot of denial, saying that some aspects of dealing with the customers weren't as bad as they were. I'm not saying I wasn't a businessman out to make a profit, which was why I was doing what I was doing. From the start I was an equity-driven entrepreneur with a primary goal of building up something I could sell. Still, I don't think people understand just how much you have to swallow your pride in the course of building your own business. There was certainly a healthy dose of that."

LYING DOWN ACROSS THE WIRE

One warning voiced by many of the entrepreneurs tells much about an underlying quality distinguishing their accomplishments: "You have to be willing to do anything to keep your company alive."

I suspect this is what gives rise to the sensational stories about various acts attributed to one or another entrepreneur. I suspect it cuts close to a quality that may explain a good deal of what it means to start and run your own business in this country.

Consider Fred Charette. He had been in business for two years. Like Ed Stevens, Fred also ended up in the software business but from a very different background. Fred earned a Ph.D. in electrical engineering, though not for the narrow purpose of the discipline. There had been the option of Harvard Business School, but Fred decided not long after he was old enough to drink legally that one day he would start a company of his own and take it public. And he further decided he would have a better chance in the climate of the early 1970s if he had specific technical knowledge rather than general business knowledge. Fred started Systonetics directly out of school with a capitalization of $200,000,

three-quarters from a venture capitalist, the balance from
the founding team of employees. Fred had a verbal agreement on the venture capitalist's second installment—until
the bull market of the late sixties was dragged through the
abattoir. Fred got a call. His venture capitalist had lost
about $9 million in the market and could not deliver. Just
another of those afternoons, Fred said, and went on. But a
few weeks later the ramifications began to hit home.

Fred is a firm, perhaps tough, man in his midforties. His
grooming is impeccable. You expect to see this sort of individual stepping out of a corporate board room. One listens
to him describing with considerable intensity his love for
tennis. One would never sensibly offer up a lob to Fred
before charging the net. But along with Fred's intensity and
competitiveness is his position as a rational businessman.
When he had only a few employees he had a level of corporate and financial planning many mega-companies might
be proud of.

But this particular Black Friday afternoon defied planning. There was no money. The founding employees had
already been deferring salary for some time. The checks had
gone out to the rest but there was nothing to make them
good. Yes, there were some receivables and some orders that
might turn, but at that moment there was nothing. Fred
had thought this company through, in the abstract, years
before he had decided on a specific product and area of
concentration. Now it appeared he was going to have to put
a lock on the door and go home. But on his way out late in
the afternoon Fred remembered something—the Franchise
Tax Board. He had a $5,000 deposit with them; it was some-
thing he'd had to do if he wanted to conduct business in the
state. Fred ran to his car and drove downtown. As he walked
through the swinging front doors of the Tax Board he
sensed they were already going through the afternoon ritu-
als of preparing to close—a typical bureaucratic office. It
was, after all, Friday. Perhaps it was a little more efficient
than some government offices . . . they were collecting, not
giving out money. Still, it was not exactly the neck of the

woods an entrepreneur like Fred enjoyed working. Fred got past a couple of counters to a manager. First he asked, it didn't work; the fellow was well-versed in the book. Then Fred pleaded with the man, which also didn't work, the employee retreating deeper into the thicket of bureaucratic dogma, complete with Kafka-like impenetrable answers and pronouncements, the sort of talk you hear at the Department of Motor Vehicles until you're driven to give serious consideration to the purchase of a horse.

Fred, however, didn't give up. In his own words, he next gave the man "the most horrific sob story you could ever imagine. I begged. I told him my life story. As I remember it"—Fred pauses slightly and measures the degree of confidence he wishes to give—then goes on. "Well, as I remember it, I might have even cried, right there in front of this guy who wasn't that many years away from a pension, I cried . . . and you know what? I walked out of there with a check for $4,000. I made it to the bank. We made the payroll and received a few checks the following week.

"There's something you need to be aware of going in. . . . If you are going to go into business for yourself you have to be willing to do absolutely anything to keep your business alive. You have to be willing to lie down across the barbed wire."

THE TRUTH BEHIND THE CAT:
BEING ABLE TO LAND ON YOUR FEET

As I'll continue to demonstrate, entrepreneurs are often individuals singularly devoted to a concept, a way of doing business or just the goal of being in business. As we'll see through some stories I relate in the next chapter, entrepreneurs are indeed often the type of men and women who stay behind and keep throwing pebbles at the log farthest out in the lake long after the others have left for dinner— men and women who stay until they finally hit it. *Determination* tends to be more the universal trait among entrepreneurs than any of the more heralded personality characteristics associated with an innovator, a risk-taker or street-fighter. For every instance of an entrepreneur muscling his dream into reality there are many more in which he has to finesse his way, including, as indicated, reining in his much-heralded pride.

At the same time I'm not about to suggest you would want to start recruiting all people who go into business for themselves for your local choir. Some entrepreneurs do come to think and react in social and business situations like middle linebackers. Many tend to compensate, perhaps overcompensate, for years of relatively powerless toil. Once they have made the grade they still don't—or can't—forget the early days. Some never do manage to adapt, even after there is no longer the need to struggle and sacrifice in the same old intense fashion. They continue to see life as the personal battle it once was. My conversations of the last few years have made it clear that those entrepreneurs who most easily shed this exaggerated sense of self-sacrifice and struggle are most often the ones who go on to manage the larger, faster growing ventures. View things long enough as a personal crusade, as you against the world, and in any endeavor, you're more than likely to end up getting what you want, jousting with windmills long after you've in fact won. What's worse, the consequence may well be that your company is stunted and kept from realizing its full potential.

So . . . if you want to be an entrepreneur, I suggest you don't start out trying to make the world bend to your purpose, or dreaming of one day paying the world back. You can't afford to waste your organization's energy on a personal crusade. If you don't learn to bend, to be flexible, you will stand a good chance of becoming an all-too-typical entrepreneur—you will most likely fail. *Flexibility and adaptability are perhaps the most underrated, undermentioned and most important qualities contributing to the success of entrepreneurs.* After all, it is not rigidity that allows one to step out of a more secure job into the buffeting winds of relatively self-determined fortune. The successful entrepreneur as renegade is a myth for a very good reason—during the early days of an entrepreneurship you work for *everyone.*

A QUESTION OF DIFFERENT TYPES OF GENERAL MOTORS?

As you read on you will continue to receive a couple of distinct messages. First, entrepreneurs come in all stripes and sizes. Second, personality and background are interesting grounds for developing stereotypes, but they have about as much relevancy to a discussion of what makes for success in entrepreneurships as shoe sizes. If you look only to background and personality traits you're not likely to find the quality characterizing the successful entrepreneur—the quality you might identify in yourself.

People also assume entrepreneurs are people who don't know their limitations, who believe they can do anything and just go out and do it. On the contrary, the majority of the entrepreneurs I interviewed talked about their limitations—both personal and relating to their ventures. When asked what they would recommend to a prospective entrepreneur, they stressed the importance of persevering, because you're likely one day to come very close to believing your worst naysayers.

Many successful entrepreneurs know a lot about rejection. Not too many are going to leave a comfortable office and chair for the unknown of a bare room. Early success along mainstream avenues might not be the best preparation for an owner-founder. Being turned down too many times when one asks to play, to join, to have this dance or for a promotion just might one day help you decide to go out and build your own world. Yet I think a recent study by the Wall Street *Journal* goes too far. It asserts entrepreneurs are far less likely to have held top positions in student government than were top corporate managers, reaffirming observations made twenty years ago by seminal studies in the field of entrepreneurial studies that claimed entrepreneurs, as a group, often lack the sort of social and political skills needed for success in more organized settings. This same study, by the way, also dwells on the different types of autos entrepreneurs and top professional managers drive. (Entrepreneurs are supposed to favor Cadillacs and Oldsmobiles; managers, Buicks and imports.)

As I've suggested, if entrepreneurs are distinguished by anything it is by the simple fact that they *act* on thoughts most everyone at one time or another has had. Please don't stop reading if you have some difficulty imagining yourself giving two weeks' notice, calling your banker and jumping out of a phone booth with a capital "E" emblazoned across your chest. Entrepreneurs are human too. As one of them said: "When things during the early days start looking like they are beginning to run smoothly, if you're lucky, you might be able to downshift to worry."

Successful entrepreneurs know how to run scared.

CHAPTER THREE

Creativity, Fortune and Hard Work

THE MAGICIAN OR RIVERBOAT GAMBLER

Successful entrepreneurs tend not to do it with mirrors, to pull rabbits out of a hat or to rely on bluff. More often than not success is founded on routinely doing business *better* than the competition, and *after* he or she chooses a deliberate, often incremental path of innovation.

An entrepreneur, by tradition, is one who does things differently—builds a better mousetrap. True enough. Even when taking an existing product, by repacking and marketing the entrepreneur meets, enhances, even creates demand, and thereby is doing things differently—finding a *better* way to do business. This can be a double-edged sword. With those I interviewed, the innovativeness or newness of their products or strategies was more often than not cited as *their biggest problem* during the earliest days of their companies. Many described the difficulty in gaining credibility and thereby acceptance for their products or strategies. It was also rare that success came from an industry's overnight acceptance of that innovation. Blood, sweat and tears—and further innovation in the form of persistent and creative production, marketing, sales and service—were needed.

For every heralded innovation pulled out of a hat to quickly find its moment, melding with a mysterious sudden demand, there is a deckful of cases of those who have earned success through less mercurial means. Theirs are the more realistic models for the vast majority of those who might set out into business for themselves.

THE OMNIPOTENCE OF PERSISTENCE

Dog owners are said eventually to begin to look like their pets. Some say we are what we eat. After spending a day with Ray Anderson I'm not so sure some entrepreneurs don't begin to reflect the productive activity, or the products themselves, of their enterprises.

Ray Anderson started out with an innovation, a 3,000 year old but little-understood metallurgical process—powder metallurgy—thirty-three years ago. To exploit the possibilities of powder metallurgy one takes powdered metals —sometimes metals that would never mix if melted to form an alloy. The procedure is to take specific powders and fill a die cavity. Thousands and thousands of pounds of pressure are brought to bear on that powder, squeezing it together with such force as to create a near solid. It is then sintered (heat treated) at high temperature to increase the adhesion. One can make a part with components as diverse as the number of metals one wishes to design into it—here greater durability, here greater strength, here a self-lubricating property. You can begin to imagine the possibilities. Perhaps with effort one could even design a part that could last long enough to keep a company alive through the lean years —even if the lean years should turn out to stretch into a decade.

In any case, someone designed Ray Anderson to last that long. Not a large man, he has the build of a gymnast and appears quite fit past his sixth decade.

Ray Anderson was a young man taking home very good money when he went into business for himself—$17,000 a year in 1953, which would be in the neighborhood of $50,000 or $60,000 today. A good many people thinking about going into business for themselves would be content to pull that down, along with the independence. But it's not always so easy, even when you have an innovation with a seemingly wide-open range of applications.

Perhaps if the war had not broken out and Ray's engineering degree from Lehigh had not landed him at the helm of a PT boat in the Mediterranean and later made him skipper of a destroyer escort off the coast of China—maybe Ray wouldn't have got the taste that turned into a hunger. True, orders came in over the radio, but there was no mistaking it—those were *his* decks. It was not long after returning to civilian life, working as an engineer and salesman for a family-owned firm in Pennsylvania, that Ray began to realize how much he missed having his orders delivered from a distance—the horizon could become limiting within a family company.

It took Ray five years, skipping vacations, to save up the stake he needed to set off on his own. His brother-in-law, also an engineer, became his partner, and together they bought some machinery—paying for it in cash.

"The biggest mistake of our lives," Ray now says. "If I were to do it all over again, having seen the last thirty years of this economy and country, I would have been borrowing like everybody else. But we didn't want to get in over our heads. We wanted to do things a step at a time and finance most of our growth internally. We didn't want to end up with unwanted partners. The last thing we wanted was to end up working for somebody else again. And we didn't, though it made things a lot harder on us."

Ray and his brother-in-law figured it would take them two or three years to match the salaries they had left behind. They worked eighty hours, six days a week, in a six-hundred-square-foot building that barely held their machinery. The first employee they hired was a toolmaker. It was hard to pay a competitive wage. In fact, their first employee came to them after a few months to complain about it. He wanted, he said, to share ownership.

"The guy was fairly honest [so to speak]. He said the only reason he had come to work for us to begin with was to steal our tools. Because we turned out to treat him pretty well he said he decided not to. We didn't feel like sharing ownership with the guy, so we couldn't come to terms, but as he left he told us he thought he knew the type of honest, hard-working and stable employee we were looking for. He referred our second employee to us, who is still with the company after thirty-three years."

As soon as they could afford a secretary they built a shack outside, but you had to crawl past a vent duct to get to the bathroom. Ray was and is not big on bureaucracy, or on official policy. He had no formal titles within the company for nine years. But one of the first policies they had to establish instructed that all employees would turn their heads when the secretary had to duck under the vent.

At the start Ray did his own bookkeeping and accounting. After five and a half years the brothers were able to build a new $32,000 facility and purchase new equipment, though Ray did the wiring himself to ease the crimp expansion was going to put in their cash flow. Which it did. If they had stopped buying the machinery, if they had stopped expanding they could have milked the situation, started taking time off, drawing a decent salary. But the minute they did that, Ray figured, they would be dead. If they couldn't keep up with their customers' expanding needs they would lose the customers. They had to keep expanding and paying the piper, each time taking matters fairly close to the edge in terms of cash flow, though they did get their days down to a mere twelve hours.

Things began to settle down through the sixties—Ray built a house on a hill and began to take an occasional day off with his wife, his three sons and a daughter. But then his brother-in-law was killed in a private plane crash in 1970 and he had to hold things together for several years before he could bring a professional manager on board to help cover.

Ray did hang in there, and he will be the first to emphasize that persistence was probably the most important reason for his now being able to sit in his modern 50,000-square-foot computerized facility with a professional president running the daily operations of his privately owned corporation, Ceromet, Inc. An entire industry has grown up around powdered metallurgy in the last few decades; there is now a trade association, with shiny marketing materials. Still, it is not exactly a household word, and each time a new client is brought on it's pretty much as it was thirty years ago—powder *what?*

Before I left, Ray insisted I wait while he retrieved a document he had at times turned to for inspiration, a quote, "Press On," from Woodrow Wilson. One of his sons had it printed and mounted and it hangs on the wall of his home office. Ray believes it goes to the heart of his success:

> *Nothing in the world can take the place of persistence.*
> *Nothing is more common than unsuccessful men with talent.*
> *Genius will not; unrewarded genius is almost a proverb.*
> *Education alone will not; the world is full of educated derelicts.*
> *Persistence and determination alone are omnipotent.*
> *No idea is worth anything unless you have the guts to back it up.*

WAITING FOR GOOD DOUGH

Sometimes, though, patience is even more important than guts—"He also serves who stands and waits," as the poet said. Leo Imperiali of Tile World, the cab driver who ran across a dream product while trying to child-proof some furniture, learned how to stand and wait. His dream product pulled a Rip Van Winkle before it began to filter into the sleep of enough customers. Perhaps the placid hours Leo now spends patiently working over the impressive stamp collection that he augments while traveling all over the world visiting tile manufacturers can be traced back to those early days.

There was only one problem with Leo's dream product: time.

It wasn't that Leo didn't have an innovation. Leo had the then-unique concept of going straight to the do-it-yourselfer. He knew he could teach anyone to do their own tiling. He knew once he had taught some he would have no problem selling others. The first pupil was himself—once he finished tiling his coffee table, he says, he figured he'd found the business he could build the rest of his life.

Leo broke down tiling into a step-by-step process and built a very simple instruction method around it. He began teaching classes in his store years before it was to become routine in home-improvement centers. But the first year was bumpy:

"I was in a small 1,500-square-foot shop I rented from the owner of a nearby hardware store. I figured being next to a hardware store would help me get a start. I spent over half my time polishing products and straightening the store. But there were just no customers. I probably should have marketed more aggressively but I was a bit ahead of the market —about fifteen years ahead of the housing boom of the seventies. I always knew the market was, and would be, there. I was having to sell to installers. It was more convenient for them to come to me than to go to the factory, but the whole business was geared to the do-it-yourselfer. I wouldn't give up on that. I could have just set up some cheap wholesale space and been a middle-man to the installers, but I would probably still be in some cheap wholesale space selling to installers today, nothing more. I knew retail could work, so I stuck with it.

"My landlord, the hardware store owner, used to come to work at seven-thirty in the morning. I was always there before him, straightening my store. When his wife came to spell him at ten, he would walk up and down in front of his strip of stores, up and down the sidewalk, past my window. One day, after walking by for about three months, he stepped in the store and asked me what I was doing. All he ever saw me doing was cleaning my store, he said. He had never seen a customer in it.

"Do you know what? That was a huge boost, to have someone notice that I kept a very straight and orderly store. It is a good part of our secret, something we continue to stress. It's just as much a reason I think customers come to us, just as much as the fact that we at the same time have more tile than anyone else at a better price. People will go down the street and pay more if they don't enjoy shopping in your store.

"I couldn't afford to hire my first employee, other than my wife, for nine years. You can bet by then I knew how to train a customer well enough that it was no problem training employees. We've got our system of instruction and we've got our methods of orderliness. We'll follow the same system in the six or eight stores we'll open this year, the same system I was following by the end of the first year in that store-front. . . . There were a lot of little things like that, like the landlord stopping in that morning. You grabbed and held onto them when they happened and you didn't let go. It was the little things that helped you persevere. I could have dropped out of the business very easily back then. I probably would have, early on, if I wasn't absolutely committed to working for myself. By sticking around, by staying alive through the thin years, I was there, knowing the business better than the newcomers, when the market picked up. Some of those newcomers were national corporations who offered to buy me out. At first they just wanted my inventory. Then they wanted to get rid of me as a competitor. Every time they ran a TV ad my business would double and I had to open another store. They made sure more people knew about tile. I made sure I had the best tile, prices and stores in town. They were doing me a favor, after all those years of being the only guy out there."

The value of persistence, whether specifically pointed out or not, was basic to the stories of all the entrepreneurs I spoke with. It's at one point or another a large part of any businessman's life, entrepreneur or not, but when you are out on your own and the stakes involve more than just your present employment you find that you have, and need, considerably more determination than you thought. And determination is not necessarily a quality one is born with, though some obviously start off with more than others. It is as much forged in the process of life as a natural gift. Even within the very most creative and fortunate of entrepreneurships, determination and patience (an old-fashioned term is "stick-to-itiveness") often make the difference between survival and empty nostalgia for what might or should have been.

Consider Gordon Moore of Intel. No one would deny the innovativeness of the Intel 1103 integrated circuit microchip. Gordon and Robert Noyce had talked over the need for a semiconductor capable of handling an exponential increase in electrical impulses, making possible ever faster and more compact data processors. We're talking about the kind of innovation that verges on technological alchemy, though those in the industry, men like Gordon Moore, who has worn a white coat and worked over a blasting kiln, matter-of-factly relate the baser elements, the incremental steps that made all these funny little boxes and screens on our desks possible. To them it is as much a matter of building blocks, of stacking one innovation on top of another as it is a big-deal breakthrough. In fact, after the technological breakthroughs that make a market thrust possible, it can take years of persistent, step-by-step research and development actually to bring products to market.

We were, though, talking about ready demand. Within four years of leaving Fairchild, after two years of development, powered mostly by the demand for the Intel 1103, sales had jumped from zero to $23 million. The next year sales shot to $60 million in pre-mega-inflation dollars and they were *still* on the ground floor. We're speaking of whiplash here. Intel had the technological edge, an eager market and the experience. Some would say it was handed to them, but demand is, so to speak, a many-splendored thing. And when it cracks it can become a many-splintered thing. You don't want to be standing too close to the semiconductor industry during a recession. You can hear the cries of pain all the way up in San Francisco from Silicon Valley. Companies are now only beginning to understand the wisdom of investing in data processing during downturns, and still the computer and peripheral industries react with lightning negativity to a recession. In the early seventies it was even worse. Intel had gone from twelve founding employees to 2,528 in five years. Then came 1974 and 1975 and what Gordon only labels "massive layoffs."

"It was," he says, "by far the hardest, most stressful time in the history of the company. That's not to say we haven't been through others, but that first one was extremely difficult."

It is often the case that the more startling the innovation, and the more a business is founded on an ingenious product development that relies on interlocking skills and talents, the more ready is the competition. Intel had not only to fend off a host of domestic industries willing to throw in the capital to get at the booming market, but the Japanese and its MITI as well. Intel has been holding its own. Sales were near a billion a year when I last spoke with Gordon, though they are now only beginning to come out of another dry cycle.

Intel absolutely relies on innovation, though Gordon Moore, who himself once was a researcher in white coat and safety goggles staring directly into a kiln, now as chairman of the board and CEO and subject to another kind of heat is frank to say: "I don't really understand what they are doing in the laboratory anymore. We hire the state of the art, the finest students and researchers in the country. And in a few years there is a new wave with a new state of the art."

How Howard Hughes Won the West

Sometimes innovation doesn't come in the shape, form or capabilities of a product; sometimes it takes the form of a strategy or way of doing business.

For example—Roy Ash, co-founder of Litton Industries. We are not talking about a storefront or starting out in a garage; we are not talking about waiting by the curb for

customers with an innovative product or building a better
data-trap and having the world beat a path to one's door.
This is the sort of entrepreneurial management much discussed of late in the context of large corporations, occurring
over thirty years ago on a scale that impresses even the
most aggressive investment banker or numbers-driven staff
analyst.

One byproduct of my talks with Roy Ash, co-founder of
Litton, as well as with Dr. Si Ramo, the "R" of TRW, Inc.,
two alumni of the Hughes famous school of high-tech entrepreneurs, was my coming to know better the patriotic con-
tributions of Howard Hughes. After assessing the impact
Litton and TRW have had on the technological apparatus
of this nation one has no choice but to conclude that the
creator of the Spruce Goose did much to strengthen the
defense of this country.

Which is not to say he did so intentionally. Howard
Hughes had other things on his mind than good intentions.
He was a man of whim. Of obsession. Not long after World
War II the United States government began to have serious
doubts about Hughes's reliability. It was becoming increasingly wary of the persona he was beginning to exhibit in his
business dealings. The men running some of his companies,
divisions and departments, de facto or de jure, including Si
Ramo and Roy Ash, soon found their own potentials frustrated by their famed employer's capriciousness. Roy Ash
was part of the so-called front wave at the Hughes aircraft
company. He had graduated from Harvard Business School
and was working as an assistant controller. When the government started backing out of dealings with Hughes, Roy
Ash read the writing on the wall and decided it was time to
get out from under Hughes's wing.

Roy Ash got together with Tex Thornton. Still in his early
thirties, Roy tried to put together a group of investors to buy
out the aircraft company. He met some investment bankers,
but the attempt didn't work out. But a short while later he
and Tex Thornton came across a small company being run
by a fellow named Charlie Litton. Litton's company was

doing about $2.6 million in sales *and* had a pre-tax profit of $1.2 million! But after the then-high taxes on government contractors Litton was kicking the walls with a mere $120,000 and all the red tape. Roy Ash put together a deal to buy the company for slightly over a million investment-banker dollars and his and Tex Thornton's management expertise.

"We weren't in the same position as Si Ramo, who had a major project, a plan to design and implement a system of radar to protect a good part of the country from Russian missiles, a major project the government had committed to. Si was able to raise the capital for a much larger and immediate start. Within the environment we were in, we did things fairly incrementally."

Roy and Tex had a relatively simple but highly innovative strategy—buy small companies on the downward trend burdened with obsolete technology but continuing to possess healthy pre-tax profits that could be put into research and development to take on new government contracts. Through such subsidized research and development, new technologies could be developed and applied to consumer markets. The microwave oven was a good example.

Under Roy, five such new projects were taken on within the company they bought from Charlie Litton. Three of them worked out and brought the company at last count over $1.5 billion in sales. Once they were on their feet, implementing this strategy in their first acquisition, Ash and Thornton went on a spree, buying 120 companies in the next 120 months, Tex striking the deals and Roy running Litton Industries as president and chief financial and administrative officer, overseeing the digestion and expansion of such growth. What was their innovation? It was not spectacular; it was quite straightforward and relatively risk-free, to Roy Ash's mind.

"Litton," he says, "just didn't sense the same opportunity. He was, after all, looking at the company as a dissatisfied seller, not as a buyer."

Like Gordon Moore, Roy downplays his own involvement

as a creative genius in the process of product innovation.

"Everyone was practicing entrepreneurial management, if that is what you want to call it, almost forty years ago at Hughes. It was a great classroom. When we started Litton Industries I didn't understand a thing they were doing in most of the companies. We kept a close watch on the checkbook and brought in some management professionals. Our secret, if there was one, was very tight control on the checkbooks and almost no control on ideas. We met with the researchers and established general project direction, then just turned them loose."

Not the stuff of which movies or bestselling novels are made—just the stuff by which a company is taken from a couple of million in sales to almost $6 billion in less than twenty years, and from 280 to 120,000 employees in the same period (before Roy Ash left private industry for government service).

Roy asserts, "I was and am no genius. I matched people with jobs, which took a lot of work and was the secret of my success. You have to be objective in evaluating situations. Once you get the right guy in, you can let him go and sit back and watch his success."

I will have more to say about the give and take involved with managing "entrepreneurial" and "state of the art" employees. It is not as simple as throwing the dog a bone; the word prima donna, for example, does crop up, with all the troubles that go with the species.

ANOTHER WAY OF STICKING WITH IT

Stanton Avery, of Avery International, is yet another example of a young entrepreneur with a straightforward but startling innovation who was still faced with the task of building a company. Who could deny the combination of the simplicity and the startling nature of Stan's innovation—a process and machine for making self-adhesive removable stickers. Yet to Stan's mind it was a logical, incremental thing to do. Adhesives existed, and could be modified. Machines to put adhesive on a piece of paper weren't that different from machines that did any number of other things. People were already using adhesives of one form or another to affix prices to products. There were others with greater mechanical and chemical knowledge. Stan Avery enjoys quoting a psychologist who has studied the nature of creativity to explain what he thinks it takes to be an inventor-type entrepreneur:

"Innovators are in some ways surprisingly ordinary people. Studies show that they are frequently smart but not too brainy; educated but not too learned."

Stan considers himself of that mold. What he did was not a stroke of genius, though many would dispute it. To him, what he did was an incremental application of existing materials to meet existing needs.

Stan had his share of good and bad breaks, but he knew how to keep his head down with the good ones and how to weather the bad. His first wife, until her untimely death a member of the board of Avery International, put up $100 from her earnings as a schoolteacher to build the first machine. He rented a work space on the top of a large refrigerator in the Los Angeles flower mart from a schoolmate. The brother of another schoolmate, and eventual partner and co-builder of Avery International, Russell Smith, was a banker who loaned Stan the $80 he needed to buy the stamps to mail an advertisement for his "Kum Klean Removable Price Stickers" to every gift store in the Los Angeles phone book, once he got his machine working. In 1937 Avery's Congregational minister father put up his life savings of $1,000 to help the business grow; Stan had the good fortune of a strong family and circle of friends. After starting the company in 1935 on top of a refrigerator and selling out his first runs of stickers, he commenced mailing advertisements to other cities and watching the orders stack up. He then moved into a storefront on East Fourth Street in downtown Los Angeles. Success looked like it was bound to stick—like a label Stan Avery was never going to have to peel off.

"Then one day some solvent in the adhesive mixing area caught fire and burned down a good deal of the new factory, including the label-making machine I had so painstakingly designed and built. For a short while it appeared as if the game might even be over. Without a doubt it was the lowest point in the history of our company, before or since.

"Fortunately I discovered a cache of packaged labels that had made it through the fire. We quickly mailed them off and waited for the receipts. There was also a little insurance money. While unable to continue production, I took all the ideas that had piled up over the last few years about ways to improve our machine, and set about building a new one.

"Out of the ashes I had the time and money to build the second-generation machine I'd been tinkering with in my spare time. The disaster turned into quite an opportunity. We were much further ahead coming out of it with the new machine than we would have been if we had kept plugging away with the old one. . . . Still, to be honest, we have never since had to make a technological advance under such disastrous circumstances."

And we are talking about some considerable subsequent technological advances. Avery International developed the label-making process that is the basis for the industry today. Stan Avery developed and introduced synthetic adhesives, stronger and much more reliable than his initial rubber-based mixes. He developed the release coating that made quick, removable labels possible. We all take them for granted.

So remember, there's hope for those of you with no more than a knowledge of the classics. Think of something that doesn't stick, or fit, or . . .

THE MYTH OF THE LUCKY CARD PLAYER

Everyone has seen the phenomenon, possibly at a card table, or watching sports, or in some other prosaic activity. It's the luck of the draw, fortune, serendipity, momentum. . . . But watch a little closer next time. One team starts to get the breaks. Except are they just breaks? Usually not. Less noticeable, preceding and underlying the fumble or tip, is an atmosphere that begins to spread across the court or field. There is a cohesiveness, a unity of purpose; concentration has been turned up a notch; the pace has quickened. Joining all this is a calm, knowing confidence—someone or some team is poised to *take* control. Oh, yes, you have to be lucky to win—just ask anyone who has lost.

You can call Gordon Moore lucky, but you'd be missing the point. Better to call him fortunate and talented, blessed with the intelligence and temperament to allow him to make his way through a school like Caltech, through the laboratory of William Schockley, through Fairchild and now through keeping Intel at the front of a highly competitive industry, at each juncture pressing on to realize both his and his company's potential. On an automatic transmission they label it "D."

That's one side of Gordon. But ask someone who knows him well and they will tell you he still keeps pretty much the same regular hours, he still goes trout fishing two weeks every year just as he did the first year he started the company. They will tell you that Gordon is not a roller coaster sort of businessman—that in fact he is steady in a roller coaster business that demands acute and objective attention.

Gordon Moore is perhaps not the best example to present in downplaying the supposed importance of pure luck. Designing a microchip and applying state-of-the-art technology to existing problems are so clearly not matters of fortune. There are other seemingly much more mysterious stories, involving the elusive and fickle logic of circumstances, in need of debunking.

I mentioned earlier Warren Dennis and Casablanca Fans. Some would say his and its story come about as close to describing an instance of fortuitous circumstances as one might hope for. But why Casablanca? There were others making fans at the time. Why not Whirling Dervishes or the Flying Agenda Brothers?

Warren does not strike one as a lucky card player. Lucky
card players are also unlucky a lot, they go in streaks; the
good ones, as we are instructed by popular country ballads,
knowing when to minimize the bad streaks. Warren does
not appear to be streaky. He strikes one as deliberate, concerned, reflective, intense in his commitment. Streaky types
aren't likely to sit down and take apart an antique slot
machine piece by piece. Warren, one suspects, could have
been a cancer researcher; he has the sort of built-in dedication and intensity one needs to push discovery forward, be
it a cell or a screw at a time. You also get the distinct
impression that Warren would work for nothing if the challenge genuinely appealed to him. Casablanca Fans started
rather like that. Warren is a fellow who needs to work at
something, to take hold of it and make it the *best,* to bring
things into their proper aesthetic order. Not surprisingly,
he now collects modern art, driven no doubt by the same
need that led him to design production race cars as a young
man in college—the same drive that led him to return to
that avocation to win a national championship after Casablanca was well under way. The same need that had him
bending over a machinist's bench along with Burton Burton
working on that first fan. Deliberate? These fellows are
natural-born perfectionists.

True, Warren and Burton had no idea there was going to
be an energy crisis. And it may have been fortuitous that
their love for fine antique machinery was congruent with a
nation's turn toward the authenticity and honesty of the
best of the past. In the middle of the seventies there was a
considerable disenchantment and disillusion coming from a
realization that everything—from presidents to wars to hot
dogs—wasn't what it was pretending to be. But Casablanca
Fans would have made it to restaurants and homes regardless of the price of oil or the national mood. Warren speaks
for himself about how the pair established themselves at the
forefront of their industry.

"There is an annual convention of the American Restaurant Association. This one was in Chicago, the second year

after Burton and I had started building the fans. We were selling them to restaurant designers and restaurants then. Burton and I decided we needed something to bring Casablanca Fans to the attention of everyone at the convention. Though we did most of our own ads, which we're quite proud of, including the designs on the trucks you might see around on the freeway, we decided to turn to what we knew best: craftsmanship.

"The ceiling in the convention center was quite high, not lending itself to hanging fans. So we decided to build a room—a fully decorated room, right in the middle of this convention with standard booths and brochure hawkers. It was outrageously decked out. We took an entire semi-rig back to the convention filled with tools and materials. We built the most fine-tuned, elaborately crafted room that you could imagine under the circumstances. We put days into it, weeks actually, designing and preconstructing it. We hung our fans in it and we blew the entire convention away. After the convention we didn't have to tell anybody who we were or how well-made our product was—here were the two founders with hammers in their hands showing their stuff. Our room at the convention ended up looking better than some of their restaurants. Our reputation and quality were cemented in their minds."

Innovation and risk-taking are undeniably important to succeeding in business for yourself. But above all, if you go into business and want to stay in business for yourself, in one way or another you are going to have to perform better than the competition. You are going to have to get down and do business better than the others—to hang in when it's lean, to build a better display, to stock more tile, to have a more orderly store, to take on a company someone else thinks is a loser, to make the tough choices and decisions when your industry is on the rocks or on the edge of change. As I've tried to suggest, it is commonly assumed that entrepreneurs either find startling niches from which to leapfrog the competition or that they manhandle, all but swindle their way over and beyond the pack. Not so.

Also, for many entrepreneurs, including some of the successful ones I interviewed, the birth and growth of their companies was not always as highly charged and spectacular as even these selected anecdotes suggest. Not all of going into business or staying in business for oneself involves hard knocks and sacrifice. There are a number of less spectacular matters crucial to survival. The myth surrounding the personality and background of the typical entrepreneur has for some time overshadowed the management practices of the typical owner-founder entrepreneur. Generally they are thought to manage with the touch of a chain-gang boss and the constancy of a diva. I shall try to zero in on specific, fundamental aspects of management practice that were given great attention by the most successful of the entrepreneurs with whom I spoke.

Though there were moments of crisis, sometimes attributed to seemingly unforeseeable events and consequences through which some unexpectedly benefited and through which others were forced to persevere, it was by performing key activities better than the competition on a routine basis that they prevailed. Real entrepreneurs may or may not eat quiche, but for sure they compete to stay alive, not just to introduce innovative products or to be modern-day swashbucklers or Cool Hand Lukes. Remember what happened to Luke—he didn't make it. Our people did. This book is about how and why.

Chapter FOUR

Starting Out:
Informed Doing is the Best Plan

It is commonly thought there are planners and doers. In one office, the lights dimmed to handle their brightness, sit the planners, men and women nowadays likely to be staring at green or amber spreadsheets on a video display. Planners are known to find deep comfort in numberized shadows of reality. At the very least planners grow attached to them, for a planner is somewhat routine, but we all have at one time or another fallen glassy-eyed under the hypnotic spell of the hypothetical's charms.

In another room, behind a cluttered desk stacked with paper (one ear much flatter than the other, or scuff marks on their heels if they work with a speaker phone), are the doers—men and women on the horn, blowing riffs across the chaos of trying to get something done.

These two varieties of business animal are known to openly question the origins of their opposing species in meetings—to resort to more primitive forms of contest in less organized and adjudicated settings.

But remember, when you go into business for yourself, you've got to work both ends of the room. There is no time for organizational schizophrenia when you are essentially the beginning and end of your organization. If you stay in the modern-day equivalent of Plato's cave too long fiddling with numberized shadows of reality you simply will never get into business for yourself. On the other hand if your planning is inadequate you could find yourself opening the tenth croissant shop in Kalamazoo, just as the first nine are folding and reopening as sweat parlors.

Detailed analysis of the business histories of the owner-founders I studied and interviewed showed that when kept within the context of doing—within the context of the activities that more directly lead to going into and staying in business for oneself—some aspects of professional planning (chiefly concerning the thought that goes into venture choice) can be extremely helpful to an entrepreneur. Some aspects of planning (especially involving numberized goals) seem relatively useless to the owner-founder preparing to go into business. Still others (chiefly personal goals and a reliance on participation in decision-making) appear to be more of the Christmas-tie management-practice variety— you might not always need them but in many cases you not only can but will use them.

WHAT PLANNING IS . . . AND ISN'T

Planning is perhaps the most misunderstood area of management practice, in large or small enterprises. Within the specific context of entrepreneurships, there is a pretty strong consensus among academic management writers that the time devoted to planning, prior to initiation, is somewhat unrelated to an entrepreneur's chances of survival or extent of success.

Yet if you take a look at the shelves of more popular business books, you might come away confused. The one area of management practice generally and consistently thought by academics to be the least important to the prospective entrepreneur, planning, is also the area about which the most books are published. Have a look. There are a number of books that offer to assist you in planning your new business. Writers know how to plan and write about planning better than anyone. Writers also spend a good deal of their time sitting in rooms—not exactly hotbeds of commerce, unless you are dealing in words.

Many I spoke with, including some of the owner-founders of companies that more quickly went on to greater growth, were relatively informal about planning. But almost all I spoke with demonstrated a keen awareness, either formally or informally, of the importance of certain key aspects of the planning process.

Let me demonstrate what I mean by planning—the kind likely to help you, and the kind likely to make less difference within the scheme of going into business for yourself.

Bill Kaufman was part of a team of three real estate development professionals who broke off from a major corporation in the early seventies to start a company from scratch. They went from the three founders to twelve employees in the first six months, from twelve to twenty in the next six months, and to over two hundred in little over a decade.

At first, title to the new company was held by its primary investor, a large financial firm. The partners had an "earn out" clause which they took advantage of within three years when the backing parent decided to divest. The three bought the company, then within another year sold it to Esmark to further their growth. Within two more years, Bill and his compatriots did a leveraged buy-out with a group of other Esmark companies, when Esmark's portfolio strategy changed, and they couldn't find a buyer. Within a couple more years, the other companies were sold off to retire the debt to Esmark, leaving Bill and his partners on their own again. Does that sound like a plan?

Believe me, Bill is not unfamiliar with business plans and stacks of contracts and paper. For that matter, Bill, thirty when he left the preserve of a major corporation to brave the radically fluctuating tide of development during the seventies, semi-retired and starting new independent ventures now at forty-five, began his career as a planner at the Stanford Research Institute. Just a couple of years out of college with a real estate degree, Bill went to work at the institute as an urban planner, evaluating land usage and the economics of proposed developments. So what does Bill think of planning during initiation?

"When we started what was to become Calmark, we had a five-year plan with financial and cash-flow forecasts. We needed the financials, just like any other business, for day-to-day operations. But in terms of project planning and overall strategy, you can have all the plans in the world but no deals. At some point you have to go out and do it. We hired a young guy from Harvard, an M.B.A., after we had our feet on the ground, and the guy used to drive me absolutely crazy, working three weeks on a plan without leaving the office to test the deal-making waters.

"We did plan quite a bit of our *strategy*. We considered everything from high-rise cemeteries to underground apartments. We talked about just what we could and should be doing and where. Geographical locations were a prime consideration. Before most, we were buying up properties to develop in Texas when vacancy rates in planned housing were 40 percent. The three of us had talked it out and figured things would definitely be getting better down there. We focused a good deal of our activity in the Sun Belt before it began to hold up the economy's sagging pants. Number-ized forecasts, tied to key indicators, would not necessarily have backed the strategy, except in the longest-range terms. The key word is *bought*—we bought the land, we made the deals and we did business, not just planned to do business."

This sentiment will be echoed throughout this chapter: well-planned and conceived doing, yes; an over-emphasis and reliance on Arabic numerals, no.

DO AS I SAY, NOT AS I DID

Having said this, let me now say why in many instances you will be pressured toward the less valuable sort of planning if you decide to go into business for yourself.

Harold Haytin, an entrepreneur who built a business importing and distributing Japanese consumer electronics goods, is now in the business of investing in businesses. California Capital Investors, a U.S. government-licensed small business investment company, has a formally stated mission, the first step of any rigorous planning process.

California Capital Investors was founded with the formally expressed purpose of targeting select companies with exponential growth potential, as a means of experiencing capital gains. More specifically, this purpose was broken down into goals, objectives and policy. A prospective company's markets should provide an environment which will permit the company to achieve sales of $15 to $35 million or more within four to six years. Using leveraged funding from the Small Business Administration, California Capital steps in as a secondary or bridge-financing alternative for existing new companies in exchange for equity positions. To quote from some of Hal's own formally stated objectives: "To qualify for investment consideration, companies meeting California Capital's criteria should submit a minimum of three years' audited financial statements, résumés of key managers, a thorough description of the company's business, and a synopsis of its plan for growth, including detailed projections of sales, earnings, and cash flow."

Now let's ask Hal how he did it himself with Telecor.

Telecor was not Hal Haytin's first business. He had several businesses before, some in the field of electronics. A couple of them went broke. He hadn't worked for anybody for a number of years. His father was an entrepreneur his whole life as well. Hal studied psychology in college but he had taken a few business courses. He has taken several business courses since he started and sold Telecor and is quite familiar with the elements of a formal planning process.

A short while before he started the company that would become Telecor, Hal remembers reading some magazine articles about changes in electronics technology and in production and organization in Japanese electronics firms. It was the end of the fifties. John F. Kennedy was about to become president. Fidel Castro was stirring up the Caribbean and soon the glow of the hotline to Moscow would have Americans digging bomb shelters instead of swimming pools out of their lawns. At the same time, without much fanfare, the first transistor radios began to appear on our shores—by present accounts a much more calamitous event.

Hal met up with a partner who wanted to go into importing and selling.

"I realized Japan was going to be factor in the electronics industry. But our planning, compared to today's, was rudimentary. There was no formal business plan at all. From a previous company, I had access to some very simple, superficial forecasts about expected electronics sales in the United States."

But how does one predict the sales of stereos if they haven't been invented yet? How to predict the sales of radios and stereos if the Beatles haven't yet been on the Ed Sullivan show?

Hal said they had no formal sales projections for their company. They had one goal, a page peeled out of the Al Davis/Los Angeles Raider playbook: Make money. Hal's business was fairly simple. He had two clerks handling the paperwork, and two shipping and receiving clerks handling the products. He bought only high-quality electronics goods from Japan and fought to convince buyers that the merchandise was first-rate despite very competitive prices. Within four years he had about twenty-five employees. Hal spent most of his time gaining access to new products coming out of Japan. (The crunch hadn't hit yet when he would have to deal more with how to distribute the flood of goods that began filling dormitories and apartments across America as the Baby Boom went to school and then work, from the late sixties through the seventies.)

Hal Haytin formalized his planning along the way as needed. Though he claims his systems were relatively unsophisticated he did have ongoing sales and cash-flow forecasts as well as closely watched sales and inventory reports.

When Hal took the company public at the end of the bull market in late 1969 the company had about sixty employees and was growing at a rate of 30 to 40 percent annually.

"We were still not on our feet, not until we went public. Before the infusion of capital that came with going public, we had to occasionally juggle the books to look more solid than we were."

But with that infusion of capital Hal took advantage of the

opportunity to increase control and planning capabilities, though once again, *along the way*. The company developed an automated data-processing/management-information system and enhanced its reporting and forecasting processes. Planning and control systems continued to be updated through the seventies to keep up with demand. In 1979, by the time Hal Haytin sold the company's core subsidiary to Matushita Electric Company of America (Panasonic), a major supplier, Telecor had 400 employees and annual sales of $140 million.

So now what is it Hal Haytin asks of a prospective enterprise coming to him for an infusion of capital?

"We want to know their business inside-out before we invest. We want to see a detailed plan."

Did he forget his own history?

Only a third of the owner-founders I spoke with actually employed formal business plans in the process of starting their companies. And of those who did have formal business plans, almost all relied primarily on external means of financing that demanded formal business plans.

In fairness, it must be said that regardless of the source of initial capitalization, the owner-founders I spoke with who initiated firms within the last fifteen to twenty years were twice as likely to have employed a business plan as those who started firms over twenty years ago.

The message is simple: The amount of planning *required* of prospective entrepreneurs has drastically increased over the last two decades. Sad but true. Business plans have entered the lexicon. It used to be you only heard that everyone had a scenario at the bottom of his or her briefcase. Nowadays, unless one has a trust fund, a winning lottery ticket, a benevolent spouse or schoolmate grown to Florida banker, one needs a formal business plan of some sort. Where it was once enough to sit down at lunch and convince a banker that your boat would probably float, more often than not to gain the funds needed to launch your craft you are now going to need a ship's log's worth of dot matrix. If you are going to start a business in the coming years, odds are you will have to engage in a formal planning process at the outset.

PICK A NUMBER . . . ANY NUMBER

Okay, give them what they want, but how much of that formal planning will be going through the motions, and how much will influence your success?

The answer is intimately related to the general misunderstanding of what planning is, a misunderstanding fueled by the increasing demand for formal business plans. Many entrepreneurs' first introduction to planning involves a painful crash course in creative forecasting.

"I think we can sell ah . . . ah . . . tell them a million widgets a month by the end of the first year. . . ."

Forecasting of that sort has given planning a bad name. But forecasting of a more reasonably calculated sort has been hiding its head of late too. Rumor has it that many of Bank of America's Third World lending practices of the latter seventies and early eighties were based on an in-house projection that oil would be selling for $100 a barrel. Whoops. Just because the equation involves a wall full of variables and influencing factors does not mean it is any stronger or more accurate than its weakest or most inaccurate input. And some of those inputs might be very ephemeral. The more one is talking about demand within a market-driven economy, the more one is venturing into the realm of volatile and inconsistent change.

I cannot think of one entrepreneur I spoke with whose initial sales projections turned out to be accurate. Everyone, of course, was convinced the company would work at the outset. Some had projections that were surpassed, including, by example, Joseph Solomon, whose marketing consultant, based on actual market tests conducted at the then two Vidal Sassoon salons in New York and a minitest in the Los Angeles area, contributed data that led to a five-year, $18 million sales-growth plan. The plan looked good after the first year's sales of $3,000. But the goal had been almost doubled by the fifth year. From the seventh to the ninth year, sales went from $35 million to $65 million in one swoop, along with the introduction of a new marketing thrust not included in initial planning and thinking. In the next two years, with a move into the international market and continued dramatic expansion domestically, sales multiplied another five or six times. Gordon Moore and Robert Noyce originally set out to hire individuals at Intel who could function as part of the management team of a $25 million dollar company in five years. They almost made $25 million within two years, the greater part of which was spent in development. Intel tripled its initial goal, well within the first five years.

I can also provide a list of some whose projections were too high and who paid the price of hanging in through the lean years. I have mentioned Ray Anderson and the newness of his powdered metallurgy. Ray learned some lessons about pressing on and sticking it out, and he has some definite ideas about the value of forecasts and goals. He and his brother-in-law projected a level of profit too high too soon.

"You know, I drive down the street and I see all of the people coming and going to and from jobs—even those that look as if they don't have jobs, and I am absolutely amazed to think how all these jobs come about. Most of them come about through free enterprise. I'm really shocked it works as well as it does. I'm really surprised there are not more people out of work. It's nothing you could plan, believe me. You couldn't sit down and come up with an equation that would describe it, let alone predict it.

"When you're young it's easy to take risk, so you take it. Business has to grow. It has no choice if it is going to survive. Planning periods like five and ten years were garbage for our company at the beginning, and in a sense they still are in manufacturing if you are a small nondiversified company. A large company can use a planning period like that as a set of markers to help them shuffle the deck when they hit a recession and have the ability to shift emphasis or divest of subsidiaries or divisions. But the minute a small company, especially a new company, hits a recession, everything goes out the window.... If you apply yourself fully you don't need to plan what you can do as an organization because you are working your hardest and achieving maximum results. When you are just starting, you don't really need a plan to tell you when you are achieving maximum results. You know when the machine is squeaking and when it is not, and you know when people are productive and near their peak and when they are squeaking. You find out what's possible in your business environment along the way because you are a totally new factor within it."

Another Anderson, John, also ended up falling short of his predictions, though he was actively using and continues to use formal planning measures within his company. John Anderson thought the ailing beer distributorship he took over would stand on its own two legs and walk a straight upward line much sooner than it did, and so gave the bank projections that showed him turning things around much faster than proved possible.

"I overestimated demand in the area of my distributorship and had to take law work on the side, to work two jobs at the start in order to feed the business until I managed to convince a supplier to let me distribute a second product. I started out with Hamm's. I tried to get a lot of other beers that were selling better at the time, but I couldn't find one that would go with me, so I went with Budweiser."

Though it had yet to dominate the market in California as it had in other areas of the country in the fifties, the addition of Budweiser as a second product finally allowed John to overcome his fixed costs, allowing the company to experience a profit which was used to expand into new territories and even more products. It was not according to John's initial plan, formulated before he had rolled up his sleeves and begun doing business, but it was, just for that reason, all the better planning. John's strategy *evolved* from feedback encountered *as he was doing business*. John kept close tabs on load factors and sales reports and as a result knew exactly what it would take to turn things around.

When it came to predicting their successes, the great majority of the successful entrepreneurs I have spoken with were dismal failures. I have yet to meet an owner-founder who won the preinitiation guessing game. You would generally do better, it would seem, guessing the number of beans in a jar. But of course guessing is not planning. Planning is not a matter of forecasting how many fish you plan to catch or what score you plan to shoot on the links. Anyone familiar with the growth of a new business knows the folly of hypothesizing any future event dependent on forces beneath the surface of the water, such as fluctuations of a market-driven economy.

And here lies the difference between planning-to-do and planning-while-doing. Useful planning should be directly linked to control processes—to feedback reevaluating the accuracy of the premises and assumptions supporting a plan. In a mature organization such planning and control is likely to be centered around elaborate management-information systems. In a new business, planning and control may be centered around a microcomputer, but the most important feedback is more likely to involve whether or not you have *a* client or customer—whether or not you even have *a* product. Feedback is likely to reflect more on the accuracy of your doing than on the accuracy of your planning.

Essentially planning boils down to sensing an opportunity and establishing the means to achieve it. It involves understanding the environment in which one operates, establishing the best way to get to where you want to be. Yes, and planning does involve establishing, to some degree, a mission or purpose, evaluating and deciding on alternatives, even forecasting some measure of progress. As for formalizing the above in a "numberized" plan—a budget— in the early days of an entrepreneurship, aside from aspects of cash-flow management that will be discussed in a separate chapter, formal numberized goals are perhaps the least important aspects of planning—the most irrelevant in making a success.

Over half of the owner-founders I spoke with had no formal goals for their businesses in a formal planning document prior to start-up. Only about a third of these successful entrepreneurs expressed a notably positive attitude toward the concept that goals were a valuable management tool. Some like Joseph Solomon of Vidal Sassoon Hair Products were quite blunt. Joseph has definite ideas about the value of formal planning. He had to come up with a formal business plan after the initiation of Vidal Sassoon Hair Products to convince outside investors of the firm's viability. Later he had to come up with formal planning documents to justify strategic thrusts into new markets. In neither case did Joseph himself need convincing.

"All those numbers were a sham. The numbers the consultants initially came up with were way too conservative. And the numbers we had to come up with, in the form of sales forecasts and all the rest, were a sham. Before we could introduce the 1-2-3 hair product line, doubling sales in two years, we had to convince outsiders again, investors and Wall Street–types. We had computer models with three- and five-year growth plans but they were just numbers constructed to make others believe in something we believed in *before* the numbers were dreamed up. You have to do that sort of thing if you are going to go public or go to the bank or investors for more capital. But I always thought, and still think, that it was just a necessary evil. You don't do it beyond the point of convincing yourself, unless you need outside money. Our strategy didn't work because the numbers looked good. The numbers looked good because the strategy was good. In fact, the numbers didn't live up to the strategy. And the strategy was good because it made sense, more particularly because it made sense for the times. I don't think the numbers helped us sell one product, beyond helping us get the capital to get the product out there. Customers don't buy a product because they think it will sell.

"Nonproduction aspects of planning, those aspects not dealing with inventory and production control, for which sales-report-based forecasts were important, were done for external parties that were not going to be involved in production or sales—that is, in making the company grow. Much of our planning was either for external financing or compliance purposes. I wouldn't have done nearly as much if I hadn't had to please outsiders."

OBJECTIVES THAT WORK: THE IMPORTANCE OF PERSONALIZED GOALS FOR YOUR NEW VENTURE

One prescription for the use of goals in large organizations suggests that organization and individual goals should be harmonized up and down the ladder. Ideally there should not be conflicts between numbers, the ways they are to be achieved and the lives both you and your subordinates want to lead. Entrepreneurs sometimes do go into business for themselves after experiencing what they perceive as counterproductive conflicts in larger organizations. Not surprisingly, for a number of the owner-founders I spoke with, personal goals were far more important than specific numbers at the outset. In fact, for some, numbers and forecasts were only a *means* of describing a path to a personal goal.

Eugene Rosenfeld was the president of a NYSE-listed builder. He left because he was certain he could make far more money doing the same thing without having to deal with the stress of the demands of the company's board and owners. Eugene set a personal goal of making $1 million a year by the end of his fifth year. He worked backward from this goal to figure what it would take as a builder to accomplish this. From this goal he developed a formal business plan with market surveys and sales forecasts, piggybacking on the work he had been doing with his former employer. It was quite a formal plan. It evaluated various geographic locations. He decided to concentrate in Southern California because the numbers were favorable—but also because *he* wanted to live there. The result: Though Eugene set a derived goal of building 200 to 300 homes by the end of his fifth year in order to meet his personal income goals, he was building 2,100 by the end of his seventh. Eugene knew how he wanted to do business, and he had a goal of *personal* reward. He knew what he would have to do to attain this goal. As a result the forecasted numbers were not shadows of reality but rather an expression of what he would have to do to reach a goal that meant something to *him*.

When Stanley R. Rawn, Jr., received an engineering degree from Caltech he already had a plan. Stan set a personal goal of going to work for an oil company but not remaining for more than five years. Those five years were very influential:

"I learned the business while I was at Chevron. I became familiar with oil recovery technology, with the location of property opportunities, both domestically and internationally, and I learned about gaps in the marketplace. It was a five-year paid education, an opportunity to observe and learn the business.

"Right at the end of my five years a friend and now lifelong partner approached me with the opportunity to become a consultant to some investment partnerships he was involved with. We developed a formal business plan, piggybacking on my experience at Chevron. I knew opportunities existed in oil recovery operations; the large oil companies could not afford to efficiently apply themselves to depleted properties. With technically altered drilling operations, making use of steam injection and other technologies, these properties could still be profitably worked by an independent. I knew where the properties were and who to talk to. We started in Kansas with a small office, contracting out work to old-time rig operators. I went to work locating, assessing and overseeing other properties until about ten years later we were able to move into international exploration and development as Pan Ocean Oil Corporation. That was always the goal, both mine personally and the investors'. We wanted to get to the point where we could tackle drilling and pumping new wells ourselves. This was not a numberized goal, though we knew the types of numbers we were talking about to be able to do it—it was a goal involving doing business in a certain manner, though the specific route and business form were not known at the start. We knew where we wanted to be, and we knew of immediate opportunities in the industry. The path was worked out along the way."

The path turned out to lead to Stan's sale of Pan Ocean Oil to Marathon Oil in 1976. As chairman of the firm he next formed, Danville Resources, Stan has continued to be successful in the energy and mineral businesses. His success has forced him to be an investor as well. Piggybacking on his five years at Chevron eventually has even led to ownership of a building on Madison Avenue, though this was never expressed as a goal. . . .

Before Bill Kaufman and his partners, mentioned earlier, got around to talking about what and where they were going to build, they sat down and figured out the *kind* of company they wanted to build.

"The very first goal was to have fun doing business. We had all worked in a large corporation and we knew what we didn't like about it. We wanted to create a management team, and above all we wanted to create an atmosphere where people wanted to work, an atmosphere in which there would not be a big turnover. All of this came before our decisions about the profit goals built into our five-year formal plan. I don't think one of us would have traded the type of company we were building for double the returns, but as it turned out, doing what pleased us was basic to our success."

It is likely that you too will remain more committed to personal goals than to numbers. Personal goals express not only where you want to be but who you are. They tend to shape the organization, not just measure its height and weight. Though most of the owner-founders I talked with did not have formal goals, if you are going to have to develop formal goals they will be far more valuable to the course of the development of your business if they are the outgrowths of more personal objectives. It is not easy to make choices among numbers, particularly when the numbers involve a string of zeroes punctuated by some big maybes. It is easier to make a decision about whether one option or another is more likely to take you closer to where or what you want to be. If your numbers are not linked to personal objectives and personality, they may very well turn out to be useless in the crunch.

REALLY, I JUST WENT OUT AND DID IT . . . REALLY, BELIEVE ME . . .

The most important aspects of planning at any level of business involve what Peter Drucker and others call the "concentration decision"—the sensing of opportunity, the deciding what to do and how best to do it. There is a great deal of agreement and common sense behind the conclusion of management writers that by far the most important determinant of survival and subsequent success is the venture or product *choice*. In this area one must plan and plan well—whether one's plans are based on numbers or dreams.

Yet the first thing most entrepreneurs will try to get you to believe, perhaps they even believe it themselves, is that they started their businesses wholly off-the-cuff—that they did not plan at all. We and they seem to value creativity that is perceived as appearing out of nowhere. $E=Mc^2$ didn't come as pure inspiration. Even Einstein had to concentrate.

Creativity does not occur in a vacuum. New ideas are the result of old ideas. Synthesis results from a thesis and an antithesis. All creativity involves some copying. Alternatives are considered and tried and rejected in part or whole until what's left appears to be something new.

"There wasn't much planning. There wasn't much to it. We simply went out and did it." I tended to hear a lot of that.

But when you start hearing that from an entrepreneur, quickly ask a few questions and you'll learn some of the reasons one business turned out to be a better choice than another, even if it's claimed to have been no choice at all.

So change the tack. Forget the word planning, which most owner-founders dislike, priding themselves on being doers. Ask them why they thought it would work. Ask them about their product, why they decided to go into this particular business, why they *like* the business, how and what they had learned about the business before start-up. And ask them why they decided to go into business at all. You are likely to find out more than a little thought goes along with the doing.

Like many of his forefathers, Merritt Sher ended up an entrepreneur. Merritt's great grandfather was an immigrant who started out selling cigars on a street corner in New Jersey and ended up with a small cigar factory. Merritt's father and uncles were all attorneys. His father went into the commercial development business in Southern California and was very successful. Merritt could have gone to work for him when he graduated from law school at Hastings in San Francisco, where he had gone to get a little further away from the family, but he didn't. He started at the bottom with someone else, going to work for a fast-food restaurant chain in turmoil as an in-house attorney, negotiating deals on new locations. It introduced Merritt to the business and was a great education. But the firm was deep in the fryer and too long under the heat lamps. It went into bankruptcy six months after Merritt left to start his own company in the Bay Area.

At first Merritt's business just involved brokering, doing numerous deals for Sizzler Restaurants, but he also ran into smaller ventures, some still in their first locations—stereo stores, record stores, furniture stores, sporting-goods stores, the sort about to burst on the scene to provide a lifestyle to the two-member and new-income family. Merritt also represented a number of midsized chains looking to expand within or into the Bay Area.

Early on something struck him. Merritt was running around looking for situations for these tenants, with an ideal location in mind. An ideal location meant traffic, ease of shopping, synergism with neighboring retailers. At the time, at the end of the sixties, there weren't many options. There were a very few scattered malls and department-store complexes. There were neighborhood shopping centers—mom-and-pop shopping centers with a supermarket, a laundromat and a Chinese restaurant. There was also the option of a free-standing building, but it didn't work for most of his clients.

To Merritt, the ideal location for a stereo store was next to a record store. The ideal location for a restaurant was very near the record store and the stereo store, where someone might stop to eat after browsing or buying, where they might have a cup of coffee or stop to think things over. And there had to be parking and comfortable walkways, easier and quicker access and better rates than in the malls. "I could see that the people who were driving two miles to buy their records, then another three miles to the restaurant, then another mile to the stereo store and so on were running out of time—after all, these were working couples that I was envisioning as customers—customers with disposable income. I was also imagining some of the other things they were going to be doing in the coming years. They would be buying houses, they would need furniture, wallpaper, decor, plants. Why shouldn't they be able to shop in one place but avoid the malls? Many of my tenants were high-promotional tenants, tenants who advertised and discounted long before entire department stores took to discounting. My clients promoted to establish an identity that helped sell products. Their goal was to build a chain of stores, but they weren't big enough to stand out in high profile from the competition in a mall. Yet they couldn't quite make it free-standing either. Besides, I already had a strong belief that they would do better next to selected neighbor tenants than if they were on their own.

"The solution seemed pretty simple. Build centers that

combined all of these tenants, often near malls, tastefully designed and constructed to reflect the tenants' and customers' visions.

"Then I had to start convincing others I wasn't a lunatic. Every time I found a prospective partner I had to explain it to someone who was content to do things the old way. Most of the tenants were enthusiastic, though many of them took some convincing too. I would get them to stage promotions, contests, in order to get the addresses of customers and inform them about their drawing radius. I would pitch how I could change that.

"The first few centers were tough. The banks were just coming off a licking in real estate and they were funding about 60 percent on our type of development. We had to sink everything into each project and sell it almost before the cement had set. There were some pretty tight squeezes in there, trying to get enough out of one project to get the next under way. We had to live with some marginal deals to establish our reputation."

As Merritt built his first centers, he continued with his promotions and analysis. It was clear it worked. Together, the tenants drew much better than on their own. Merritt can show numbers that allow him to use the word synergy without pulling it out of a book. But the important point is that it was the understanding of the key dynamics of his business that led to the numbers. Numbers do not breed numbers. Understanding, combined with action, breeds success, which is verified by numbers.

Even with the numbers, some of Merritt's clients still weren't convinced. Some people don't trust numbers, even when they are results, not predictions. Well, Merritt just had to prove it to them by further doing—if they didn't believe him after he had proved it then he put them into business. He bought into their businesses and gave them free rent. He built out their spaces and gave a few money to buy inventory. He helped propel Le Petite Boulangerie from a few stores to a sale to a Fortune 500 corporation and nationwide expansion. He became the owner of a chain of record stores, part owner of a number of other sprouting chains.

"It turned out to be the right idea for the time. The centers allowed new businesses to expand much more quickly than they could have on their own, moving into existing free-standing space in less than desirable locations. I put together a center with a major tenant, like Oshman's or Big-5 Sporting Goods, Pacific Stereo, Toys 'R Us, Cost Plus Imports, eventually Mervyn's, the Gap and others, and the smaller tenants fed off them. By the end of the seventies people were coming to me to ask about the concept, from Southern California and eventually from all over the country. I taught a course about it at Berkeley, though I myself wasn't much of a student. Most business truths are pretty simple, even if dealt with in a long-winded way by academics. I was usually too impatient. Anyway, now you can't go into a developing area without seeing the sort of center we pioneered at Terranomics."

THE SECRET: A MAGNIFYING GLASS, NOT A CRYSTAL BALL

Terranomics had its financials too. They were required. In most cases you couldn't get a loan on a center until you had projected costs and rental income over five- and ten-year periods. Which meant some of the fingerling businesses Merritt was signing up as tenants had to be taught to plan—well, at least to *act* like businesses.

"Some of the guys who were starting record and stereo stores and furniture stores and the rest, the sort of businesses I was having to turn to to fill up the centers at the start—during a recession, as a matter of fact, before I could afford to rely on established nationwide tenants to come to me to want to get into our centers—well, some of them appeared to have learned most of their business in the underground economy if at all. You asked a guy like that how many records he was going to sell and he was likely to take off his headphones only long enough to yell "millions," then hurry back to his bopping. I put a vice president from an established record chain into business and a year later he just flaked out. I did business with another fellow once who also disappeared, not just from a business but from his *family*. I had to give a lot of first-time entrepreneurs help in putting things into a more proper order. I was all but showing some of these guys how to tie a tie on the way to the bank.

"One of things I learned early on was that the guy who was going to make it did sometimes plan a little better than the others. At least his cash flow. More, the guy who made it from scratch just plain put more into it. He was the guy who came up with an angle that would generate cash flow. He was the guy who generally understood how business worked and understood how to apply that general knowledge. He made sure he knew what the competition was charging. He went over there himself and found out. He or she knew what was selling and not just at his or her store. The ones who made it knew what would sell, knew more about their customers than their suppliers did and let their suppliers know so they could get what they needed. They not only knew *what* was going to sell; more important they knew *why* it was going to sell.

"The successful businessmen I have dealt with have been very sensitive to demand. They have known what people were likely to buy the next year. They were always thinking about it. That's a lot of what we did and still do. What's doing well, what's not . . . how are other things changing. Retailers and developers sometimes take a bad rap. People think they have a one-track mind: sell, sell, sell. But at the same time we were developing those first shopping centers we were constantly talking about what was going on in the rest of the nation and world. We had some pretty good debates. I can't separate some of the consideration that went into those debates from our success. We talked nearly as much about trends as we did specific numbers of deals. Our business, after all, depended on the national economy, and the economy depended on politics—not just domestic politics. That's the way the world works. Our country is a free-market economy, despite what some think, despite real encroachments in certain sectors. At the level of retail, where I deal, demographics are next to godliness. The businesses that rocketed in the seventies catered to the Baby Boom, and those customers are continuing to change as consumers. We couldn't wait to read about it in the magazines. You have to be sensitive to the public spirit, the public will in the political sense, to gauge broad trends and consumer patterns. You have to be more sensitive to the public spirit and will than to numbers extrapolated to describe immediate economic trends, important as they may be.

"That's the sort of planning I depend on. When we sit down to try to come up with the best mix for a center, now that we are free to deal for the most part with proven, reputable and reliable clients, we talk it out. We look at the numbers but we also focus on factors you can't describe so easily. It's not really intuition, it's a belief in an idea that incrementally develops along the way as a result of trying to satisfy your customers and your customer's customers— in my case, satisfying the needs of the businesses I bring together in a center. It only comes across as intuition when so many others don't at first share the idea. Intuition is just the ability to stick with what appears to be a sensible idea. Intuition isn't whim. The idea's the same, before and after the bandwagon, though I've got to tell you, it is extremely satisfying to turn out to have been right. . . ."

Another retailer, Howard Morrow, who might have done well to meet up with Merritt Sher back then, said his decision to go into the particular form of nut business he chose hinged on a number of considerations.

"I knew I could sell nuts. I had seen others in my family do it in conjunction with other products in stores. All I really did was modernize the business. I could look all around me and see the franchise concept being used. I also

thought the key would be in specializing, in just selling a
selection of products, nuts and candies, by themselves
rather than nuts and candies in a larger store. Now everyone specializes. I'm not sure exactly why I thought it would
turn out that way. Specializing, to me, meant quality, and
I suspected it would mean quality in the customer's mind as
well. I knew buying patterns were shifting toward quality,
I could see it in my generation and the one just behind
me . . ."

When asked about the planning that went into the two
strategic moves that catapulted Vidal Sassoon Hair Products to sales in the hundreds of millions from a first year
of $3,000, Joseph Solomon is as definite as he is about the
value of forecasts.

"It wasn't really planning. We knew the opportunity was
there. The sales force and productive organization were in
place. We were too busy to think about it. We were very
lucky. The strategy was bound to the time, and I don't think
we could have done it again, not with the same dramatic
growth with the same products. The time was right. The
public was ready for the do-it-yourselfer concept. People
everywhere, with all kinds of products, liked the idea that
they could bring the beauty salon into their homes. And
they were keyed into the designer name. They especially
liked the thought that they could bring Vidal Sassoon's
salon into their homes, with all its connotations of wealth
and fame. We were well aware of these trends, and I was
convinced the product would sell once we got it to market.
Other than this, there was really no planning or preparation prior to the move."

No preparation? But what about the thought that goes
into sensing such an opportunity? Break down Joseph Solomon's concentration decision and you have another example of a clear and adaptive understanding of the key dynamics in an industry—a key awareness of not only present but
future demand characteristics, including a keen awareness
of demographics. These are, after all, the core ingredients
of sound planning. Numbers mean nothing if the fundamen-

tal understanding of the business and its environment is not
sound.

So you get the picture. The aspects of planning that appear to be most important to the early days of entrepreneurships have to do with the quality of thought that goes into
the concentration decision—the decision to do one thing
rather than another, and in one way rather than another.
This planning must come first. It is probably more responsible for the fate of the business than any other decision an
entrepreneur can or will make. Quality thought and consideration, at this point, is invaluable. Aside from the sort of
entrepreneur who comes up with a dream product or innovation, the vast majority have to wedge their way into an
economy through better service, quality, price, methods of
doing business and most important, by a better understanding of the business—which is what is meant when it is said
they simply have to do business better than the next guy.
And doing business better than the next guy usually ends
up meaning knowing the other guy's business—and often
knowing the industry top to bottom. That is why so many
entrepreneurs go into business in a field they have learned
working for others.

All right. So far I've suggested that the most important
planning you will do will involve the thought that goes into
your concentration decision, not the numberized fictions
you will most likely be required to manufacture for potential investors, lenders, etc. I have also suggested that when
it comes to goals one is better off having them simple and
personal.

THE BEST-LAID PLANS AND OTHER SLAM DUNKS

Other stories indicated some further key aspects of planning important to the owner-founder of a newly initiated
firm that could turn out to be capable of continuing to assist
a company to survive and grow.

Fred Charette was born both a planner *and* a doer. By his own admission, he is probably more a planner than many planners. Fred has more than once had a hard time hiring planners and controllers, he claims, for the very reason that candidates are often just not detail-conscious enough for him. Without a doubt Fred planned his business more than any other entrepreneur I have ever met. But wait until you hear not only *what* Fred's product ended up being, but *how* it ended up being the source of Systonetics' survival and success.

While a student at Caltech in the sixties Fred Charette took every business course offered. He minored in economics. He could have and almost did opt for going to the Harvard Business School instead of pursuing his Ph.D. in a technical field. But even then Fred was planning. He figured a technical degree would be more valuable to him when he'd be ready to start a business.

For a year and a half between receiving his B.S. and M.S., as well as during summers as a student, Fred worked for North American Rockwell. They gave him a fellowship to complete his graduate studies, hoping to encourage him to sign on after he received his doctorate. While at Rockwell Fred found himself coming up with new ideas and products but not benefiting from them. He found it frustrating to hatch an innovation only to see it taken away and turned into a producing idea by someone else—and to see his idea adding to someone else's coffers. He worked at the Jet Propulsion Laboratory for a while as a student too, and found himself constantly thinking about going into business on his own. Three or four years before he completed his doctorate Fred began to think up more specific ideas for a company. Any company. Just get me out of here. . . .

"I would say I thought through somewhere between fifty and a hundred companies as a student. Totally thought them through. Product, organization, growth, personnel, financing. The works. About two years before I graduated I became even more serious. I read everything I could find on planning and running a company. As a student I was reading two to three books a week outside my technical field, almost exclusively business-related. After starting the company I continued to read thirty to forty journals a week at night and while on planes. I still read voraciously today, and I really believe I would have been in deep pucky many times during the course of building the company if I hadn't kept informed and taken the business courses.

"I had one false start as a student. I put together a tech-oriented company with a founding team primarily made up of other students, but it fell apart almost at conception as a result of differences within the team.

"I came up with the specific idea for Systonetics one night while sitting in my office at Caltech talking with an associate who became my partner. His specialty was programming. Mine was systems engineering. We sat up that night and worked the whole company through, including coming up with the specific goal of going public within five years. We were still students, you have to remember, waiting to receive our diplomas. But we weren't just talking. We officially founded Systonetics eight months after leaving Caltech.

"We prepared a very formal business plan for venture capitalists. It was specifically spelled out that half of the business would be in software products development and half would be in systems engineering. The plan included prospective budgets for the first five years, pro formas describing cash flow, return on investment, profit, etc. I would say for the time it was about as formal as you would want to get. When I was at Rockwell there used to be something called 'unk-unks,' or unknowable unknowables. It is very hard to plan for unknowable unknowables. And all it takes is one to throw a new company out of orbit.

"We were capitalized with $200,000, $140,000 of which came from venture capitalists. But the venture capital money always just trickled in and had to be pried away from them."

I've mentioned what happened when the venture capitalist reneged on a second funding and Fred had to take the next step beyond blood and sweat to keep his firm alive, but here's what happened to Fred's business plan a few months after the company was founded.

"We had five employees at the start. I was the oldest, at 32. The others ranged in age from 26 up. Everybody in the company, except our secretary, had a masters or better. Two had Ph.D.'s. We all worked very well together. We grew to ten by the third year. The crisis with the funding was in the second year. But that was nothing compared to what happened the month we started the company. Almost within days of receiving our commitment from the venture capitalist, based on our formal business plan, including the discussion of products in the systems engineering sector, the greatest recession since the depression started. All government systems engineering monies dried up. Three months after we officially founded the company, from the great height of my used desk chair in front of a desk I had built by putting a door across a couple of sawhorses, I had to throw the entire business plan into the wastebasket.

"We threw out everything and gambled on one specific software product that seemed to be the most innovative, a tool for planning, of all things, that could be sold to larger high-tech firms and government contractors, allowing them to track program and product development. I had to take over all marketing and push this one product very quickly or we would have gone under before we had even really got our feet wet. We had one sale the first year while the product was still under development. We had five sales the second year, ten sales the third year when we went public ahead of schedule and thirty sales the fourth year. These were decent-sized five-figure contracts each. I worked fourteen hours a day, seven days a week for the first two years. I took my first day off the third year. I don't think I had planned for that."

All those years of thought and planning—after a detailed formal business plan and enough calculations to please a planner with a habit for the hypothetical—and in the end, having to toss it all out. One might conclude this is a strong argument for taking the planning process lightly. It is not. The formality and elegance of Fred's plans might have lost something at the bottom of a wastebasket, but the *thought* that accompanied his planning was not wasted. What if Fred had not decided to concentrate in two areas to begin with? What if Fred's plan had not included *alternatives,* allowing him to adapt within a changing environment; what if they had chosen to concentrate only in systems engineering to begin with?

Which brings us to another important aspect of planning for entrepreneurs during the early days of their firms: adaptability and the preparation for it.

The most important thought or planning that will go into your business will be the choice of product or service you will choose to deliver. But second most important, intimately wrapped up in the first, may well be the alternatives and back-up options you consider—the "what ifs." The what-ifs are really just an expression of how well you have thought the business through. They involve the most important dynamics, inputs or outputs affecting your business, and they need not necessarily involve brass-tacks forecasting. Brass-tacks forecasting can be dealt with by brass-tacks adjustments in production, marketing and organizational practices. Most entrepreneurial firms react very quickly to those sorts of changes in the environment. But the type of change likely to sweep you up or off the floor often involves broader shifts in an environment. The entrepreneur who best understands the general workings and influences within his court, and best anticipates and reacts to them, is most likely to survive.

TWO OPEN EARS CAN BE VISIONARY

Sorry about the mixed metaphor, but I'm trying to highlight the news that you don't have to be clairvoyant to cover the what-ifs of entrepreneurial planning.

Michael Bobrow was a director at an architectural firm

and on-track to be the top man as the sixties came to an end. But wanting to control his own destiny, he decided he wanted to break off and start his own firm. How did he plan his new company?

"I simultaneously started off on my own and became involved in a program called Project Enterprise at UCLA. It was a program designed to hook up successful entrepreneurs as mentors with individuals just starting out. The goal was to come up with a business plan. During this planning process I went through two firms that didn't work out before I was able to found my present firm. We've got about 120 employees now."

Like some of the other successful entrepreneurs I have mentioned, Michael Bobrow centered his formal planning around personal goals.

"The plan I came up with was very formal, but it was primarily formally designed around the life style I wanted to live. There was a five-year financial plan, but to me the most important parts of the planning involved the more general goals we formulated as a means of describing what I thought would be important concerns of the business. The five-year-number goals were surpassed in the second year. These goals were conservative, expressing what we expected but also what we thought we could get by with— what would support the business. More important, we formally established priorities to guide *how* we would do business. The first goal was to focus on collecting clients. A secondary goal, after we had achieved a sufficient client list to keep us alive month to month, was to concentrate on diversifying the types of clients and building we were doing as opposed to strictly building the business in terms of raw sales. Though it was a bit scary at first, the first goal was attained fairly easily. The second goal was much tougher because we tended to find a niche in a certain type of building that we became known for. But it was and is an important goal that has taken much longer to achieve. It's a goal we're still working at. I still believe it is the key to long-term success and survival. Diversity is not something that should be left to conglomerates. There are lots of smaller ways to diversify within any concentration strategy."

Michael Bobrow relied on the assistance of a mentor program while formulating his business plan and initiating his business. As his business survived and continued to grow he did not drop this effort to augment his own intuition and reading of market trends.

"After receiving the input of my mentor and the program at UCLA, at which I now myself have served as a mentor, I put together a formal advisory board made up of respected experts, architects and others, and they gave and continue to give me very helpful suggestions along the way about how my business should be run, about directions and strategies I might consider. We still keenly listen to what they have to say about the marketplace and trends.

"But some things you can't plan for," he says happily. "My fourth hired employee became my wife. We now take turns being chief executive. In 1979 some legislation was passed that brought about a great acceleration in the construction of health-care facilities, a market niche we had established. We doubled the size of our office space and took on a significant number of new employees."

Michael Bobrow and his wife, Julia Thomas, of Bobrow-Thomas Associates were not the only entrepreneurs I spoke with who made specific mention of the value of consulting with others outside their firm for valuable input about the environment they were doing business in.

As mentioned, most of the successful entrepreneurs I spoke with started businesses that piggybacked on knowledge gained working for others. Men like Jim Collins, who start off in entirely different fields and build very large organizations, are the exception. But something about how Jim went about it still argues the importance of early care in exploring a business. By training as an architect, Jim took one look at the McDonald brothers' hamburger stand in San Bernadino and could see it was a terrific idea. But he also knew enough to know he didn't know straight up about how to run such a business. So he went to work for a man in Long Beach who was already working off the concept. He saw the customers come and go. He dealt with deliveries and suppliers and established contacts. He saw what worked and what didn't. He saw the type of employee that worked in such a business, and he got some ideas about how they should be managed, both for their good and the good of his business. He also saw that such a business could work in a geographical location not too different from the area in which he would be operating.

Jim planned his business while he was doing it. First, he made a commitment. He acted and reacted and thereby created a business capable of survival and growth. Jim left his other job to learn his new one. He stepped out. He had no choice except to make adjustments, to continue to plan, because he was in business for himself the moment he took up his father-in-law's suggestion. He acted as he planned, and learned in the process.

After Jim had built up a string of stands he was approached by a white-bearded gentleman from the South with a penchant for crisping chickens. It was 1963. On the basis of a two-and-one-half page contract, Jim's company became the West Coast franchising agent for Colonel Sanders. Jim had to reorganize the company to sell and supply franchises. Along the way, he ended up buying back many of the franchises he sold.

Before he signed on with the Colonel, Jim went to talk to some people who were doing the same thing in Chicago. And for over a decade Jim has received advice from *competitors*. He meets regularly with a group of owner-founders and presidents, with a formal council that sometimes brings in a management consultant to talk to them. And across the table from Jim often sits Carl Karcher, owner-founder of Carl Jr.'s chain of fast-food hamburger restaurants. They trade few secrets about special blends of herbs and spices, but they do talk over common problems they face as an industry.

"The most important thing I had to learn at the start, and when I set up the company in '63, was the concept of the business I was going to be entering. That part of the business I wanted to know inside-out—how the business *worked*. Who bought and why, and how the product or service was best delivered. I had no formal plans or numbers to tell me how I was doing. My only goal when I started was to open one stand and make a bunch of money, though I now know I never would have been truly satisfied with one or a few stands.

"I thought I knew the right way and the wrong way to do it from what I had seen. I copied a concept someone else had developed, but I also did my best to understand *what* I was copying. That's why I went to work for someone else first. I understood why the McDonald brothers and others were doing it right, and I tried to develop my own methods of enhancing the concept. You can have all the numbers in the world, but if you don't understand how a business works you'll be lost. And if you don't continue to stay abreast, if you don't continue to work to understand your business and industry as they grow and change, you're no better off than at the start."

In 1962 a group of businessmen in the area of Ninth and Los Angeles streets in downtown Los Angeles near the garment district came to Leonard Weil. They had some ideas about investing in a bank but they had no credibility in the banking community. Leonard agreed to leave the safety of his position with another bank to become a founding partner, shepherd and president of the bank, walking it through the intense planning requirements of government regulators. There were packages of financial data, personnel background and the intended organization and activity of the proposed bank. There were fairly rigorous regulations to assure that a bank will survive, as we know, but not all do. Of prime importance was the concentration decision made by the bank that resulted from a rigorous process of elimination conducted by the founding partners. The decision was to focus on commercial lending. That was the key to Mitsui Manufacturers Bank's present success, not the formal goals of reaching $50 million in assets with 1 percent of assets-profit ratio within five years, which were hugely surpassed.

And once the bank was founded, consultation and participation did not stop. Sophisticated planning and reporting systems don't guarantee against bad decisions. Entrepreneurs are typically described as autocratic megalomaniacs quick to shoot from the hip and operate seat-of-the-pants. But I did not find this to be the case for many of the more successful entrepreneurs I spoke with. Many showed a keen awareness of the value of soliciting different opinions, of hearing what customers, advisory boards *and* employees had to say. When a company is small, this, of course, is easier to do. Like some of the others I spoke with, Leonard Weil set up a formal mechanism for insuring that various opinions would be gathered before he made decisions.

"From the start we had formal weekly management meetings and monthly meetings of the entire staff. We made a point of designing the meetings as problem-identification and solution sessions. We wanted individuals to stand up and voice problems and we wanted to hear what others had to say about them. We worked in an open-office environment, and the meetings were just an extension of this."

At Intel a similar policy was carried even one step further. A research and product development–oriented organization, Intel was designed with a formal matrix/project structure from the outset. To counteract the problems that tend to arise when information and authority are not channeled up and down hard, not-to-be-crossed lines within an organization, Intel developed a system of coordinating councils. When I talked to Gordon the system had evolved to encompass ninety of these councils, through which, among other things, information was gathered and input was solicited as part of the decision-making processes.

The message seems clear. The most important aspects of planning for the prospective or newly initiated entrepreneurship start with questions of what and how, not how much or how many. The more options considered, the more alternatives thought through, barring the odd instance of trouble-free demand, the more likely the owner-founder is to be better prepared for managing the business. Don't spend too much time worrying about spreadsheets predicting hypothetical performance. Do them, sure, but don't worship them or get too dependent on them.

Do be concerned with what and how you are going to perform. In a later chapter I will cite stories testifying to the importance of strong control once you're under way—stronger control than is usually prescribed for owner-founders of new ventures. Control and the sort of feedback mechanisms that also serve the planning process are certainly something to be concerned about, but at the outset concentrate on understanding the concept of your business, about understanding your industry and your competitors and most of all your customers. A vast majority of the owner-founders I talked to either formally or informally polled or talked to customers before starting their businesses. Make some calls. Be a customer yourself. Think like a customer. As Peter Drucker suggests, find out about your customer's customers. Watch them as if they were different animals, as if you were an anthropologist or sociologist. Try to think about them objectively but also try to identify with them. How do they think? How do they feel? What moves them? What do they now show a preference for, and why? Answers to these questions are basic. So you missed the Baby Boom's consumer-jolt of the seventies. But what will the Baby Boomers do with gray hair? How will they differ in life style, with fewer children, from the families they grew up in? You don't have to invent products, technologies or services—these will be invented anyway. You can combine and/or augment technologies. You can help others understand a technology. You can supply a high-technology company's low-technology needs. There are businesses that *dust* computers. Once at Caltech, having a look at a gravity-wave detector, a series of lasers transversely trained throughout a warehouse meant to prove Einstein's theory of relativity by detecting the slightest pulse in the universe,

I peered closely at some rubber washers cushioning one of the laser targets from less ethereal vibrations and saw that they were nothing but squashed rubber cars bought at a five and dime. . . .

As Ralph Crump said to me, "Ideas are cheap. I could sit here right now, without being especially creative, and come up with two or three ideas that would work for anyone's particular background if they wanted and needed to be an entrepreneur, if they were willing to follow through and figure out what it would take to make the idea work."

Believe me, if you are more intimately familiar with the ins and outs of your business plan than the psychology, needs and wants and potential *future* needs and wants of your customers, you're starting your business with a blindfold.

Chapter FIVE

Entrepreneurial Employees:
To Have or Have Not?

By now everyone has heard about the importance of entrepreneurship in American business. All of a sudden we are all being asked to become more entrepreneurial. Our competitiveness has suffered. Our economic survival is at stake. We have supposedly grown soft since the Second World War. It's time for everyone to rev up the engines and begin working 110 percent again!

So far this call for a reinjection of the ways of the entrepreneur has centered around the notion that we need more risk-taking and innovating in our economy. To continue to be competitive we need to work more daringly and creatively. We need to come up with better ideas within our struggling corporations. We shouldn't just sit back and accept things the way they are. We should stink the place up a bit. Moreover our corporations should create environments for us to make waves in. What we need are entrepreneurial employees!

Let me be more precise about the sort of animal I'm talking about. Though many I will discuss are indeed daring and creative, mostly I'm talking here about the employee one often finds working in an entrepreneurship—who often goes to work for an owner-founder during the early days of a new business—a species that will have a good deal to say about whether your company turns out to be one of the fittest that survives.

But also don't tune out if you are a manager in a large corporation. Some of my talks with successful entre-

99

preneurs reflect the realities of managing creative and daring employees in larger firms as well. Many times the sort of employee who goes to work for a new or small firm has either lost, not yet developed or will never develop a taste for working in the corporate world as currently structured. Some are the sort of employee enlightened larger corporations are now, at last, doing their best to live with.

Of course, I don't pretend to believe one can cast a broad net and categorize the sort of person who goes to work for a new venture during its early days. Many, maybe even most, of these employees hardly differ from their cousins working for Big Blue—perhaps even for certain more efficiently organized encampments of Big Red, White and Blue. Most meaningfully to a manager, owner-founder or not, there are many types of employees—at least as many as there are clichés describing the types. But for the sake of describing a large part of the experience of each of the owner-founders I spoke with, I'll risk a few more clichés about types of employees.

Employees are often permitted, even encouraged, as much by circumstance as design, to be more themselves in a small firm. Which leads a certain sort of person to work for a small new firm. An owner-founder can benefit from the characteristics of such employees. And later as the firm grows the quality that was positive during the founding days can become a negative to the owner-founder looking to further growth. Whatever, there are few areas of management as important to an entrepreneur's survival and success as the early relationship with founding employees—as well as the ability to *transcend* this early relationship at a later stage of growth.

GETTING MORE THAN YOU PAY FOR

No question the most frequent cause of the entrepreneurial employee and owner-founder getting together is the scarcity of cash. Which means that what one gets is at least in part a labor of love, in part someone relatively inexperienced willing to work all sorts of hours to *learn*. The result is you get way more than you pay for.

Paul Griffin of Griffin Homes was raised in the home-building business. Both his father and grandfather were builders. But both were "passive" entrepreneurs, as Paul chooses to describe them. They never made an effort to expand their building activities into an organization.

"I worked for my father as a boy and I always knew I would be going into the business. I studied engineering at UCLA and was in an ROTC program that included some management courses before starting my own firm, so I had a pretty good idea from the get-go that I wanted to build a larger business if I could. There wasn't much planning. My motto was bigger is better. I just wanted to build the business.

"At the start, I couldn't afford to use head-hunters and other personnel recruitment services to attract proven professionals. I hired inexperienced people with brains, young people who were intelligent but hadn't worked in the industry. I gave them an opportunity to learn the business for less than the going rate. It was a totally 'can do' atmosphere. I tripled the size of my father's business in my first year. I was working about fifty hours a week but I didn't take a vacation for the first five years. I had one person helping in construction management, one with records and finance and one in sales. I started the business during an extremely favorable time, in 1960; our biggest problem was figuring out how to mass-produce the product. We could sell them as fast as we built them. The people I had working for me were workers and doers. I would meet with them in the morning and they would take care of business the rest of the day while I trouble-shot. I was giving unskilled people a chance and that was enough for them. It was a situation of real teamwork. I worked extremely closely with them, and was extremely close *to* them. There wasn't much that went wrong that I couldn't blame on myself. If we had problems I would sit down and talk with them and we would straighten things out right then and there. We had fifty employees by 1963, but we were not exactly a professional organization.

"There's a four-year cycle in the housing and construction industry. Now I know enough to see them coming and plan for them. At the start when things turned down I would lay people off and start doing everything myself. It took me three cycles to figure out I should be keeping the people on during the downturn so that we could go out and bring in new business—so that we would have a professional organization poised to quickly take advantage of more favorable circumstances when things turned around. At the start, I didn't know enough to go about things the way we do now.

"The funny thing is, of those three first employees, although they all stayed with the company ten to twelve years and were great employees and people, none could handle the more professional larger organization. Two left because they didn't like the idea of a new level of management inserted between myself and them. Another was promoted and given an ownership position, but it turned out he couldn't delegate and really didn't like the people-demands that were being put on him. We went from a scratch start to $90 million in sales and five levels of organization. I had to buy the third original employee out and help set him up in business for himself. We're still best friends, but he just wasn't suited to a more formal organization."

I heard the same story from many others. Someone just wasn't "a hundred million sort of guy." "She left when she found she didn't like working under a general manager. . . ." "Things haven't been as good for him, now that we don't see as much of each other. . . ." Though many unskilled or slightly skilled employees do often stay with a company from its inception on, early employees often have a harder time than the owner-founder in making the transition to a professional, growth-minded organization.

Sometimes it is a matter of competence. Sometimes it's attitude. Warren Dennis of Casablanca Fans hired a good number of what he described as "ex-hippie sixties-types" because of their craftsmanship and desire to work on a quality product. But as the company grew many of them developed attitude problems because of lingering prejudice against big companies. Of the employees Warren tried to promote into management in the more formal company almost none made it.

"Most of them became lost, they couldn't or wouldn't handle the change to a more structured environment."

UNCLE MERRITT WANTS A FEW CHEAP SMART KIDS

Merritt Sher of the Terranomics Group has developed a fairly accurate characterization of what many budding owner-founders are looking for in an employee—in any event what they usually end up with when starting out:

"What you want is good young cheap smart kids—don't try, you'll never get an acronym out of it. But it's that simple. You can't afford to hire professionals. And you don't want anybody who doesn't follow through. There are people who aren't aggressive enough, and there are those who're too aggressive. At the start you're willing to put up with the too-aggressive so long as they understand and tend to share your ideas and vision. You can't make it at all with those who are not aggressive enough.

"Ideally you would hire people past their twenties. Generally they are reasonably mature at that point and have made some life changes. Their expectations are more realistic and stable. They might be married and have a family and be more settled. They've experienced the word *no* outside the home. In a word, rejection. They've been bruised and they know how to get up and get on with their lives. When you hire someone right out of school they're going to want the job to change with them every year or two, both in scope and reward, and sometimes it's hard to keep up.

"But at the start the sort of more mature employee you could afford to hire would not be enough of a go-getter so

you're forced to deal with the ups and downs and changes
of the younger, cheaper but intelligent and ambitious first-
timer."

I have previously suggested that entrepreneurs are often
individuals who themselves have heard the word "no," have
experienced rejection and know something about compromise and sacrificing pride to the larger goal. At the start
they are forced to hire young men and women who have yet
to learn such lessons. Merritt Sher has what appears to be
one of the all-time good-cheap-smart stories.

"I was managing a friend's political campaign out of my
office in the financial district of San Francisco in the mid-
seventies just as I was getting my first project under way.
My friend was running for a directorship of the Bay Area
Rapid Transit District, not a highly political office but a fun
local race I was involved in as a hobby. I put an ad in the
paper for campaign workers and was surprised by the mob
that showed up at the door. Most of them were willing to
work for nothing. It was like being descended on by a band
of gypsies. One of the guys who was living in a Volkswagen
van turned out to be the heir to a sizable fortune. He was
taking calls about disbursements from the family foundation. Another guy started at $25 a week, though I boosted
him to $50 a week at the end of the first week, mostly out
of guilt. He was putting his body and soul into it because he
wasn't busy and didn't want to go to work in a regular job.

"Well, it's a little like that Mark Twain story, about how
Twain purports to have been visiting the gold fields of California as a young journalist and how he went to work for a
fellow with a gold mine for nothing just to prove his worth.
He worked so well and hard for nothing that it got so he was
such a good deal that the mine owner couldn't afford to let
him go. He ended up offering him the mine to keep him.

"After the campaign I offered this guy a job, if not the
store. He was smart and dedicated and a really hard worker.
A Swiss boy, honest almost to a fault. Get this, only a year
or so earlier he had been personally studying with Herbert
Marcuse, Angela Davis's mentor, the fellow the French stu-

dents placarded all over Paris in 1968 along with Mao Tse-tung. Don't ask me how we ended up developing commercial shopping centers together, but we did. With just a part-time broker and a secretary and a part-time bookkeeper and this young-smart-cheap kid we developed from the weeds up and sold two centers in less than two years at a time when hardly anyone was finding it possible to get a building up.

"This kid didn't wear ties. He wore the same blue corduroy Levi's shirt as a sports coat every day. He had an untrimmed beard. Well, in a way that was traditional for the development business—old-time land owners we purchased land from, contractors and subs, small businessmen opening up their first storefronts—they aren't pin-striped-suit types either. But this employee of mine didn't wear ties when we were on the twenty-eighth floor of the Transamerica or Bank of America building either, when we were dealing with top management people. He never used an umbrella, he had a war-surplus poncho that wasn't exactly 'in' on the streets that year, what with the Patty Hearst–thing and the rest of what was going down during the time. Just to break the ice I used to have to make jokes about how they would have to be careful or he'd sneak up on them on the crepe soles of his desert boots.

"But after they had done business with him for a very short while they didn't care. He was *sharp*. He was also honest and polite and careful. You could put him in a meeting with a litigation attorney who had been featured in *Time* magazine the week before, or one of the most aggressive attorneys out of West Los Angeles, the sort they keep on a leash until it's time to negotiate, and he wasn't impressed. He would just sit there with his understanding of what was and wasn't a fair deal and say no to them. It was as if he was personally insulted by the fact that someone would be trying to take advantage of us. He understood things pretty well, he had a natural sense of business and what was and wasn't a deal, and he had a knack for smelling crooks.

"The downside was he wasn't too good at compromising,

and compromising is business. As a matter of fact he was *horrible* at compromising. He hadn't learned to battle hard and let bygones be bygones, you know, to at least pretend to be civil in order to continue doing business. You could feel the hair rising on his back whenever he was forced to live with something he didn't think was right. And if there was some slight change in world politics"—Merritt laughed—"we would end up talking about it for hours.

"But I developed and sold my first two centers with his strong help. Two years before he had been reading some of the most arcane writings on Western civilization, and let me tell you, he was one hell of a contract administrator as a result. He monitored our loan agreements, purchase and sale contracts, leases and dealings with tenants. He stayed on top of things very well, and he worried until things were right. In many ways the perfect young-cheap-smart kid. He could give his all negotiating a contract or legal dispute worth millions of dollars, and he was being paid $800 a month and sleeping on the floor in a small apartment—at least at the start.

"But there's a problem with such kids. It's nearly impossible to make the transition with them. How are you going to provide the environment they can mature in, considering that well over half of that maturing is going to involve matters that have nothing to do with their work lives? This guy turned down my offer to double his salary, which would have had him making $30,000 a year in 1976 at the age of twenty-four, plus deferred-ownership incentives that would bring him a guaranteed $100,000 cash in five years . . . to live in a bread truck and pick apples and write poetry in the state of Washington.

"We're good friends now, and he's in business for himself and admits to his immaturity at the time. Those were pre-yuppie times. Now you have the opposite situation, when every young guy who has taken a few business courses expects to make at least $30,000 on his first job. What you sometimes give up when you take on someone who is so keyed into the corporate world from the start is that edge that makes an employee entrepreneurial. The corporate

world is only now beginning to figure it out. We entrepreneurs have known this for a long time, and that's why
we often find ourselves in the position of hiring employees
who may not be in and of the corporate mold. A lot of
entrepreneurs themselves are either not keyed into, or no
longer want to be keyed into, a particular corporation. So
we understand these sorts of employees. We also suffer
them.

"Now that I can afford to I hire older, more experienced
and settled professionals for key positions, but I'm still
looking for a guy who wants out of a situation and is willing to take an ownership position in lieu of part of his compensation—a guy willing to work to determine his own
rewards . . . But I've got to admit, every now and then I like
to bring in a good cheap smart kid to keep everybody honest.
Besides, they remind me of myself."

MARITAL BLISS, PEACEFUL CO-EXISTENCE AND OTHER LESSER STATES OF EMPLOYMENT

The key word to describe the relationship between the entrepreneur and his first employees is *personal.* In some
cases, as I learned, the relationship can become *very* personal. As I mentioned, Michael Bobrow and his fourth employee became husband and wife and co-chief executives.
For a good many other owner-founders, experiences with
some of their early employees added to some of their most
vivid memories, both good and bad, from the early days of
their firms.

Warren Dennis describes his first employees at Casablanca Fans as having been his friends as much as his employees. They spent whole days together. They ate lunch
together. Warren had built the first ten fans himself, and
most of his first subordinates were also involved in the production process. One of his first employees built the next 100
fans. His fifth employee, a young man in his late twenties,
built the next 1,000.

"He was the kind of guy you just wanted to do things for,"

Warren says. "He was just an all-around nice guy. He was divorced and had a child and would do whatever he had to do to make ends meet. He never complained or let anything get in the way of his work. It took some convincing, but I finally talked him into going back to school, knowing it would mean he would leave Casablanca. Eventually he became an optometrist, and the last I heard he was doing very well."

Warren had another employee, a young woman who had dropped out of school when she was sixteen to have a baby. "She came to work on the assembly line, but I could tell she had savvy so I offered her a job in the office. Her child had one crossed eye, and a doctor wanted to do an operation. She was wary of the whole thing but was afraid to ask questions. She came to me for advice and I offered to go to the doctor with her. It was sort of like the United Nations . . . she'd vaguely express concern, I would translate it into a pretty demanding question for the doctor, who would give me an answer I tried to interpret for her. The operation happened and, thank God, was a great success. The woman has moved out of the area and remarried and is doing just great now."

Warren worked side-by-side with his first employees. Two of the first ten he hired are still with the company. One young woman he hired within the first few years is now purchasing manager for the company.

"It was very rewarding to help employees at the start, to help better the person's life. I got a lot of satisfaction from this but I also had a few lessons to learn. There was an awkward period for me—I was about 29—when I had to stop being one of the guys and start being management. People who had been my buddies, especially the ones who had been there from the start, began to take advantage of our history —that we used to work so closely together. They began coming late and loafing. I had to take each one aside and have a long chat with him, pointing out that they were now senior employees and needed to set an example for the others, describing a problem I thought *they* could help me with. What I was especially doing was saying, subtly, I hoped, that things had changed. I was having to make the transition from being a doer to being a delegator.

"It worked out with most of them. It didn't hurt that we paid about 20 percent above the going rate and were as selective as we could be in hiring. We were looking for motivated employees, and we did everything we could, considering the nature of the work, to contribute to that motivation. We had a regular policy of profit-sharing that involved bonuses distributed four times a year and amounting to an extra two months' salary. We wanted people who would take pride in their work and the product and company, and for the most part this worked out."

(I will have more about what many owner-founders had to say about problems and their solutions in the transition from doing to delegating. It would be nice if the only problem an entrepreneur had to face involved establishing authority with for the most part productive employees. Truth to tell, when starting from scratch many owner-founders are forced to become personally involved in the lives of their employees with considerably less than positive results.)

Warren Dennis, along with many of the entrepreneurs I met, considers the worst kind of employee the one with a bad work attitude. "One guy early on had one of the hugest chips on his shoulder I've ever met up with. We did a lot of polishing of parts, and he had been hired as a buffer. We wanted people with pride in themselves because that usually went with pride in their work. This guy, though, just couldn't understand why he wasn't playing shortstop for the Yankees. He thought the work was beneath him. A prima donna. One day he walked out in the middle of his shift and then came back. It seemed he had just called OSHA to complain about our production line. OSHA arrived shortly thereafter and went over the entire plant from corner to corner and congratulated us on being in full compliance. I called the guy over and told him we were in total compliance and that the job still had to be done and if he wanted it, it was his. If he didn't, well, he knew where the sun shined. The guy walked over to his station, picked up a part, buffed it, set it down, turned around and walked out. We never saw or heard of him again. I stopped looking for his name in the box scores a long time ago."

Leo Imperiali of Tile World actually closed down half the stores in his chain because he was fed up with certain employees. "There was a stretch toward the end of the seventies and start of the eighties when we were having a very hard time with theft, drinking and drugs. I don't know what it was. We were hiring the same way we always had but the young people coming to work for us were very confused about life and living it, I thought, in a very unhealthy and unproductive way. It was the worst period during the company's history. I just didn't want to deal with it anymore. It took me a year or two and some much more positive experiences with employees to convince me to expand again. So far we are having a lot better luck attracting young employees with better attitudes, and we've been trying to screen a little better too."

Ray Anderson figures his worst experience with bad attitude was an early employee who insisted on scheduling his own breaks. What came to the surface was that he was breaking machinery so that he could get a breather while it was being fixed.

Early on, the best entrepreneurs tried to do something about work problems. Ralph Crump of Frigitronics says he was a "real social worker" the first few years. "At the start if an employee otherwise performed and was important to the operation I put up with a lot of extra-work personal problems. I dealt with medical, marital, social problems— you name it. A young woman had a miscarriage at work and I took her to the hospital, stayed with her and paid her bill. I had one employee who drank and I sometimes had to drive out to his house and pull him out of bed and sober him up. It got so bad that I wouldn't pay him on the same day as the others just so I knew he would get some of the money home to his family. Now I put up with a lot less of that even though I'm isolated from it. I've learned there are certain things you just can't help some people with. To assume you can help is presumptuous. I've stopped asking questions that involve personal, psychological problems . . . like 'Why weren't you here?'

"An exception involved one of my first managers, an engineer I had promoted up through the ranks. He had stock options about to expire and I knew he wouldn't exercise them because of his religion: He and particularly his wife were members of a fundamentalist church that didn't believe in profiting from anything except their own labor. His wife thought the notion of stocks and her family making money from them was *evil.* I tried to take him aside and explain it to him but I was having no luck. I went out to the house and talked to his wife, saying that no one had worked harder with his own hands and mind than her husband to make Frigi work, but she seemed to think I was the devil incarnate. I finally all but tied him down with an attorney and the paperwork to make him see how he was about to throw away a very sizable chunk of money, money that was *his,* stock I had given him because I couldn't pay him what he was worth—yet here he was about to throw it right out the window. I *made* him sign, and his wife never talked to me again. . . . And you know what"—Ralph smiles and shakes his head—"the son of a gun ended up using the money to go into business for himself."

What you first notice when you enter the reception room at the corporate headquarters of Frigitronics, an NYSE corporation with sales of $125 million, are not the fancy PR materials, though the company has a very attractive annual report. You notice the plaques and trophies—softball, bowling and other sports; plaques and trophies honoring the accomplishments of *employees.* There's a genuine feeling of family in these halls.

While we were talking a little later in the day Ralph glanced out his open door and through his secretary's office. He jumped up from his seat as he saw one of his employees walk by and gave chase.

"Have you quit smoking yet?" he called out down the hall. The answer came back, "No, not yet," and he told him he'd better and so forth.

Returning to his desk, Ralph qualified his new attitude

toward not involving himself in his employees' lives. "That's one social work I haven't given up. I'm on a campaign to make every employee in the company quit smoking. Used to smoke myself. There's nothing worse than a reformed sinner. . . ."

Jim Collins got very close to many of his first young employees as he was building a chain of hamburger stands. He learned some lessons that served him well as he made the transition to being a franchiser and supplier of other fast-food restaurants.

"I was like a father figure to many of them. I wouldn't let them continue to work if their grades suffered. I came to know many of their parents. Most of them turned out to be real good kids. Most were fun to work with. My first assistant manager was a fifty-year-old Christian Scientist. He stayed with me fifteen years, moving up to become first a stand manager and then my operations manager. But every Saturday night at five, just about the busiest hour of the week for us, he would leave to go to services. I used to rib him about it but I kept him and worked around him. For the most part it was a string of positive experiences. I made one woman manager of our second stand. She stayed with me until she tragically developed cancer. Twelve of my early employees stayed with the hamburger part of the business for ten years. The only real problem I had was with a couple who drank, and I would use the job, threatening to fire them, to keep them in line.

"Early on I learned the vital importance of enthusiasm. I worked hard alongside them and led by example. Enthusiasm motivates. Even after I was up to three stands I continued to work one day a week in each stand, *under* the manager, to monitor and control but also to keep up the enthusiasm."

STRAIGHT FROM THE BOSSKI—PEOPLE LIKE TO WORK

Even when the owner-founder sets out to establish an objective, professional environment from day one there is still going to be close social interchange in a small firm, if only because of the few bodies involved. An owner-founder in any size organization probably has a limit to just how many people he can talk to in a day. But at the start of a company that limit often includes the entire organization, top to bottom. Such interchange influences overall morale. The boss is around. You see him. Moreover you see him working and there are few doubts about who is working the hardest. He's there when you arrive and he's there when you leave. Besides that, it's his neck on the line. It's his personal and sometimes singular success that fills out your paycheck.

The pace of activity in a new firm can become extremely exhilarating. The word "teamwork" is a byword. The word "family" actually applies.

Karl Marx, whatever one may think of his ideology, made an observation early on that's worth noting—that man is essentially a productive species, a being who produces his particular nature or life as he produces his means of living. Man's nature, he said, dictates that he find the best form of organization as a means of productively functioning alongside his fellows. There's considerable difference of opinion, needless to say, about what makes for the "best" organization of productive activities, but Marx had something when he talked about man being a working animal. People really do derive more fulfillment from work than from play. Especially when that work is productive. As most of us know, some of our more rewarding moments in life come while exerting ourselves, while stretching our limits alongside fellow men and women doing the same toward a common purpose. It is perhaps the true potential and beauty of a successful marriage and family. And it is certainly one of the great satisfactions that comes to both the owner-founder and employee during the building of a new company—a level of activity and excitement older and larger firms often gracelessly attempt by way of hype and mechanical motivational tactics.

In addition to the satisfaction that comes with being productive under duress (generating a type of comradery that flourishes in war-time environments as well), there is also, as mentioned, the enriching and bonding mentor relationship that often forms between owner-founders and some founding employees.

Fred Charette claims one of the most rewarding relationships of his life was with a fellow he promoted through the ranks to vice president of operations, eventually to vice president of marketing.

"I felt like a successful parent. I was able to watch him grow, taking on challenge after challenge and always giving 110 percent. We never openly shared our feelings about things or socialized, and yet it was a very close and satisfying relationship. He left to become president of a firm. I know he will do well wherever he goes, and I am proud that he learned a lot of his business with us."

PRIMA DONNAS—AND OTHERS
WHO WORK FOR MORE THAN A SONG

While owner-founders may have fond memories of those who struggled through the early days with them, often the most productive members of an entrepreneurial team are not always the easiest to live with. Witness Fred Charette's comments about some problems that developed with an early founding programmer at Systonetics.

"At the start, it was more like a forced march than a business. I worked seven days a week, fourteen hours a day. It wasn't unusual to see everyone there at ten in the evening. I led and exhorted more than managed the first employees. It was as if I was driving everyone toward the Promised Land. Everybody was already busting their rears because of their extremely high self-motivation, but we still had to do better. Survival, because of the nature of some of the obstacles we faced, was nip and tuck. I had to fire my first employee after three months. I had to fire my first founding team member within the first year because he couldn't handle the job we needed him to do. It was extremely traumatic. And there was an ongoing conflict with my initial partner, the programmer, who was an absolute genius at product development but who by nature fought sophistication in any shape or form.

"Even when we were working on sawhorse desks, even when I was doing everything myself, cleaning the coffee area, sweeping the floors—I didn't ask anybody to do anything that I wasn't willing to do—even then, to the outside world I made a point of projecting a thoroughly professional organization. If our customers didn't come right to our office, they always assumed we were a large established professional organization because of the way we conducted ourselves. I knew how important that was to the business.

"I admit I helped create the monster by catering to my tech partner at the start, but he was so crucial to product viability. He was absolutely crucial and brilliant and highly creative, but he had a *massive* ego. He didn't understand or want to understand the overall challenges of building a business. He expected that the world would adapt to him. He was on a different wave length, he expected not only the world but reality to adapt to his perceptions. But he always gave his all and the company wouldn't have made it without him. He was fantastic at solving problems, even if it took an entire team to clean up after him, to refine his solutions. He wanted to keep things small and unsophisticated, and it was a constant source of conflict at the beginning. Things became easier for us both when I promoted a team member to vice president of operations. While I was out selling on the road he pretty much ran things and served as a buffer between the tech partner and myself. The tech partner ended up staying on for nine years, then went into business for himself as a consultant, which allowed him to work entirely on his own terms. . . ."

Roy Ash had had his run-ins with a few scientists while still at Hughes. Science may be, as some claim, the twentieth century's art form, but it has spawned a whole new breed of super egos. Take any child and encourage him to fix his energies in one direction, leaving not as much time for the socializations by which we all acquire the bumps and bruises and confidence that will help us get through life, and you are likely to end up with someone with a certain idea of the *right* way, if not the right way to communicate it, on the tip of the tongue. Often the sort of person who excels at difficult disciplines has excelled for some time. He or she is accustomed to high grades and being accepted at elite schools, at winning and having things his or her way within a narrow realm of expertise.

Many corporate managers like to brag about the fact that they don't tolerate prima donnas, that no one is irreplaceable (though of late a new tune is beginning to be sung in the corporate halls—Do it your way, just do it better than the competition . . .). But it's also true that if the prima donna's expertise results in an important innovation, a manager also tends to learn to tolerate the mercurial and demanding behavior, especially during the early days of an entrepreneurship.

After founding Litton Industries Roy Ash also found himself with buildings full of scientists. As Roy Ash and Tex Thornton continued with their strategy, evaluating and acquiring small government defense contractors constrained by the profit limits then put on them by the government, Litton's ranks of scientists grew. From the start Roy and Tex sensed there were "unlimited possibilities" in following their strategy as long as they had sense enough not to meddle too much in the affairs of the researchers.

"When we bought Litton we bought 280 employees. I set up a headquarters, personally hiring all the headquarters people. I hired controllers, accountants and attorneys. At headquarters we spent a good deal of our time monitoring the work of employees through financial reports. We gave them a checkbook and a budget and set them loose. Duties were not spelled out for researchers the way they were for people in headquarters. These were, we felt, entrepreneurial types. So we managed by exception. As long as progress was being made, everything was fine. We agreed on a general direction, and after that I would meet informally with them, maybe twice a month to hear how things were going.

"There were tremendous opportunities for doing interesting work and for making money. We made twenty men millionaires in our first few years. If someone didn't find that enough incentive to stay on track, they were quickly let go. We didn't tolerate the type who couldn't stay productive under those circumstances. But of those who remained productive, well, we had to tolerate all sorts of things.

"I had a particularly hard time with one extremely brilliant person who couldn't understand why the world was behind him. He was a visionary. In the fifties when they were still making computers on entire floors of buildings, we took him to a computer company conference and he just walked in and started high-handedly talking to the scientists and executives about how backward this roomful of computers was and how it wouldn't be long until it would be sitting in a little box on a desk. They almost threw him out the window. He used to disappear for a week at a time, and if you had to find him to talk about something you had to take your shoes off. It usually turned out he was just walking up and down the beach, thinking.

"We kept him, sure, but it wasn't easy. He did very well for the company but he wanted to do things his way, and at his level. In most companies you succeed by being able to deal on the company's level. If you're a researcher you still have to understand corporate matters and politics and you have to be able to translate your work for others. With this particular researcher we had to call on a translator. He just couldn't get along with people the way he could with ideas. What I finally did was interject an entrepreneurial manager with stock-incentives between the researcher and headquarters. This manager could better deal with the researcher's eccentricities and keep him on track. He had incentive and could better deal with the negative side so that we could have the advantage of the positive side without being driven crazy.

"I would say in general that scientists tend to be spirited horses that have to be managed with loose reins. And that is the way we wanted it. We wanted group leaders thinking about their projects and nothing else. We didn't want them worrying about accounting or patent issues. That's why we quickly hired a full professional staff of controllers and attorneys. The only thing close to meddling that we did was reserve the right to hire managers one level below the group leaders reporting to headquarters. I felt this was necessary to assure that we were all thinking along the same lines. The prime reason for doing this was to reduce organizational politicking and keep the scientists doing science. We didn't want anyone to think the grass was greener anywhere else, so we offered tremendous financial incentives and degrees of independence. We didn't always understand what the scientists were doing, but it was fairly easy to understand whether or not they were applying themselves to their fullest abilities. We decided, unless an individual really went around the bend, to clear out the problems that could get in their way, stand back and let them go."

HE WAS THE BEST OF EMPLOYEES, HE WAS THE WORST OF EMPLOYEES

Each of the owner-founders I spoke with was asked two specific questions about their early employees: What was your best experience with an early employee, and what was your worst experience with an early employee? For one entrepreneur his answers involved the same employee.

When the entrepreneur started his company he brought along a top manager who had worked under him at their previous place of employment. The entrepreneur matched his subordinate's salary and gave him stock in the company, though the entrepreneur himself drew far less than his previous salary from the fledgling company. At first there were just three employees—the entrepreneur, the man he had brought along and a secretary. The first year or so was spent in product development.

"We were working six to six-and-a-half days a week, ten to twelve hours a day. Our product development phase involved a great deal of work on a computer and both of us were self-taught. You didn't just go out and hire programmers in those days. The skill didn't exist in great numbers outside research institutes and large research-oriented companies. . . . There were tremendous satisfactions that came with acquiring the skill together, working side-by-side and helping each other along the way.

"Those first couple of years were very exhilarating. We were working very efficiently. We added a few more employees, I think we had six at the time, and rented an office across the street. Most of us were still concentrating on product development. To keep costs down we didn't even rent a phone in the other office. We had a system of two differently colored vases. We would put one in the window if there was a phone message for someone, another if a meeting was being called. Paul Revere stuff. We were getting great amounts of work out of a very few people. Morale was very high. There was tremendous team spirit. People were shouting down the halls when a problem was solved or a new customer was signed on. It was an awful lot of fun. There was a tremendous sense of accomplishment each day. No one felt they were working for money. It was more like a family than a business, and I now know part of the problem that developed probably came from these early days when bonds formed that later got in the way of more organized management decisions.

"Within a couple more years we were up to twenty-five employees, and the manager I'd brought with me from my former employer was made a vice-president. By the time the company was seven years old he had sixty people under him. He was a very bright and creative guy, but he was getting restless, uneasy in a larger company. Part of the problem was mine . . . I was out taking care of customers and delegated too much without having good control of the situation. I had brought him along, the two of us in effect built the company, then all of a sudden I was off dealing with the business of the business. I had moved beyond product development, and he was left behind on his own.

"This guy . . . and it's hardly a knock . . . was the sort who *always* needed new challenges. That's a terrific strength when you're starting a company, you're lucky if you find people like that for key positions. But eventually you hit a stage when you're taking on more and more customers with one particular product and it's time to settle down some and service them. You can't just start and then move on and expect to keep customers. But this vice-president wanted to take on a new product direction. He got bored by routine, started to look for distractions both at work and in his life whenever it seemed that things were settling. I can't say I'm all that different, but you've got to discipline yourself when distractions go counter to the best interests of the company you've work so hard to build.

"Finally he convinced me to take on a project neither of us knew anything about. It involved hiring someone familiar with the product, someone older than both the vice-president and me. I don't know whether the age thing had anything to do with it, but what happened was that neither of us really knew what the guy was doing. The project went nowhere. I should have fired the guy after three or four months but because it was the vice-president's project he backed it up, even though he didn't know what was going on. I should have let him go too. The project lasted two years and we had to hire another guy to come in and sort out the first guy's work, to find out we didn't have anything we could take to market.

"Look, even if you know better, it's hard to let someone go who has worked right alongside you from the start. They think of the company as their company too. After all, you encouraged this at the start. I should have faced up to it. I should have fired him as soon as it was clear he was hurting the company. I guess you have to be willing to do that, just like a regular old corporate manager. But starting your own company means leaving that world behind. It seems you have to relearn some of the old corporate ways when it becomes necessary for survival. I am sure the guys who go on to build Fortune 500 corporations from scratch wouldn't have hesitated to have made the move on the spot. But there are entrepreneurs and entrepreneurs. I still tend to give people the benefit of the doubt, and frankly I like myself better that way."

Undoubtedly, some employees prefer working in small, entrepreneurial environments, because they specifically prefer a personalized work situation. Some seek out the sort of work bonds and satisfactions inherent in entrepreneur-ships, work bonds and satisfactions often restrained in other work environments. The price they are willing to pay is their hard work. From one perspective, perhaps the perspective of some professional managers, a desire for such satisfactions in the workplace lacks maturity or an acceptance of how the world works. Nevertheless, such satisfactions and desires are a fact of entrepreneurial life—both a fact with regard to the desires and motivations of employees, and in some cases a fact with regard to the desires and motivations of more than a few owner-founders, when they first start out. During the course of my conversations, more than a few owner-founders specifically described a personal desire to get away from the politics and back-biting of larger firms.

The irony, of course, is that the satisfactions of start-up working conditions that lead to success and growth can lead to miseries down the line, can evolve into tragic situations for founding employees and owner-founders as well. A good part of the transition I will later discuss that's demanded of owner-founders as their firms grow past survival focuses on changes in the kinds of satisfactions and goals the organization needs to pursue to promote *growth* after the early days.

WHEN THE CHILDREN LEAVE HOME

There are also employees who go to work for small firms to escape the division of labor, the specialization, in larger firms. They don't want to be pigeon-holed. They crave and enjoy the opportunity to have their hands on all the parts of a business. Too many corporations, for them, are like department stores, a different product or department on every floor, and never the floors should meet.

But there's a snare if not a delusion lurking. As the young firm grows and seems to demand more specialization, these early employees are pushed to specialize. They resent having jobs taken away from them. Often more experienced professional managers are brought in as middle managers above or alongside them. It's a little like going to the door to see your parents bringing home a new baby brother—and a baby brother that happens to be older and bigger than you to boot. Full circle: The old employees now find themselves plagued by the same irritants that moved them to seek out a start-up company.

All the entrepreneurs I spoke to had a story about at least one employee who became dissatisfied as the company grew and his or her job became more routine and specialized—an employee who eventually left because the company just wasn't the home it once was.

Regardless of why an employee goes to work for a new firm, one upshot is that at least some can't help but learn about starting a business. Working in a small entrepreneurship is a daily primer on what it takes to start and manage such a firm. Many go on to start companies of their own. As each family teaches, promotes and reproduces its particular ways, entrepreneurships spawn successive generations of entrepreneurs.

NONE OF THE ABOVE AND OTHER PROBLEM CHILDREN

There are also employees who go to work for new ventures for none of the above reasons. Some can't find other work, just stumble into it. Some of the more frustrated, perhaps in the manner of Warren Dennis's frustrated shortstop, come to resent the perceived freedom of the entrepreneur and are likely to develop the kind of attitude problems mentioned above, least tolerable for an owner-founder caught up in building something in a constructive manner.

But in *any* of the above cases, often the result of the employee's motivation in going to work for a small or new venture, the owner-founder does come to be perceived as something of a savior or protector—at the least a dominant figure in the employee's life.

As a result, and not always fairly, owner-founders are frequently criticized for being paternalistic toward employees. My own estimate is that they tend to be drawn into a paternal role by the employees themselves, employees especially attracted to strong, independent personalities that create a sort of father image—especially for those looking for one.

At this point—more later—it's safe to say that many of the problems that develop between early employees and owner-founders do center around acts of rebellion—early employees resenting the fact that they eventually lose the sort of personal relationship they once had with the owner-founder; coming to resent the very personal nature of the relationship; regretting the loss of the satisfactions that came within a smaller company; or deciding they want to strike out on their own in any case.

The good news is my conversations made clear that there are ready means for minimizing at least some of the problems that tend to come up between owner-founders and their first employees. See to it that the employees are entrepreneurial themselves, not allowed to hide under coattails and only vicariously sense the rewards. Push them out in the sunshine, or shadows, sharing the risk along with the

satisfaction of hard work, *providing* they also experience
some of the financial incentives and rewards as well.

BREEDING AN EMPIRE VS. PROTECTING A KINGDOM

One of the clearer findings of my study was that owner-
founders who called on extra-salary incentives, either in
addition to *or* in lieu of a competitive salary, went on to
manage greater growth in a shorter time. Over two-thirds
of the entrepreneurs I spoke with did call on extra-salary
compensation tools.

I've mentioned Roy Ash's use of stock-incentive plans.
Also Warren Dennis's and Casablanca Fans' use of quar-
terly bonuses for production workers. When you pay less
than the market and don't offer other incentives you're
obviously asking for trouble . . . turnovers, morale crises.
Watching you alone benefit from everyone's hard work
wears thin.

Ralph Crump can hardly be described as a bleeding heart
or soft on employee matters. He is decisive and has not been
afraid to let the ax fall, something he perhaps learned as
captain of a ship in the navy. Ralph's method of hiring
marketing representatives is legendary, for both those who
passed and failed the test.

"My general strategy was to hire people who were
smarter than me in a specialty. The engineers I hired were
well checked-out and were highly educated and creden-
tialed individuals."

Ralph did all the initial sales and marketing himself,
delivering products to doctors and standing by as they
tested the equipment. He knew how crucial the position was
so he personally selected and trained all his initial marketing reps himself.

"My interviews with candidates were held very early in
the morning. All they knew was that we were in the medical
instrumentation business and we dealt with ophthalmologists. I would give instructions for a candidate to meet me

on a specific corner at 6:00 A.M. This showed whether they at least could find their way around a city. They would assume we were meeting for breakfast so their stomachs were empty when I then took them directly to an operating room to watch an operation using our equipment—essentially watching a human eye being opened up. If they didn't faint during the course of the operation, I took them to lunch. During lunch I would ask them to write down any new words they had heard that morning, to see whether they had really kept their heads or had just been struggling not to faint. If they had some questions and a pretty good list, then I took them over the next hurdle, taught them how to demonstrate the equipment on a pig's eye. We developed an excellent marketing program as a result."

Ralph was demanding of his employees, but he also made sure that there was incentive to match the demands. When Ralph founded Frigitronics he paid an attorney to go to Washington, D.C., and push through the first registered employee stock-option program in the country after changes made in such programs by the Kennedy administration. Ralph had worked for a small firm that wasn't going anywhere, and he had learned a lesson. The owners had not wanted to share ownership with Ralph, though he was all but running the show. From the start Ralph paid his production workers competitively and gave all his engineers stock in the company in place of a competitive salary. From the start he *insisted* that all key employees own stock in the company.

Similarly Joseph Solomon, at the outset of Vidal Sassoon Hair Products, gave stock to his first employees, shipping and receiving clerks in a small warehouse in Canoga Park, California. Some might suggest that extra-salary incentive-based compensation is not the domain of a small or struggling new entrant, that any examples are exceptions: companies with great growth potential in high-growth environments with reasonable assurance that growth would allow shared rewards. Not so.

I mentioned that Merritt Sher of Terranomics continues

to be on the lookout for entrepreneurial partners. From the start Merritt used ownership positions as a way of hiring others to help on his projects as consultants in lieu of his ability to pay market salaries. Now, though his firm is capable of attracting and compensating proven professionals, Merritt still prefers to use this method of bringing key employees on board—he often first enters into a ownership-share, contract-partnership on a deal or two with a prospective employee to get to know them. Once an employee is on board, Merritt's approach doesn't change. The president of the brokerage division of the Terranomics Group owns 40 percent of the company and shares in the profits generated by his efforts.

When Jim Collins began to have trouble with his fourth hamburger stand that was located a considerable distance from his first three he tried to solve the problem by traveling back and forth between his other operations and the trouble-prone stand. But what made it work was hiring a couple, friends of friends, and cutting a profit-sharing deal with them by which they would keep the *majority* of profits above rent and expenses. The stand turned around and became profitable.

"The situation was unacceptable, running a losing stand. Once it was turned around it hardly bothered me that I had made an arrangement by which I was in fact the junior partner on the stand. Ever since, I've had a policy of sharing the opportunity for success, helping others become entrepreneurs, and it's paid me back many times in return. I helped many people open franchises over the years, and as a result they would come to me to sell out before they would go to the parent corporation. So, in addition to our franchising and supplying operations we've built up a vertically integrated company owning hundreds of franchises. It turned out that helping others realize opportunity was a very profitable strategy for both the company and me personally."

Fact is, it's next to impossible to describe a work situation in a market-driven economy for which incentive-based com-

pensation can't be creatively employed. The trick isn't in
giving up profits or ownership strictly as a means of enhancing benefits. Ownership for key employees should be related
as closely as possible to the *results* of performance. And
there are many ways to do this short of stock options or
profit sharing. . . .

Once Baldemar Rodriguez had built up an investment
portfolio of apartment properties he found himself managing an organization of some fifty maintenance people under
eight foremen. Their chief duties involved painting, repair-
ing and landscaping apartments, preparing them for new
tenants when others moved out. This was already a fairly
professional organization, as the standard in the industry
went. Baldemar's subordinates were provided uniforms.
There were job descriptions and procedure manuals in both
English and Spanish. There was an apprentice system, by
which a maintenance person could progress to being a lead
worker, then a foreman, then a supervisor of foremen. Compensation was based on a survey of the hourly wages being
paid in the area for comparable work. Almost always it was
a better job to have than what many of the individuals
might otherwise find. But that wasn't enough. Rod didn't
mind sweetening the package if the end result was his being
able to hold his employees to higher standards of work reflected in professionally maintained properties that allowed
him to achieve low vacancy rates and the best rental rates
the market allowed. He also wanted to keep his employees
motivated, thinking positively of the company. He bought a
vacation home that employees could sign up for. He bought
sporting event tickets.

He then went about figuring how he could more directly
improve the performance of his maintenance organization.
Rod didn't see profit-sharing as a reasonable incentive for
maintenance personnel. He had already instituted a commission system for apartment managers that tied bonuses
to lowered vacancy rates. For his maintenance personnel he
came up with the next best thing to—some would say a
better incentive than—money: time. Maintenance person-

nel were assigned specific tasks and time allotments for each—based on his doubling the time it would take him to finish a job himself as a motivated owner. Jobs were handed out at the start of each day. If an employee or employee team finished before the end of the day, and the quality of the work was assured by the inspection of foremen and supervisors, the employee or employees were free to take off. They could then work on the side, so long as it didn't interfere with their work for the company, or enjoy their leisure, or go on to the next day's tasks and earn time off that could be taken in the form of long weekends.

The lesson is pretty simple but basic: Whether you're dealing with nuclear physicists or grounds keepers, there's a way to create incentive-based compensation systems. In a small start-up entrepreneurship there's not only a way, there's a great opportunity—after all, there is still no entrenched bureaucracy or mass of employees with conflicting interests complicating introduction of such a program throughout the organization.

Such incentive-based compensation can serve as a ready buffer against some of the problems that crop up between the owner-founder and founding employees. Profit-sharing and ownership-sharing leave little room for excuses when it comes to conflicting or counter-productive work behavior. Activities are either directed toward the goals of the company, or they are not.

When some of the initial exhilaration begins to wear thin, the company is usually beginning to stabilize, which often means it is beginning to be profitable as well after weathering the usual initial storms of cash-flow and so forth. At this point, rising stock prices or bonus checks can go a long way to soothe a nostalgic heart.

Later on, as new employees come on board, after the initial days of exhilaration have long passed, there is a ready means of harmonizing the goals, performances and rewards of the early employees who still carry the founding perspective and the new employee who is apt to have a much more calculating and unsentimental eye. Initial employees who might have professionals hired over them still have their piece of the company and the rewards that will continue to come with shared ownership.

Finally, should founding employees not find it possible to function productively as the company continues to grow, they can cash in their stake in the company they have helped build and take off, even if it's to their own greener pastures—not just skulk out the door but take a chunk of their efforts with them.

A little competition, after all, inside or outside an entrepreneurship never hurt an owner-founder. And who knows when your home-grown entrepreneur might one day down the road combine with you to mutual benefit.

Chapter SIX

The Underrated Importance of Control

So you have an idea. You start a company and hire some aggressive employees willing to brave the seas with you, perhaps in exchange for the opportunity to share in potential profits. If you are still in business after the first year, barring "luck," a variant we have already dispelled, you probably spent and continue to spend a good deal of time and thought on understanding your industry, business, competition and competitors. Formal or not, you have a strategy. You know why a product or service is likely to sell and you know how to go about selling it. Your sales are building. You can expect growth.

Undoubtedly others have begun to sense your opportunity. If you do not possess proprietary technology you either have or soon will have competition—not just competition from other small entrepreneurships but often from some big boy down the block who sees a good thing and believes he's got the marbles and bucks to send you packing with your pockets turned inside-out.

What at this point is going to help assure that you are going to be in business at the end of the second, the third and the fourth year?

First, continued innovation. You might have to come out with a new or improved product just about the time your competition is using their size and economies-of-scale to duplicate your product or service at a lower cost.

Also, though it may not seem an innovation in itself, continuing to focus on the *quality* of your product, delivery or service—in particular focusing on the quality of the customer-related aspects of your business—may be the most immediate and cost-effective innovative approach you can take. It will be appreciated too. Customers and clients are always complaining about a lack of timely, competent service in their business dealings. A continuing emphasis on the quality of product, service and customer relations is the most fundamental level of innovation, especially when one's competitors refuse to address these issues in an aggressive manner. When the chain of command stacks up with more layers than a wedding cake, communication, enthusiasm, discipline and individual initiative often get lost. You've got a chance just on the grounds of not having grown too unwieldly and fat and smug to put out service for customers and clients.

Insistence on quality service and product, and all that it requires in the form of motivation, should indeed be the easiest and cheapest task to accomplish within a young entrepreneurship. It's *small*. There's no squabble about who the captain is. The organization is flat, and there are few if any lieutenants to gum up the works. Politics are not tolerated, let alone allowed to become a way of life. The young entrepreneurship's chief assets are flexibility, adaptability and the speed with which it reacts to changes in the marketplace.

Still, there does come the day when the young entrepreneurship must begin to exert some *control.* The early advantages of being young can become liabilities if a balanced approach to professionalizing control systems within the enterprise isn't given a chance.

It's said that the successful entrepreneurship succeeds because it ignores the awful paper work. Formal control is at a minimum. But a potential consequence of control-to-a-minimum is control below an adequate level.

To *continue* to survive, to continue to innovate in a fashion necessary to compete, you will need a pinch of organization, a pound of leadership and, most important, a conduit of adequate capital and credit. I'll deal with aspects of leadership and organization in later chapters. In this chapter, the focus is on control. Without adequate control, not only of cash flow and credit management, not only of production and delivery but also involving feedback on less "numberizable" (awful word) aspects of the marketplace—on not only the how muchs but the hows and whys—you stand a good chance of becoming an all-too-typical entrepreneur, the sort of entrepreneur who was *once* in business for himself.

To Grow or Not to Grow?— It's Not Really a Question

Each of the entrepreneurs I interviewed was asked an open-ended question toward the end of our conversations: What would you recommend to an entrepreneur just starting out? The results of my poll were not even close. In first place by a well-struck fairway wood, accompanied by a healthy share of heavy emphasis, was a clear warning: Pay particular attention to credit and cash-flow planning during the early years.

Growth was characterized as a matter of survival by many of the entrepreneurs I spoke with. Growth was something that had to be accomplished to recapture the costs of start-up and survival. Though a surprising majority of the entrepreneurs I spoke with expressed a belief that they could have remained smaller and survived, for almost all of them growth was described as a given—growth seemed to be perceived as something that either by necessity or desire naturally unfolded, like a child's growth, out of conception.

Ray Anderson puts the necessity of a new venture's growth this way:

"For a number of reasons you have no choice but to grow. You have to grow to satisfy your customers' growing needs. If your product or service is a good one there will be demand. If you don't meet demand, if you choose to stay in the garage, someone else will satisfy that demand and you will lose customers.

"But you also have to grow to support your organization.

Many like to compare a company to an equilateral triangle, with you the entrepreneur at the top. But it's not just a matter of making the base grow, of being able to hire and compensate more people. As the base grows, as you satisfy demand and find yourself hiring more people, the triangle has to broaden farther up too. You have to provide a future for good people. You want to be able to attract and hire the best you can, and future considerations and opportunities are important to anyone worth hiring into a key position. This isn't, as I say, simply a matter of providing more money. You have to be taking on new challenges as a company to provide new challenges for employees."

Another entrepreneur I spoke with, one who is still struggling through his first few years, put it succinctly:

"There are two kinds of businesses in my industry—established businesses and newcomers. There are no 'tweeners—not for long, anyway. Either you are taking a run at the established businesses and you succeed, becoming established yourself and threatening their position, or you make a run and fail and peter out. There's *no* such thing as making a run and *sort* of succeeding. If you don't continue to compete you wither, unless you're just plain stubborn and manage to wedge your way in as a mom-and-pop—unless you are the cockroach-type of entrepreneur who is just going to hang in there and scrape and pick up the crumbs from a very narrow crack. Most people aren't that tough—or crazy enough to want to fight it out for nothing. If the company grows, life should become better and easier. That's why you go into business for yourself, to work hard but to gain something for it."

So if you don't fancy yourself heading back to some personnel officer or headhunter with your pockets emptied, and if you aren't the type cut out for dodging the regular attack of your exterminator-competitors from a narrow crevice in your industry's wall, you are simply going to have to grow. Often you are going to have to take on growth with capital demands *far greater* than those it took to start your business.

A specific area I focused on during my study was described as "the first major expansion." My own experience was soon verified by others, that early on there is often a period of dramatic or condensed growth for many entrepreneurships. Often this first period of dynamic growth can make or break the enterprise. Many of the entrepreneurs I spoke with described opportunities within their early years that led to a doubling or tripling of sales, facilities, employees or some other measurement of their organization within a year or two. For most successful entrepreneurs, often within the first five years, almost always within the first ten, there comes a decisive moment—a moment offering the opportunity for drastic expansion. For some this moment appears more as a matter of necessity. But in either case the trials, tribulations and progress made during the course of this first spurt of growth have much to say about just how far and how fast an enterprise continues to grow in later years. If an entrepreneur learns to allow and promote an incremental, balanced efficient professionalization of key aspects of the organization, his company usually continues to grow. If he develops a case of white knuckles trying to hold on to the old ways, it can be a debilitating, shrinking process.

To meet your first major expansion head-on you are going to have to risk more than you risked when you started your business. Now you are for real and you have earned not only the opportunity to move out of the garage but the opportunity to *lose* the garage as well.

Over three-quarters of those I spoke with relied primarily on external financing from either a bank, financial institution, partners or other private investors during the start-up and survival phase of their business. For just under three-quarters, banks or financial institutions, meaning credit lines, continued to be the primary source of capital used for growth subsequent to start-up and survival during the first year or two. Rarely, if ever, can even the most successful budding entrepreneurship live, let alone finance growth, out of cash flow.

An entrepreneur can have an innovative product or innovative approach to customer- and organization-related aspects of management practice, but if he doesn't keep control of the company, even within a very favorable market, he can quickly find himself back working for others—at the very least scratching for new ideas and investors willing to ignore failure.

Too often management "experts" downplay the importance of a young entrepreneurship planting the seeds of sound control during the earliest stages of growth. Too often the emphasis is on growth of sales. Some say an owner-founder shouldn't *worry* about cash flow during the earliest days, rather that he should concentrate on gross growth. Cash flow is bound to be negative early on, and cash flow can only be made positive through sales, sales and more sales.

That's the road to imbalance. The most successful entrepreneurs I spoke with all showed a distinct concern for *financial* control during the earliest days of their firms—a much greater concern than the popular, prevailing wisdom would suggest.

Speed Thrills . . . and Sometimes Kills

And on the other hand . . . sorry about that, but every truth tends to get naked . . . dramatic and dynamic growth can also generate a dilemma. Initiation and survival are exciting; subsequent growth can be exhilarating. Survival, that in-between fight for your life most companies experience for various durations, is as inspiring as it is cash-thin. Now here comes relative gravy, even if the hounds are not far off your heels.

With the proof that you appear to be sticking it out, both to yourself and your customers, comes credibility. Credibility is a spring-board. Sales can double, triple, more. Cash flow appears to be a river, when watched from one bank looking only *upstream*. Morale is no doubt high. Hills and mountains are daily, hourly, scaled. It may seem that by the time you've seen the control-related balances of your replicating growth on paper they are already history. The pace is captivating.

At this point, there is a great temptation to ignore the control-related details of your history, to assume they have little or nothing to do with your getting where you are. As an organization you are going to be tempted to fix your gaze on the speedometer and odometer and shout out how fast you're going and who you've passed. At best, you are going to keep an eye glued on the results of your growth, assuming the other gauges must be doing just fine. However, if you don't glance now and then to the battery, water, oil and gas—well . . . it's a long walk back into town.

The control practices of the typical entrepreneur who is riding for a fall are most often characterized as rule of thumb, informal, reactive, personal and intuitive—quite simply, they are most often characterized as not professional or capable of supporting the sort of growth and activity demanded of a surviving, established firm. He/she delegates little in the area of control—sometimes developing a chronic case of second-degree chin burn from all the looking over the shoulder. Formal, professional control is said to involve modes of thought and action just not up the alley of the innovating, risk-taking sort of son-of-a-gun who strikes out on his own. The typical entrepreneur isn't a natural bean counter, and so forth.

Some entrepreneurs, including a few I spoke with, acknowledged as much. Merritt Sher of the Terranomics Group made no bones, or beans, about it. . . . "I am not a bean counter. But fortunately I have always known just how *lousy* a bean-counter I am. I have a firm understanding of the numbers that make a deal. By now they are burned into me. But from the start I had a hard time keeping a handle on the brute administration and accounting. Within my first year I knew I had to have people working for me that were better at the details than I am. Control is something I don't even like doing, and if you don't like doing something you aren't going to do a good job of it, no matter how hard you try. I think it almost boils down to different sorts of personalities. I made a point early on of making efforts to bring people on board who liked to count beans and dive into the detail. The more capable these people were, the better we did. I could have a great idea for a center, a near-perfect idea, but if we didn't have a handle on the project it could end up looking like a very bad idea. You can make some not so good ideas appear better with good control early on. Ideally you have both, and you keep them checked and in balance."

The focus of the myth of the daring, creative, gambling entrepreneur suggests that owner-founders excel at managing the splash and the dash, not the cash. Those are the entrepreneurs we read about. But, again, most successful entrepreneurs cannot afford to be caricatures. What they lack in sensational profile, by practicing a little solid bean counting, they make up for in the curve of their growth.

Of all the areas of management practice analyzed during the course of my study, control stood out as the most positively correlated with the speed and extent of growth—with an entrepreneur's success. The results were conclusive: The more professional (though not necessarily formal or complicated) the control practices were within an organization (and usually this meant control practices instigated and managed by the owner-founder), the more likely was that organization to go on and up.

Put simply, successful entrepreneurs *do* count beans, in a balanced, contextually appropriate fashion. Moreover most dedicate high priority *and* worry to securing adequate control systems even during the first days of their enterprises. Successful entrepreneurs know the math as well as the marketing. Sometimes they may keep some of it in their heads—which has led to the misconception that entrepreneurs tend to control "intuitively." But we are not talking about internal divining rods. They know the math. Throw some numbers out at a successful entrepreneur sometime. He might not have the most elaborate computer packed between those entrepreneurial ears, but you might be astounded to hear the clarity with which his calculator whirs. The successful entrepreneur knows the key numbers—they are programmed into him, all customized for his business. Some people mistakenly refer to this as a knack for the bottom line. But the bottom line does not appear out of thin air. The bottom line is a sum or product—what separates the successful entrepreneur or entrepreneurial team is a handle on the key inputs and outputs of the business.

In fairness I should qualify these observations. I did not talk with any failed entrepreneurs. I can't say that most entrepreneurs or entrepreneurial teams fail because they fail adequately to gain control of their organizations during the early days. In fact, this probably isn't true. If you do open the tenth croissant shop in Kalamazoo, just as the first nine are folding and industrial America is heading south, provided you don't have some unique innovation or tenacity that marks your venture it won't matter much how well you count what crumbs there might be.

But I am assuming, and will continue to assume, that success is not an isolable phenomenon. Success is a chain of interrelated pluses, a chain of successfully performed key activities and management practices that are as much an integrated way of life as a way of doing business. The activities and approaches uncovered in my conversations are not so much secrets or keys as they are *links*.

Among the successful entrepreneurs I spoke with, I *did* encounter more than one who experienced real problems—sometimes organization life-threatening problems, as a result of inadequate control processes. More often than not control was at the bottom of all of the problems cited by entrepreneurs who had successfully made it through initiation and early survival.

And when comparing even successful entrepreneurs in similar businesses it became even clearer that the entrepreneur who made a conscious point of securing sound control systems during his very first years most often went on to greater and quicker growth with fewer problems. Went on, that is, to be more successful.

SOUND CONTROL: THE PULSE, THE PAPER AND . . . THE PAINT?

With control, as with planning or any other management function, it first needs to be made clear what is the heart of the practice. Again, it is important to distinguish between the pulse and the paper of the management practice—between the formalizations or tools associated with a practice area and the basic reason behind the organizational need.

We all know what paper is worth once it stacks up to be more important than performance. The key to the success of the entrepreneurs I spoke with often centered around a performance-focused measurement and evaluation of the key indicators of their businesses. The successful entrepreneurs did not necessarily have one of each control tool in the book, though it was surprising how many did call on rather sophisticated control tools during the early days of their businesses. But the successful entrepreneurs I spoke with had a penetrating sense of the heart of the matter. For example:

Jim Collins, after he had opened his first hamburger stand, had a pretty good idea about what could hurt and help his business. Lack of demand could hurt his business, but the lines outside were pretty good. Not having enough help when he needed it (operating a not-so-fast food stand), or having too much help when he didn't need it (operating an expensive human bumper-car ride) could definitely threaten survivability—particularly as competitors began to wield spatulas down the street. And theft, spoilage, lack of supplies could all hurt his business, both in the short term and, if mismanagement became chronic, in the final term. But there isn't much room in a hamburger stand for desks and in-boxes or clerks. Jim opted for paint over paper.

"I ran the first stand myself, opening it at 11:00 A.M. and closing it at 1:30 A.M., sometimes later, six days a week. I made the patties, readied the French fries, filled the shake machines, all of it. My employees at the very start were part-time employees. And there is a definite knack to hiring and managing part-timers. Our organization hires over 7,000 of them now. Part-time people have other things in their lives. Most of them are still living at home and going to school. You have their attention for a small fraction of their lives. They are not usually as dependent on the income as a full-time employee.

"You screen the best you can. I got to know most of the kids' parents, establishing a link with the home, hoping some of the values of the home would be kept up on the job. Most of my early employees turned out to be really decent, really good kids. But these are kids. Some of them are still learning what it is to be an employee. They haven't yet realized what it takes to get ahead, and sometimes they try to take shortcuts.

"I developed a system for keeping track of supplies as well as for forecasting demand and scheduling part-time employees. Whenever there was a delivery we would count the buns and pounds of meat and figure out how many burgers we should be able to make. We wrote it right up there on the wall. Register sales were checked daily and broken down by hours. By comparing the two we got a pretty good idea about when anything was going out the back door.

"The same system also allowed me to predict staffing needs. Not only could I look back to see how much we sold at any given hour the prior week, giving me an idea about how many employees I might need on hand for a similar period, but after a while I could look back at months and years to similar days and hours and get quite accurate in my predictions.

"When I expanded to other stands and no longer could keep track of all the walls it was just a matter of making a form and having it filled out by the assistant managers. We kept daily inventory reports and projected needs for purchasing and staff, looking back over the years, months, days and hours. We had monthly profit-and-loss statements for each stand, daily sales and a balance sheet for the whole company almost from the start.

"After I met up with Colonel Sanders and became the

West Coast franchising agent and reorganized to set up a
company to develop, support and supply franchises, I stuck
with the same basic reports. We were growing rapidly then.
I had to set up a real estate division to scout locations and
construct stands. I sold the franchises myself. I hired another guy to set up a team to train the franchises. And I had
another team that would go in and open a stand, serving as
management and staff until I could sell the stand. We were
opening a stand a week at the start. If we hadn't had those
basic, simple but crucial reports on the key indicators we
wouldn't have been able to do it. With these reports we had
a pretty good handle on each stand. We knew how each
stand was performing and progressing and what might be
called for if standards weren't being met.

"Control really hasn't changed that much for our company. We track the same basic inputs for each of our compa-
ny-owned franchises and restaurants now—we use the same
basic reports to track almost half a billion dollars in annual
sales. Both those initial wall writings and the reports that
evolved out of them measured performance. They measured
how successful *each* stand was. No matter how many stands
you have, no matter how complicated or sophisticated the
organization becomes, someone still has to keep track of
what's going in and what's going out, and at what rate. You
can't just look at the larger total numbers at the top. Stands
and their performance have to be held to individual standards, and your control and reporting mechanisms have to
continue to maintain this level of tracking as they evolve.
Control can't be allowed to evolve into abstract measure-
ments of success. Control has to stay *performance*-focused
and to stay focused at the site of that performance."

BUDGET FOR A MINIMUM OF FOUR SYLLABLES

This may all sound fairly simple and commonsensical, but
you would be surprised how many new ventures fail to get
to the heart of their control problems. You can pick up any

number of business-management books that will talk to you about sales forecasts and cash-flow reports and budgets and the rest. Each of these may prove to be helpful, maybe indispensable to your company. But each company is different in product and service. Cash may be cash, but it's also directly related to the particular nature of the particular business. One man's widget is not another's, at least in the particular use it's put to by your customer.

More important than going down a checklist and making sure that your organization has one of every control tool will be figuring just what sound control needs to be for *your* organization—just what the key inputs and outputs are for your enterprise and how most efficiently, with an eye to tomorrow, to track them. To do this it's helpful to understand what sound control is, at bottom, meant to achieve.

The heart of performance-focused control is not one or another specific tool, it's an approach or concept—the cybernetic model. Unfortunately the simplicity of this cybernetic model is often left to more advanced management courses and writings. I suspect it has something to do with the term "cybernetics" striking fear in the hearts of those who shy away from anything with four syllables and a 'y' in it. Fear not. The simplicity and elegance of cybernetic control is betrayed by its moniker.

The cybernetic control loop is based on four very simple and logical steps. These same four steps are found, whether consciously practiced or not, whether efficiently practiced or not, in all living organisms and organizations, from individual cells to individual animals, humans, families, communities, companies, nations, planets.

First, information or feedback is obtained on performance.

Second, this information discloses variances from norms or standards.

Third, variances lead to adjustment of standards or corrective action.

And fourth, or first again, the loop is closed by further

*information or feedback on performance, reflecting on
adjusted standards or corrective action.*

This is how a bacterium maintains equilibrium. It is also
how a small company can keep from being infected and
overwhelmed by the residue of unknown forces or factors.

Most important within the context of a young entrepreneurship, the cybernetic control loop is not just a means
of *maintaining* equilibrium—it is also a means of maintaining the equilibrium of a dynamic, *growing* organization.
Control should not be viewed as some kind of static anchor
that simply lets you know what you have done. Cybernetic
control is supposed to point you not only toward what you
are doing but, as Peter Drucker suggests, what you should
be doing.

It's really important to view control as a loop. Breaks in
it can be as life-threatening to a young concern as they are
bureaucracy-breeding to the large one. A report, budget or
forecast is in itself meaningless if the loop is not continued
and closed with adjustment or correction.

Michael Bobrow promoted a managing architect, something like a general manager, about six years after starting
his firm. Part of this person's task was to improve the control processes within the firm.

"We had incredible formal reports. We got deeply into
computers, keeping track of the hours of our architects and
job charges. This person was an incredible planner and a
great communicator in meetings but did not adequately
follow up with people, so all the sophisticated reporting was
not helping. No correcting and adjusting was taking place."

Control is not simply monitoring. Control is not simply
compiling reports and stacks of papers. Control is not just
a reactive but a *proactive* process—an ongoing process
through which an owner-founder not only monitors but influences the performance of his company. The further monitoring and correcting are separated, the greater are the
chances for each respective function being performed inef-
fectually. The more an owner-founder designs and practices

the monitoring function primarily for investors and the bank, the more an owner-founder corrects with off-the-cuff, sweeping actions as a reaction to not fully understood hotspots and fires *after* they occur, the more likely he is to find himself running in circles—at first small and then slowly growing circles. It's like a baseball player/manager trying to compensate for a gopher-ball pitcher and porous infield by continuing personally to hit home runs.

But even when an owner-founder realizes the importance of sound control there are pitfalls built into the young entrepreneurship's terrain that make sound control a considerable challenge during the first years of his firm. A sales or any other report is virtually worthless as a measurement of performance until there are standards or norms to compare it against. Standards can include goals and objectives established in planning but they become much more meaningful once they consist of realistic markers of past performance—markers against which future performance can be predicted and judged, predictions based on an understanding of what has been done and what is being done—learning through doing that leads to more accurate postulating of what can and should be done.

But of course entrepreneurships often don't have much of a past. Not surprising that entrepreneurs tend to fix on the present. What's happening today! What's happening right now! That's the cry. And so new ventures tend to ignore the past—at best to spin romantic yarns about it. They become so accustomed to change change change that they sometimes even tend to overlook the value of the present as an operating record. New orders are coming in, new machinery and processes are being taken on. Just one new employee can drastically affect both the process *and* the results of the business. An owner-founder can quickly fall under the spell that it's through his own and his company's so far sparkling actions, through sweeping strategies and changes that could never be captured on a report, that his company survives and succeeds.

Cash flow looking bad? Inventory not up to demand? Not

only open palms but clenched fists at the backdoor? Not to worry. Have I got an idea up my sleeve . . . wait till you hear this one . . . this here entrepreneur still knows how to scatter the numbers and turn the accountants on their pointy heads.

In fact this perception may very well be true, either for an entrepreneur or entrepreneurial team. But a tendency to refuse to adequately control or track the process of these so far sparkling actions can lead great men toward great troubles—even terminal ones.

When the business begins to hit a more stable stage, when finer points of the past, present and future must be better understood for the present to be truly tuned and shaken into optimum performance, the bad habits of the early days—relying on sweeping changes and dynamic growth and performance to overcome weaknesses in control—sometimes come back in glaring red sheets to haunt you all in a rush.

To survive, most companies must continue to grow. In order to grow, without creating an awkward and ailing monster careening toward a premature end, the activities of the hands and the feet, the head and the heart, need both to be *understood* and *coordinated*. Often out of a fear of slipping into the bureaucratic stasis he fled in the first place an owner-founder will deliberately avoid taking on issues of control. The typical entrepreneur tends to continue to control through personally shaking things up, by relying on drastic reactions to variances he's stumbled upon. The typical entrepreneur is said to trust his instincts just a bit too long. But please, altogether now, with harmony . . . the ty-pi-cal en-tre-pre-neur ty-pi-cal-ly *fails!*—or, at the very least ends up leaving the company once it struggles to grow past him.

Just as they understood their innovation, just as they understood their business and industry and customers, successful entrepreneurs also appear to understand what the key inputs and outputs are, what their relationships are and how much they need to be monitored for the company to survive and thrive at each successive level of growth. Again, like planning, successful entrepreneurs seem to understand the core of the practice long before they understand or have learned to apply sophisticated management tools associated with the practice within a larger organization. Many of the entrepreneurs I spoke with appeared to derive their own early personalized control tools from a fundamentally sound understanding of what good control is meant to do.

All of which is to say: Successful entrepreneurs do not do it with mirrors—successful entrepreneurs think hard, they work hard and they also worry and keep track hard.

WHICH *SHOULD* COME FIRST: THE CHICKEN, THE EGG OR THE SCALE?

The successful entrepreneurs I spoke with, particularly those who went on to run the largest corporations, didn't wait for the rain to buy an umbrella. They did not all formalize control top-to-bottom from the start, but they did demonstrate a keen awareness of the aspects of their businesses that demanded more formality, as well as those best left for later formalization. And when aspects of control were left for later greater formalization, they still tended to formalize those aspects *before* absolutely required.

For its first decade Casablanca Fans was faced with greater demand than it could supply at each stage of development and after each successive expansion into larger and newer production facilities. There were half a dozen other budding entrepreneurships making fans when Warren Dennis and Burton Burton started out—but they weren't making fans equal in design or quality. Most of them never made it out of the garage. Though Casablanca's only goal was to produce the best fan and shoot for the high end of the market, they soon found themselves—as a result of their commitment to those objectives—offered up a larger and growing wedge of their emerging industry's pie.

Out of a small machine shop, with the switch from custom

fans for restaurants to the production of their first commercial fan in 1975, Casablanca moved into a 10,000-foot facility. The building seemed massive. Warren took one look, uttered a word and heard "cavernous" echoing back at him. At first the entire company parked its cars inside. You could have fielded a couple of baseball teams and had a good game without breaking any windows. Yet by the end of their first year they had already outgrown the building. Warren and Burton were forced to rent a number of closely located buildings, to branch out and divide the manufacturing process. By 1979, before a move to a customized 180,000-square-foot facility in the City of Industry, Casablanca had spread into eight separate buildings within a four-block area.

In 1976 as the company began spreading into the different buildings Warren sensed that greater control was in order. Remember, the company was at this point only about a year old in terms of its commercial production.

"I spent some 40 percent of my time acquiring the proper computer and software and making it all fit together. Then I spent a great deal of time cramming it down everybody's throat. Burton was all for it, but just about everybody else in the company had to be convinced. This was a totally integrated on-line system by 1978. At any moment we could punch in and access the status of orders as well as a list of parts needed to fill orders, projected nine weeks in advance. The nine-week period was dictated by the constraints of the computer, or we would have had it even further.

"The resistance I met with was incredible. I had to run the system parallel to our manual reporting tools for a year, during which time we found only six mistakes—all in the manual system. We called the system 'Monday,' because every Monday we would churn out reports on the status of all orders, inventory, delivery dates and the rest. From the orders and promise date the computer worked backward and spelled out right then and there what had to be ordered and done to meet the promised delivery dates. Every Tuesday morning we would have a meeting and go over the printouts."

Beyond problems involved with control of the logistics of

production and inventory, Casablanca also faced a crucial and continuing concern over quality control.

"Quality control was always a problem area. Not that we weren't shipping the highest quality product on the market, but because we wanted to *continue* to ship the highest quality product on the market. Early on there was always a debate over whether to have quality control under production or separated out. We knew large companies always separated it out, but the question was whether we could afford to set it up like that at the start. Production had a natural tendency to want to meet the demand, to sacrifice quality for numbers. But the minute you ship junk, your image is ruined and it can't be recaptured by simply not shipping junk the next time. It takes years to recapture a lost image of quality. At the start I personally checked the line. As we grew I had someone break down a randomly selected fan each day. Our next step was to hire a full-time purchasing agent who was familiar with quality control processes and who, though not through formal reports, managed to keep standards up by confronting suppliers head-on with unacceptable parts. As soon as we found the right person we moved to a separate quality-control department."

Warren and Burton were not worried about what sales were going to be two years down the line because their biggest problem was meeting existing demand. They intuitively forecasted sales one year ahead, based on past performance. But it wasn't because they thought demand would be never-ending.

"From the start we assumed we were in a fad business that could dry up in ninety days. In a sense this was an assumption in our planning. We never extended ourselves beyond such a time frame or took on more growth than was indicated as necessary in the short-term. It wasn't until about 1978 that we felt we were financially there to stay, regardless of whether the fad died out or not. By then, with the help of the computer, we were set up so that we could react to changes on demand, either to maximize a growing market or to cut losses without much of a lag. We were in a seasonal business. We tended to sell a lot more fans during the summer. With the system in place we could tell more about how the seasons were going. We could gear up and down more gradually.

"Besides helping us prepare to run the business, addressing control early on helped us to prepare to sell the business. The strategy from the start was to build up something we could sell. When we decided to grow in a big way about a year and a half before the move in 1980, we were thinking of what it would mean to the value of the company. We were definitely thinking about selling the company then.

"Without having addressed our control needs before our major expansion in 1980, when we moved to the larger building, we never could have done it without a tremendous increase in staff and a loss in productivity. Because we had a good handle on control before we expanded into the building, we were able to go national, to double our productivity, to go from $20 million to $65 million in sales while only going from 110 to 150 employees. This was a forethought. We knew that getting a handle on control, keeping the company efficient as sales went up, would make the company more attractive. We didn't have to sell low because we were turning over a company we had lost control of to a larger company who thought they could get hold of things and make them work with their big-company methods and manners. We were turning over a lean machine that was probably more efficient and in many ways more productive than some of our suitors. We sold a company that had just been moved into a 180,000-square-foot facility, a company that had just tripled sales in the span of a year or two *and* a company that was running smoothly. It was definitely not a case of a lot of chickens running around with their heads cut off. In effect, we turned over a cash cow when the grass was greenest."

The refrain in the above: Getting a handle on control *before* growth and expansion, not during or after, verged on being a phobia for some of the entrepreneurs I spoke with.

Some refused to grow until they felt secure in their control systems. Of those who didn't, many acknowledged they'd learned their lesson.

Eugene Rosenfeld had worked for a large NYSE builder, and had been promoted all the way up to its president. The last thing Eugene wanted was to have his company grow into the same kind of headache-territory he had previously experienced. If he was going to grow, it was going to be *controlled growth.*

Eugene Rosenfeld is very strong about controlled growth.

"From the start we had formal budgets and cash-flow reports like any large company. But the most important factor in our business is tracking the sales of the homes you have built. Related to this is your overall effort in pricing homes—not only in pricing homes but in deciding what homes you are going to build and where. All of this goes into the planning before a decision to go ahead with a project, but at the same time you have to monitor the decisions you've already made. You have to monitor how well your homes are selling and try to gauge why some are selling better than others so that you can adjust."

Another builder, Paul Griffin, is frank about some early weaknesses in his control mechanisms.

When Paul's company was two years old he went from one to six tracts in a single year. The market was booming. Paul could sell them as fast as he could build them. So things worked out well until the next downturn, when Paul found out just how little control he had over the financial aspects of his business. He claimed to have come close to setting a world record for self-taught accounting once he learned he was actually losing money for a short period. The experience would motivate Paul to bring on a consultant and professional controlling staff, kept on during good or bad times, as the core of his company. He regrets he hadn't known enough to do this from the start.

"When things are going well you don't pay as much attention to efficiency as you should. At the start if things aren't going well it doesn't matter. You may fail, but you haven't invested much. So many who do succeed do it just by having started at the right time. During good times you don't realize the importance of financial control."

Eugene Rosenfeld had the advantage of watching a few upturns and downturns from the helm of someone else's ship. Before he would even consider undertaking his first major expansion, entering three national markets after having built in just one, Eugene first put together a strong central staff of accounting professionals.

"I dipped *deep* into cash flow, far deeper than I would have for any other reason, to bring a full-charge controller on board. I spent a good deal of money putting together a centralized financial staff. That way I could take on entrepreneurial joint-venture partners in other markets and have a way of keeping tabs. Up to that point I had relied on hiring young, ambitious, inexperienced and inexpensive employees and they had worked out. But I wouldn't even think of expanding without having adequate control in place. That's just asking for a nightmare."

Ed Stevens seconds the motion. Before doubling the size of his company through an increased marketing effort, Ed hired a part-time business consultant who had worked for a Big-8 firm. In exchange for stock in Ed's company, the consultant professionalized the control and planning processes, acted as a liaison with the company's outside accounting firm, supervised the preparation of all reports to the company's primary investor, a bank, and introduced formal planning methods to control expansion, including a financial prospectus with goals and budgets.

I'm walking a fine line here. Earlier I've said that successful entrepreneurs tend to formalize *what* they need to formalize *when* they need to formalize it and to save the rest for later. Successful entrepreneurs do tend to allow later formalizations—they do not tend to let nostalgia or a personal attachment to the early days and early ways get in the way of later formalizations. As a matter of fact, as I'll detail later, successful entrepreneurs seemed to be relieved that they had made it through the gate and left the early days behind. It was interesting how many of those I spoke with who had gone on to less growth, or who had disengaged at an earlier stage, tended to have much more to say about the joys of the early struggle. The successful entrepreneur formalizes control practices at least a half-step ahead of the need—doesn't formalize unnecessarily (meaning inefficiently or when one can't afford it) but will sometimes make financial sacrifices to formalize ahead of schedule in order to avoid more expensive problems down the road.

"If you don't have advance control," says Paul Griffin, "and if you don't have trust and confidence in your control systems, sufficient to be able to delegate, you're trapped into personal involvement and monitoring no matter how much you try to delegate. Adequate control frees you to delegate and concentrate on the planning that should go into growth."

I'll have more later to say about problems and solutions regarding delegation and personal stress. Owner-founders are often criticized for not delegating enough. For now it's enough to point out just how dependent delegation is on adequate control systems.

I emphasize control mechanisms and practices for the entrepreneur because too often they're slighted, but they're not intended to be at the expense of entrepreneurial aggressiveness.

Ralph Crump had co-managed a successful manufacturing firm before striking out on his own. He knew the value of strong financial control. Ralph sought out and was introduced to a professional accountant who became an early partner. Frigitronics early on had all the formal financial tracking tools in place. Ralph still relies on a system of formal accounting and other reports as he oversees a geographically dispersed portfolio of companies. Information from earlier years is bound in leather and stacked amid his bookshelves. But Ralph's early emphasis on control, his early move to an accountant-partner, did not stifle the firm's entrepreneurial verve. Ralph's partner did not pull

down the green visor, get out the tweezers and control the
works to death. He in fact did a little entrepreneurial business himself. He was in charge of accounts payable. Really
in charge. He drove around in an old car with a big wad of
cold cash in his pocket and cut favorable deals with suppliers for payment on the spot.

Control does not have to come at the expense of movement. Control is sound when it facilitates and guides,
doesn't impede, the speed of growth.

FOR EVERY CONTROL THERE IS A SEASON

Which is just to say that control should follow or mirror
strategy.

Two of the entrepreneurs I spoke with, both in high-technology ventures that experienced exponential growth, had
quite different emphases and approaches to entrepreneurial
control during the start-up and first year or so of their
companies.

Roy Ash, as mentioned earlier, along with Tex Thornton
devised a strategy for acquiring and building small high-
technology government contractors into a diversified corporation with consumer-product lines in addition to defense
and other government contracting. At the outset they acquired companies with established contracts. The prime objective was to encourage these organizations through research and development monies supplied by the government
to branch out in new directions. Roy Ash wanted to *free*
scientists to discover and invent. He had no idea exactly
what he wanted them to come up with, but to allow them the
freedom Roy had to establish disciplined, centralized financial control from the outset. It wasn't really a question of the
chicken or the egg. Tex was out there negotiating so fast
("One of the most brilliant negotiators I have known," says
Roy), it was more a matter of Roy building up a professional
organization of controllers, lawyers and accountants fast

enough to keep up with him than deciding whether or not to formalize.

"You have to understand how fast we were growing. One hundred and twenty companies in 120 months. A company a month for ten years. At one point the acquisition phase of our strategy was functioning so efficiently that we found out we had a company under us that we didn't even know we had acquired. So many were being integrated into our system that one just slipped in.

"Our entire approach was founded around relatively loose idea control and extremely tight financial control. I spent most of the first days setting up control systems and monitoring the work of employees through financial reports and budgets. We didn't let anything slip by with regard to checkbooks. We hired experienced control people and kept a very close watch on the numbers. As a result it wasn't so necessary to be reading reports on exactly what they were doing. We agreed on general direction and then set them loose. I would meet with a project director or company head maybe twice a month, but it was more a matter of touching base than minutely reviewing the step-by-step progress with research. Program strategy was all oral, and could be so because financial control was extremely formal. If there was any secret to our success, it was that we combined the freedom that came with self-control and incentive on projects with a very disciplined, professional and state-of-the-art approach to financial matters at headquarters. We had an incredible amount of data on products, distribution and program budgets, but we didn't track the people themselves.

"Because we provided such great opportunities for bright researchers to tackle interesting problems, because we made a point of creating incentive we had no problem when we encountered variations. Correction was quick. Decisions could be made almost on the spot when it was clear someone wasn't doing the job or wasn't doing the job correctly. Opportunity was to be taken, not fooled with."

Because Roy Ash wanted to encourage the broadest innovation and entrepreneurial activity among the researchers, for whom he said he had the greatest admiration despite his claim not to have really known what they were doing, he opted for little control on ideas and more control on purse strings to assure they would stay in business while heating up the greenhouse.

Roy Ash's modest preaching follows his practices:

"Don't overrun your funds and jeopardize your strategy. Don't undercapitalize your company, and *never* take on an underfunded strategy with hopes that it will somehow work out."

At Intel, things were different at the start. Gordon Moore and Robert Noyce had talked things over informally with three other members of the team of five they put together. They came up with one product strategy—an advanced memory chip—which they strongly believed would gain wide acceptance on the market. Now the only problem was designing it—designing and manufacturing a specific product from what was a specific idea. The technology was there, with some twists, but it wasn't something one accomplished over a long weekend. They were definitely still talking laboratory science and development.

It was in the company's third year—though they had brought other chips to market—that the breakthrough came that catapulted Intel from forty-two to over a thousand employees. In 1971 M. E. Hoff, Jr., a young engineer at Intel, took the microchip technology one step beyond the large-scale integration of thousands of microminiaturized transistors on a silicon or polysilicon chip by inscribing a photo-reduced computer brain or CPU on one of Intel's chips. Such a general purpose, single-chip computer could run a calculator, a telephone, almost any gadget you can think of or have encountered over the last ten years. A ten-dollar Intel microprocessor could perform many of the tasks once delegated to a roomful of computers with a six-figure price tag.

Because of the extent of product definition at Intel from the start, the control emphasis that developed during the initial days at Intel *focused* on project, program and people control. The organization was formally designed as a matrix from the outset. Though there had been no business plan, the majority of the company's seed capital was raised by a venture capitalist, the same one who raised the seed money for Fairchild Semiconductor. In addition, Gordon and Robert Noyce each put up their entire stake in Fairchild, and Noyce's alma mater, Grinnell College, anted up a sizable chunk. Because of the personal nature of the investments, there were not the normal, pressing needs to reassure investors with volleys of reports. Still, formal program controls were set up at Intel from day one. Duties, tasks and time schedules were spelled out in writing. There were formal progress reports on different aspects of the research and technology going into the product.

The approach to financial control was more relaxed. At first, the scientists did the books themselves. An accountant was brought in after a month as part of the founding team, but Gordon preferred that he report to him orally.

"We had budgets and all the standard financial reports, but I didn't read them. Mostly I would just ask whether we were in the red. Direct questions looking for simple answers. At the end of the first year, a year devoted primarily to research, we had sales of $3,000. Of course we were in the red. Since most of the seed money was our own and we had faith in the product and our efforts, we weren't burdened by unnecessarily overexplaining our expenditures. The formality and detail of our project control in itself exerted great control on expenditures.

"As sales multiplied we had to bring on more professional accountants and controllers. I am sure they devised any number of more sophisticated reports somewhere beneath me, but I was still interested in simple answers to simple but important questions. I tried to keep the stacks of reports away from my desk. I wanted accuracy, but I didn't need to see it demonstrated so long as things were running smoothly."

THE ART OF CONTROL
BEYOND TRACKING BY THE NUMBERS

Michael Bobrow of the Bobrow-Thomas Associates architectural firm made a particular point of the inadequacies of control systems that are too focused on broad results and numbers.

"Part of the problem with formal planning and control is that it's not always focused on what the capabilities of your organization are. I would recommend that a brand new entrepreneur make a point of planning for downtrends, that he make a point of having the numberized plans and be in a position to react when things turn sour. You have to make a point of gaining fiscal know-how. You should have all the standard reports for the bank and investors. But you can't allow yourself to be misled by those reports. Those reports may not accurately reflect what you can really do. You have to have a way of knowing what you can really do *beyond* 'general accounting principles.' You have to know what you can really do beyond the bank's 'bottom line.' "

Often monitoring what you can really do is not just a matter of better or more realistic operating versions of the same sorts of numbers. The trick is in coming up with methods of monitoring the most direct performance-related aspects of your business. These are the aspects, the key inputs, that will end up making the numbers. If you just monitor the numbers, you lose track of how you *achieve* the numbers—which is closely related to being out of touch with what changes have to be made to change the numbers. For example, an emphasis on monitoring the amount of sales may not be as important as monitoring the number of sales calls. And an emphasis on monitoring the number of sales calls may not be as important as monitoring *how* sales calls are being made. A young entrepreneurship must quickly learn just what the most important areas of control should be at any stage of development—just what feedback is most important to the business both at that moment and just over the horizon. One must be as innovative in building control systems as in discovering a product or service.

In the building industry, as mentioned, sales forecasts based on feedback on ongoing sales activities are crucial. But just as a builder needs to know what is selling, he also needs to know why it is or is not selling. The successful entrepreneur not only needs the input of front-line numbers assessing performance, but he also should attempt to control what causes those numbers.

In the housing business successful companies closely question prospective and actual customers about what they are looking for in a new home or condominium, the sorts of fixtures and floor plans and features that sell in today's and tomorrow's market. Without that sort of feedback, as well as the more obvious needs to control cash and quality, a builder can have some temporarily paid-for white elephants.

One of Eugene Rosenfeld's first three employees, a secretary/administrative assistant, spent a good deal of her time talking to customers. In any business failure to solicit feedback and respond to information concerning not only quantitative but qualitative aspects of demand is a terminal weakness.

And to do this properly an entrepreneur cannot rely solely on "intuition." Judgment must be made on the basis of objective observation, both of the results or numbers and of the workings or "doing" of the business. Because the owner-founder is often in a position to see enough of the workings of the business to have a pretty good idea of how the numbers are going, it is sometimes falsely claimed that the owner-founder controls intuitively. It is forgotten that control and business are not natural or intuitive acts. No one intuits that there are not enough parts on hand to meet orders. One comes to the rational conclusion, sometimes based on a report, sometimes based on a glance at the parts shelves. The owner-founder learns what the key inputs and outputs are and sometimes through personal observation is able to make judgments on their status. The successful entrepreneur *knows* his business, he doesn't dream it.

It is also said that the typical entrepreneur often continues to control through personal observation to his detriment, that he sometimes becomes too accustomed to personal observation as a means of control. Yet one thing I observed as a result of my conversations was that successful entrepreneurs not only allow more formal control systems to evolve but also continue to get out there with a pair of open eyes and observe their businesses. The secret to making the transition to a more stable or established but still entrepreneurial enterprise is not in dropping so-called entrepreneurial practices but in facilitating them—the successful entrepreneur formalizes control so that he is free to remain personally involved with the key aspects.

I mentioned that Leo Imperiali believes the secret to Tile World's success has been rooted in standards of order and presentation within his stores, as well as simple methods of training both subordinates and customers. Leo trained his first salesmen after years of training customers to install tile. He trained his first salesmen after years of handling all the sales himself. Leo had it down to a science. Leo's store managers now train their subordinates according to the same methods by which they were trained—it can all be traced back to those first days, to Leo as he waited alone for customers to one day fill his storefront.

Leo can now sit back and watch the numbers compiled from Tile World's daily sales reports and mostly smile. Or he can occasionally personally stop in at a store to see that subordinates were good students—not as often, granted, because he has other things to do involved with running a larger company, but neither has he developed the distance of a middle manager in a non-entrepreneurial corporation.

It's also true, of course, that an interventionist end-run around managers by an owner-founder can be destructive. The owner-founder who meddles or wastes time poking around otherwise well-running areas of his business is a boor and a fool. A delicate balance is the ticket—one to be struck between observing and snooping.

Despite the fact that Merritt Sher has established a capable staff of "bean counters," he continues to visit stores at his centers, to walk through the stores and talk to store managers, not only to ask but to see how business is, to not just rely on financials provided by higher-ups and monitored by his staff.

"It is one thing to read a number that says sales are down or not what you expected," Sher said. "It is another to see a store and the customers in it. You should be able to tell that sales are down or are not what they should be just by looking at it. At the same time you should be able to get a few ideas about what can be done to change things. Sometimes I am able to react more quickly than the store manager's higher-up at the parent corporation. Sometimes I pass my input along to both the store manager and his manager back at headquarters. I want them to succeed as much as they want to.

"If you watch the numbers too closely and lose track of the reality of the business, the actions you take to try to change the numbers stand a good chance of being misdirected. What's worse, they stand a good chance of being too late."

Tag along on the odd day Merritt spends on the road every week or so, and you are likely to stop in for a tie at a clothing shop, a roll at a bakery, a video from one of his record stores—you will not just hear about but see—*experience*—Merritt's business.

Merritt continues to run promotions himself when he can't encourage the entrepreneurs in his centers to do so, thereby keeping an eye on the overall drawing power of the tenant mixes he has created. He goes to other centers to see how new businesses and ideas are working out. He has developed more formal control systems and reporting—he doesn't strictly *rely* on personal observation—but he hasn't given it up either. He has maintained his entrepreneurial practices while formalizing as needed a growing organization.

Baldemar Rodriguez has employees conduct phone polls of competitors in the apartment rental business to assess local vacancy rates. If he is considering purchasing a project in an area in which he has not operated he makes sure he knows how every other competing building in the area stacks up.

"When I read in the paper that some government agency or industry group says that vacancy rates are going up in this area or that it's too late. We're not only concerned about vacancy rates in counties and cities but on particular corners. We have our own dailies, we know about vacancy rates, collections, overdues and legal actions. With our new computer all of this is on-line for each of our units and tenants. But we also keep track of the number of prospective tenant contacts as well as the number of marketing contacts in the area with realtors and companies and corporations likely to be bringing employees into the area. We want to stay aggressive, and the only way to do that is to train your employees, give them the methods and then make sure that they are not only performing but that they are performing the right way. We hire marketing consultants to randomly pose as prospective tenants to see that our training has been successful. We hire consultants to train our apartment-marketing personnel in everything from makeup and clothing to sales methods. And after putting the resources into all of that you can be sure we follow up and make sure we aren't wasting our time and monies."

When it comes to the major inputs, including demand trends in your industry, it is better to sense changes before they show up on the order desk—before you hear about it on the news—before change begets crisis. It is better to attempt to influence or *control* these inputs—it is better to integrate them into your feedback, evaluation and so-called action-loop.

A FINAL WARNING:
DON'T EVEN TRUST YOUR AUNT

I can't stress it enough. I really do think that the various aspects of control described above may come as close to distinguishing the entrepreneur who will meet with the greatest success as any other influence I came across, even beyond initial product or service choice.

More than one successful entrepreneur was honest enough to share some of the problems that plagued his organization.

Howard Morrow, of the Betty Zane Corporation, founder of a chain of Morrow's Nut House franchises recently sold to Tenneco, characterized his early control practices as less than professional.

"I'm not the world's greatest bean-counter, and we actually *sell* a lot of beans—jelly beans. I went broke in an electronics business because I didn't keep a good enough eye on what my partner was up to. Starting Morrow's Nuts amounted to finding a vacant store, remodeling it, supplying it and running it long enough to sell it. I continued to scout locations and start and sell stores as fast as I could at the start. That was and will always be my strong point—sales.

"As soon as I could afford to I hired two elderly married women, one to train the people buying the franchises and one to keep the books. Cash flow was always the problem. I was always broke. I was always sinking whatever was free into the next store and being faced with debts on the ones I had remodeled and sold. I had to babysit each store until I had a buyer.

"I was single at the time. I had a pickup truck and I would drive around delivering nuts. I used the same truck for dates. It didn't even have a radio—we're talking late sixties, not the depression. One time I wanted a particular sports coat so bad for a date I sold two suits to a used clothing store and threw in another twenty dollars to get the sports coat. I was definitely living out of my pocket.

"I never looked at the books the little old lady was keeping. I didn't know how I really stood for two years. I would just sit down with a pile of bills and wad of cash each Friday and decide which ones we could pay. I would take a little of whatever else was left as salary. Some weeks it was twenty dollars, some weeks it was five hundred.

"It turned out that this little old lady, one of three older married women I ended up hiring at the start—they were like aunts to me—had been writing checks on the side for two years. I didn't have any regular formal reports. I just asked for one when I needed it for someone else.

"I'm sure I would have done better with a little more formality. I stayed ahead of the game by aggressively selling and raising the prices of the franchises when things began to look thin and the market would bear it. But the fact is, if there is one problem that continued to be our weak link it was a lack of sound control. After sales were up to over twenty million I found myself losing money one year when we shouldn't have been losing money, and I had to spend a great deal of time trying to find out why and without the best consequences for my health."

The entrepreneur capable of overcoming the more stereotypical traits attributed to the entrepreneur, who manages against such tendencies, who within the context of preparing for future exigencies even begins to experiment at acting like a professional manager during the early days, particularly in the area of his control practices, stands the best chance of making the transition to becoming the top manager of a larger, more established—and more successful firm.

CHAPTER SEVEN

Benign and Malignant Neglects

So far I've identified two areas of management that success-ful entrepreneurs practice before the fact: thinking through the business during the course of start-up and sound control put in before expansion. At the same time I've said that what separates the haves from the once-hads is an ability to formalize practices along the way—an ability not to get too attached to early ways of doing things, to go with the formalizing flow so long as it's the best means of increasing that most important of flows: *cash.*

If there is one particular attribute that distinguishes the successful entrepreneur and his approach to management, it is the ability to practice a mixed bag of tricks—to, in a word, be flexible; to be open to change. For an organization to stay flexible and thereby open to fortune, it has to learn to mix things up from the start.

For successful entrepreneurs there's no contradiction in early-on formalizing control of some aspects of planning while maintaining an informal approach to many aspects of training and delegation. They sense it is only through change that they can maintain control *and* grow.

It isn't entrepreneurship versus bureaucracy. You need to move beyond the one-dimensional myth of the typical owner-founder without succumbing to an across-the-board campaign of formalization that could destabilize the organi-zation.

EARLY ON: "WHAT" AND "WHEN"
ARE MORE IMPORTANT THAN "WHO"

To your customers, what and when are *always* more important than who—providing the particular who handling their business knows *how* to deliver the what when it's needed. The quality, the timeliness of delivery of the product *are* the business. How *well* you do something should in fact be *what* you do. You should not just be in the business of making ceiling fans, as some of Casablanca Fans' early competitors were. You should be in the business, like Warren Dennis and Burton Burton, of making the highest quality, most efficiently produced and dependably delivered and backed-with-service fan on the market.

As you grow, of course, it will take more whos, or employees, to do what you do according to the same standards. In some large businesses, sometimes even in medium or prematurely aging small firms, the whos can begin to pile up, to get in the way of the what and the when or the how-well of the business.

In a young entrepreneurship *you* are who. At the start, if your company is very small, you might find yourself many times personally answering the phone. In any event your suppliers know who you are, your customers know who you are—everyone knows who you are (except perhaps your spouse and family).

Ralph Crump gave me the title for this particular management ditty. Ralph did almost everything himself during the early days in Frigitronics' first 400-square-foot facility. He spent time in the lab working on application designs for the microrefrigerant technology he had decided to pursue before he hired his first engineer. He followed up leads on potential applications, talking to experts and prospective customers as he narrowed engineering design toward product prototypes.... "What if I made you a thing-a-ma-jig that would do this? Would you buy it? And how much would you pay for it?" . . . Ralph made calls and visits all over the country. Once he began developing prototypes he even wrote his own patents. The only area Ralph delegated to others from the start was bookkeeping.

At the start almost all headaches were production-related: parts that weren't built to specs; even worse, parts that were built to specs but didn't work. Ralph's first employee was an engineer. As the product moved toward a prototype, design personnel were hired. As they moved the prototype toward production, production workers were hired. Ralph had what he described as a generous private investor who didn't want things to be too tight at the start. The company was adequately capitalized. When they needed to hire someone, they did.

From the start, Ralph didn't want quality control under his production supervisor. So he personally handled the quality control as well until he was able to hire an experienced QC person and set up a separate department.

Once he had delegated an area he rarely stepped back in unless there was a major problem, but Ralph still continued to fill the gaps as Frigi grew: As engineering and production began to stand on their own two feet, for example, he upped the level of marketing.

"The who was always very informal during the early days," Ralph says. "Keeping the who informal was our only means of assuring that our more formal what and when schedules and quality would be met and sustained."

Clearly, the owls have it, when it comes to being a smart new entrepreneur.

FORMALIZING WITHOUT FORMALDEHYDING YOUR ORGANIZATION

As mentioned in the previous chapter, there comes a day when it is no longer as simple as ringing the alarm and broadcasting orders for all hands on deck. There comes a time when individual whos and departments of whos must be held responsible for their own decks—when the company must be organized so as not to greet difficulties with a Keystone Kops act.

How do successful owner-founders do this—how do they formalize organization without surrendering their entrepreneurial sword?

Most of us are personally familiar with the trappings of formal organizations. Professional organizations are supposed to call on a number of formal tools to keep order—organization charts, job descriptions, information flow charts, authority charts, responsibility charts, procedure manuals, formal accounting controls such as budgetary authority descriptions, personal parking spaces(!), corner offices, offices beneath the stairwells or HVAC unit. There are plenty of ways to keep people in their places and make sure they understand just what those places are. But the more an organization begins to envision its enterprise as a Chinese puzzle of individuals filling places, horribly complex methods for fitting individual pieces obscure the organization's *purpose* and *strategic thrust*. The organization is now dancing toward paralysis.

Especially in a young entrepreneurship, purpose is king. The entrepreneur often doesn't even have to state that purpose in a formal way. It's *there* for everyone to see. The very activity of the place defines the purpose. Communication is open, the business takes place before everyone's eyes. Purpose is also something you can, at this stage, not only see but feel. Success is something you may not yet be able to taste but you may definitely be able to imagine the sweet smell. Which leads to high morale and the sort of in-sync group effort that propels a young entrepreneurship through the high waves of start-up and survival.

But how does one maintain cooperative dedication to a group purpose while at the same time dividing up the kingdom to local rule once the size of one's lands demands greater specialization and autonomy?

The answer seemed fairly simple for the successful entrepreneurs I spoke with: Aspects of formal organization that emphasized the chain of command were early on borrowed from the big guys and correctly practiced, aspects of formal organization more concerned with drawing hard and fast lines around who does what—those thousands of seemingly harmless thin strings with which the Lilliputians managed to pin Gulliver to the earth—were left for other, later developed, realms.

Successful entrepreneurs do not carry on a crusade against formalization. At the same time they are distinguished from pickled bureaucracies by carefully formalizing *one step at a time*.

ORGANIZATION CHARTS—MAYBE.
ORGANIZATIONAL PARALYSIS—DEATH

For a classic example of hovering in the breach, consider the entrepreneurs I spoke with who had the presumably obligatory organization charts during the early days of their companies but also pointed out how unimportant these charts actually were to their organizations. Almost a third had a formal organization chart prior to their first major expansion (again, a period described as their first doubling within a year or two—for most a feat occurring within the first five years of entrepreneurial life). Almost half had a formal organization chart *before* the conclusion of their first major expansion. But . . .

But, again, the question of the pulse and the paper rears its head. Just what *is* an organization chart? What can it *do,* and what *can't* it do? For most successful entrepreneurs I spoke with an organization chart was *not* a diagram they posted in the halls or held over subordinates' heads. It was not a static method of describing some settled, mature and even decaying beast. It was more a means of thinking through key activities, of classifying, grouping and assigning activities in a rather more organized fashion. A chart was a way to identify gaps and new needs—a tool for *thought.*

When Ed Stevens began to realize that a major marketing expansion was needed to secure the number of radio-station customers needed to bring his automated data-processing system for the broadcast industry toward profitability, he

quickly sought out an individual with greater organizational experience. In exchange for stock a part-time consultant from a Big-8 consulting firm was hired, an individual
experienced in operating companies, to help plan Compunet's expansion. Milestone charts were set up, prospective
organization charts were designed to define personnel and
the amount of outside experience they would need to bring
in to accomplish the expansion. Through this process Ed
came out with more concrete *ideas* about what would be
needed to create quickly a marketing organization. It was
decided the effort needed a marketing manager with experience in the industry. Ed immediately set out to find the
right person.

Once this individual was located the organization chart
and other planning materials were ready tools to be incor-
porated into briefings related to the particular task at hand.
The chart was *not* meant to remind captains and lieutenants who were generals and who were privates. The chart
was a means of designing new organization as the company
grew, not a means of pouring concrete around individuals
already on board.

The point: An organization chart should be a tool for
reevaluation and change, not hand-maiden of static order.

How Can I Describe You When You Won't Stand Still?

With the above in mind, there's a further important re-
minder concerning organization charts. During the early
days of a successful entrepreneurship you would be well-
advised to draw them with pencil on erasable bond. Don't
waste money on fine graphics. Before you've had a chance
to appreciate the beauty and balance of your work, someone
or something—more often the pace of change itself within
a growing entrepreneurship—is likely to make you reach
for an eraser or a bottle of White-out.

Consider job descriptions. They were almost universally

ignored by the successful entrepreneurs I spoke with for long periods within their growing enterprises (only about a quarter of them had job descriptions by the end of their first major expansion). Most could have very easily sat down and in detail described what should and had to be done, but few found purpose in putting blinders on a corralful of green colts and fillies with incentive to jump (or run through) fences for the good of the company *and* themselves.

Job descriptions are a means of establishing continuity, a tool to be used in training a person to fill a slot or to inform a superior, who might be brought on board to supervise an unfamiliar position and unfamiliar methods of work. On the other hand most aggressive employees, even in larger firms, manage to rewrite their job descriptions during the course of proving themselves worthy of moving up or on. Job descriptions are better called job guides. Even for larger firms the major value of job descriptions comes at the time an employee is hired, used as a means of matching people with tasks. Rarely within large organizations are they used as they should be—to reevaluate qualifications and assignments, to determine further needs for training.

Since many owner-founders find themselves looking more for general qualities and work attitudes than specific experience, job descriptions are especially irrelevant during the early days.

Ask Bill Kaufman about writing a job description in a young entrepreneurship. For more than one of his early employees, but particularly for one woman who came to work for him during the first years, it would have been a total waste of time.

When Bill and his partners struck out on their own to start a residential development company, they moved into a 2,000-square-foot office with no partitions. Communication was, by design, open. They had just departed a high-rise chock-full of rules and regulations and job descriptions.

Right from the start the three partners were able to secure adequate capitalization and a line of credit. Dealing with their growth became the biggest problem—assuring that they did not grow up to act like the monster they had just left.

"We went to twenty employees by the end of the first year. In some ways we were formal about hiring. We had an organization chart and we used outside personnel agencies. All three partners talked to each applicant. We ran ads. We had a policy with a local college by which we arranged to talk to top grads each year, whether or not we or they were looking. We wanted 'A' players—strictly people who found it an interesting place to work and wanted to move up. We set an example by working hard ourselves, by staying off the golf course. We did everything we could to bring employees along. We monitored their work through regularly scheduled weekly staff meetings, at which anybody at the professional or subprofessional level was present. We steered away from one-on-one meetings for monitoring operating matters. We wanted communication and learning shared among everyone. The youngest and newest guy might only talk five minutes, but he would be asked to talk, and he would get an education listening the rest of the time, and he wouldn't be so worried about what was going on behind closed doors.

"We used something like rough job descriptions with the agencies to guide them when they were searching out applicants for us, but once we had an employee on board we just didn't find them useful. We wanted people who would take things on, not just accept a description. I hired one woman for $400 a month as a secretary and she was absolutely the worst secretary in the world. She wasn't even worth the $400 a month. She wasn't worth $200 a month. But before I could let her go she had already convinced me to let her take something else on. As a result she continued to move up in the organization. She's now making close to a quarter of a million a year working with a financial organization. On the other hand we hired a guy who had worked for the Federal Housing Authority and was intimately familiar with job descriptions and nine-to-five. We thought he would be an asset, having experience in the field. But he had been tainted by his experience. He knew more about how the FHA worked than about how an entrepreneurial employee in the field *should* work. He didn't last three months with us.

"Long before you find the need for job descriptions, you are probably going to suffer some of the less productive outfall they tend to promote. The backbiting and politics are going to find their way in, you're going to find your way battling them soon enough. As soon as you find yourself promoting people, creating new levels of organization responsible for supervising the work of others you're going to find problems developing with misused authority. There's no sense creating the problem ahead of time. Keep the group purpose first, and as soon as you see the in-fighting cropping up you have to deal with it. We promoted a very loyal and competent secretary to be an office manager, but within a short time found her lording it over the others, trying to control the flow of information—even divulging personal information from executive correspondence. I had a talk with her and tried to straighten it out. It didn't improve so we let her go, but not soon enough to have prevented all the damage. As you grow larger it becomes more and more a problem. Eventually, maybe you have to spell things all out formally to keep people in line, but as long as you can remain vigilant and stay away from the negative effects of having to totally formalize everything, you do."

Most of the job spelling-out that's needed in a young entrepreneurship during the first year or two with less than some fifty employees, can be handled orally when such matters as conflicting jurisdictions come up. Informality, though, is the ticket. Only a quarter of those I spoke with had weekly staff meetings before their first major expansion. Two-thirds of those I interviewed said their plans, instructions, job assignments, etc., were almost exclusively oral *through* their first major expansion.

Generally making clear responsibilities and duties isn't a big deal for young companies. People aware of the group purpose and the growing list of challenges surrounding them tend not to stray from the path. Those few who do are let go. The deadly virus of *any* organization is political fever. On the other hand, an owner-founder, usually not faced with such problems, can sometimes overreact in setting out to avoid counterproductive internal vying.

In large organizations that have begun to exist in and of themselves as a purpose—thereby threatening to supplant the primary purpose of the business—there's probably a positive aspect to the anchor such an outfit puts on the hands-on policies of singular managers. *Maybe.* Change is the constant of all living organizations, but one of the ironies of large companies is that in spite of their greater financial and productive capacities to deal with change they're often set reeling by needs to adjust to change, far more so than newer, smaller, more adaptive firms. The larger the organization, the harder it is to find consensus. People out near the ramparts are bound to get a little more jittery when they begin to smell a new thrust. Sometimes their jitters turn into activities that in fact make it difficult to change policy or performance. Obviously change for change's sake is helter-skelter, but people bred in routine tend to fall in love with it, accept it as a steady mate. The result is stagnation.

Owner-founders of small firms may bristle at even the suggestion that such a state of affairs would be allowed within their companies. Anything that might make change and flexibility less possible is cursed. Entrepreneurs understand that swift strategy implementation often marks the difference between the life or death of a strategy.

However—ah, always the "however"—none of this is to say that being totally informal will *help* you succeed. To prepare for the day when the organization will have a need for more formality, wise entrepreneurs don't twirl their six-guns and say "make my day" to *all* aspects of formal organization. Some get to be a little too proud of their non-big-guy informality. Some begin to poke their chins out just a little too far and end up with sore jaws. The successful fellows walked a fairly sensible line, staying loose but not to the extent of risking chaos.

Vice Presidents of
Shipping and Receiving and Other Tall Titles

Some three-quarters of the entrepreneurs I spoke with had formal organization titles at the time they promoted or hired their first intermediary—which is to say, at the time their organizations first had three levels. Moreover, those who went on to the greatest success used titles that said just about all anyone needed to know in the way of a job description: stand manager, production supervisor, lead maintenance worker, director of engineering, director of programming, marketing representative.... None of these titles was exactly innovative; some might have been borrowed from larger organizations in which an entrepreneur and his employees had worked, in which case they inferred certain duties or position-guides as well. The point is, however subtle the difference, there is a right way (using descriptive, functional titles) and there are wrong ways (either concentrating on establishing the more power-related aspects of hierarchy or using no titles at all) to use formal titles. Many entrepreneurs hate titles. They had that stuff in prior incarnations. But it's clear that those who personally had a hard time taking this first small step of formal organization—who delayed using formal titles for as long as seven or eight years until their organizations had as many as four levels—were hurting themselves and most often ended up with smaller, slower-growing companies.

Understandably, some still believe that formal titles can be devastating to an organization, a belief rooted in a fear that with titles come rigid divisions of status and territory and all the backbiting that can go with them. But it needn't be so. The point is to use titles to indicate who knows and does what, not who has the highest walls and the deepest

moat and the most retainers. Not to mention the key to the
executive john.

Clearly, calling your first promoted employee a vice-president just because he's next in command and because he has
been with you from day one is a mistake. One entrepreneur,
a very successful fellow who sold his company and from the
start harbored a dislike for the formal, bureaucratic organizations and their ways, gave an initial employee a vice-
president's title even though his duties consisted of supervising shipping and receiving in a small warehouse—a task,
as it turned out, he couldn't carry out as the company continued to grow. Though this might have seemed like an
"unbureaucratic" thing to do—to call someone a vice-president because he had been there on board from the start and
was about to become a more important right-hand man—
such an act can lay the groundwork for personnel problems
as incremental formalization takes place, as it must, with
growth. Titles can help make clear reporting, information
and duty lines without spelling everything out in fine print.
Incorrect use of titles, or no use of titles, communicates the
owner-founder's own disrespect for the notion of lines.
When this happens it can actually create a climate for bureaucracy. Without decent reporting lines the owner-
founder must continue to be an octopus-like hub with a
hammer in each wiggling tentacle; comes the day that's no
longer enough and the company is actually riper for the sort
of problems the owner-founder had originally set out to
avoid.

Besides being a good means of preparing your organization for more formal coordination without gumming up the
works, generating descriptive, functional titles can be instructive. Correct use of functional titles can assist your
organization in many of the same ways that correctly used
organization charts, descriptions and the rest can assist a
larger firm without the feared bureaucratic side effects. A
descriptive title for a new position helps give existing employees a handle on just what change is about to take place,
more tangible than all the assurances. Such titles may be

the only formal organizing tool you need the first year or two. And again, comes the day when the organization does need more, there will have been a precedent—it won't be as if you were bringing in a consultant and shoving formality down your organization's throat.

SPECIALIZATION FOR SPECIALIZATION'S SAKE

Appropriately used titles can introduce another notion into your business—departmentalization. Some specialization will be inherent in job activity. While you don't want to go overboard about chalking tasks and hierarchy during initiation there's nothing wrong with beginning to use titles to spell out key activity areas.

Both Gordon Moore of Intel and Fred Charette of Systonetics divided up key activities among the founding team. This established the key departments and a precedent for growth. If one founding partner or team member was assigned a research and development focus there was a good precedent for giving him a title like director of research and development as well as good strategy for hiring on research and development people under him without spelling out in detail just who they reported to in formal documents. It may sound silly to have a director of research and development working on a sawhorse-supported door next to the director of marketing next to the production manager all in the same small office or warehouse, but the use of titles to clarify some departmentalization will make sense to the new employee who might otherwise walk in the door to meet Dolores, Harry and Ned—and spend months trying to find out what they *do*.

All this means a thinking-through of the business, not a drawing of lines around kingdoms. Nothing is to say the director of marketing can't be called over to help pack a shipment or plug a leak in the ceiling. Though the owner-founders will be required to wear many hats and wield many tools, it seems apparent that the more successful are distinguished by an early understanding of their roles as generalists—as top managers whose specialty soon enough becomes *managing* the specialists. The use of titles to establish departments-to-come can help the whirling dervish entrepreneur get a hold on his own impending larger responsibilities.

PERSONNEL PRACTICES:
THE SKULL AND CROSSBONES,
AND OTHER TALES OF THE HIGH SEAS

Consider the climate of Silicon Valley during the seventies. Most of us have found ourselves daydreaming about waking up one morning to find ourselves in demand like a star athlete. Most people have to plough through want ads—to find a job doing something *someone else* wants them to do. In Silicon Valley in the seventies high school graduates who ten years earlier would have had to leave town for work were being trained to perform functions that previously had only been performed in the laboratories of the world's most prestigious research institutes and universities. They couldn't be trained fast enough. Once you knew how to coat a wafer or bake a chip you had an ace in your pocket. The work-place usage of the word "shift" was given an entire new meaning, as a supervisor might bring along his or her entire crew in moving from one employer to the next that cropped up down the road. The phone would ring at all hours of the day. The incentives piled up clean and crisp and varied—great salaries, bonuses, profit-sharing, stock options, exercise facilities.

Gordon Moore is frank about what Intel had to do to build up its work force as they found themselves going from five to over twenty-five hundred employees in five years.

"We pirated our former employers, Fairchild Semiconductor. We hired away as many capable people as we could. In fact, after we pirated Fairchild, for both management and production personnel, Fairchild pirated Motorola. It's common practice in a new industry."

They may as well have built a leg of San Francisco's

BART train between the older and newer concerns in the valley. And by older and newer concerns we are not talking archives or carbon-copy dating—in some cases we are talking about start-ups during different seasons of the same year. Formal personnel procedures had to be put in early on, just to keep track of all the movement. Besides, once you had managed to shanghai a crew, you were then faced with the task of trying to keep them on board.

"For key employees we made things very attractive, both in terms of salary and stock incentives. Beyond this there was the question of building a company that was the type of place people wanted to *stay* with. Early on this was often a question of benefits and atmosphere. More recently and after the industry went through a few cycles it has become more a matter of proving that you are and are going to continue to be one of the thriving survivors."

Intel did go out of its way to reinvent the modern corporation. Though growth demanded strict formality of project planning and eventually an aggressive and organized approach to personnel matters, getting straight who did what *under* whom in an overly formal manner was cast on the nearby rugged western shores—and left on those shores well after an amount of growth that would have sent most companies into a fit of spelling things out.

To manage this there had to be a very formal matrix organization from the start, including organization charts, that helped make it clear who was doing what with whom on each project. Aspects of both the formal and informal organization relating to power and hierarchy were left outside, didn't even get a look-in. At Intel, there were no corner offices, and to this day Gordon works within a partitioned cubicle on an open floor just like the other managers. There are also no private parking places. Which didn't mean that Intel wasn't a very highly organized entrepreneurship. In order to operate such a large and growing company without the plague of certain undesired formal trappings, Intel, as mentioned, developed its system of coordinating councils to assure that information continued to flow to the proper parties. Beyond this, Intel went out of its way to make sure that both new and old personnel did not lose track of the company's purpose, its core philosophy, its general approach to doing business. Intel's philosophy about doing business became as important as the products they were inventing, producing and marketing. Though there was and is a lot of equality at Intel, considering its size, everyone was subordinate to *concepts* framing the determination and drive that propelled the company into the international microchip wars. At Intel you were supposed to solve not just your particular challenges but find time to attack others as well. You were supposed to figure how to put yourself on the line without tripping others. You were supposed to contribute, not just show up, and these "supposed tos" were regularly discussed, rehashed, refined and, most important, renewed at company "culture" sessions held for *all* employees—mass meetings to which the troops were summoned, sermonized and made to feel they were part of a program.

Steering away from the snares and delusions of too much formal organization did not mean that Intel wasn't *thinking* about the organization, about the best means of setting up for current and future growth. And being vigilant about organization didn't always result in formal organizational tools at the start.

Such vigilance does have to be a recurrent, a *conscious* process for an owner-founder. You can shuck off the trappings but if you also toss out the process of thinking and rethinking, creating and recreating your optimum form of organization for your entrepreneurship, pirate or not, you can find yourself on the rocks, along with the annoying formalities you tossed overboard.

This May Sound Like a Phone Commercial, But . . .

Word-of-mouth and happenstance is mostly the way entrepreneurs hire at the start. With more high-powered starts involving venture capitalists there may be much thought and even headhunting that goes into putting together an entrepreneurial team, but most of the people I interviewed weren't so calculating.

Early employees were often partners, part of an entrepreneurial team, people the entrepreneurs had got together with in the act of starting the business. They tended to match up with others whose strengths offset their weaknesses. An owner-founder can't safely take the "anyone can be replaced" attitude some narrow-minded corporate managers like to boast about in describing their attitude toward personnel—especially not during the first year or two when, so to speak, the cost of shifting horses might mean being left at the gate.

Still, as mentioned, many entrepreneurs do run into partners or early key employees through coincidence, industry contacts, family or school associations. Some had worked together before, some were referred by others. Fred Charette's first key employees and partners were classmates. Ray Anderson's first key employee was a co-founder and manager—his brother-in-law. Roy Ash teamed up with industry associates. Gordon Moore and his partners left as a team. I previously worked with my first partner at a corporation, though neither our jobs nor the corporation we worked for had anything to do with the field we were entering. Stanley Rawn paired up with an old friend. James Collins eventually brought an old classmate on to be his second in command. Ralph Crump was introduced to an accountant partner by his major private investor. Ed Stevens hoisted the flag and took a manager from his previous employer along with him when he left. Leonard Weil put out feelers and gathered together a proven group of banking professionals from friends and industry contacts as he shepherded a fledgling, privately chartered bank through the regulation process.

Dan Chandler followed the same strategy as Merritt Sher, hiring a young man right out of college, a young man recommended by a friend. Dan needed a bright, ambitious and inexpensive young employee to help during a start-up period of thin cash flow. Dan had an earlier experience trying to start out with a peer broker, but the partner was trying to run too much of the firm himself, making decisions that weren't his—what's worse, making *bad* decisions that weren't his to make.

"It has been extremely satisfying," Dan says, "to have taken a kid right out of college who didn't know anything about business and to have brought him along to the point where he is a part owner and running some aspects of the business on his own. One of my partners at the brokerage, where I still serve on the board, is sending his son to work for me just so he can learn the business as a trainee who might work his way in. That is darn rewarding, to have someone in your industry respect you enough to send his son to you."

Maybe that would be called piracy once removed, if the brokerage firm Dan left had its sights on second-generation employees. In any event it appears that an objective approach to screening and selecting initial employees did not especially distinguish the entrepreneurs I spoke with who went on to be successful. As the management writer Harold Koontz points out, even the most sophisticated and formal approach to selecting and screening employees only indicates what an applicant has done or might be *able* to do— screening rarely divulges what an employee *will* or might *want* to do (his motivation, ambition or drive).

WHEN RIGHT NOW MIGHT BE TOO LATE

I hope I've made it clear that you may want to think about hiring professional accounting or control personnel *before* you need them. The extra expense justifies itself as you grow. The extra experience and precaution added to your organization may *facilitate* that growth. Depending on your business there will be other specialties of particular importance to you that may demand the early introduction of outside professionals—such as, for example, engineers.

But what about upper management people? Experienced managers who can step in and deal with a growing organization and numbers of subordinates beyond, frankly, the scope of initial employees who have been dragged up the ladder with you?

This rather cold assessment of the chances that early employees will grow along with the company to fill top management slots isn't just mine. With a few notable exceptions, the entrepreneurs I spoke with—members of a species not known for its *own* ability to handle the responsibilities and tasks of a larger more established firm—as a group had a hard time promoting initial employees into upper management positions.

Those who didn't start out with experienced personnel acquired through friendship or industry contacts often just hired inexperienced people and taught and promoted them along the way.

Leo Imperiali, for example, often found himself hiring individuals referred by tile installers, apprentices who wanted more security and steady employment. Leo didn't mind. These workers only had to be infused with the ability to communicate an enthusiasm for the product, to be instructed in the particular methods of training Leo had developed over the years.

Leo has had good success promoting employees through the ranks, from sales to assistant store manager to store manager. His first store manager was promoted through the ranks. His general manager started in sales. But Leo's experience is the exception. His organization is *structured* around apprenticeship and training. Tile World has grown through the repetition of a pattern practiced with each new store. But most businesses grow through metamorphosis; they start out focusing on a production specialty, then in a few years find themselves looking at demands to initiate, separate and organize other functions equally important to the original production specialty. Many successful entrepreneurships survive in the start-up because they service their customers better than the competition (which often

means producing a more innovative or inexpensive product
or service). If they succeed, one day such organizations find
themselves wrapped up in *new* problems demanding *new*
skills and talents unrelated to research, development and
production—new skills and talents also unrelated to the
beginning promotional or marketing strategy. Such organizations then either reorganize or create new aspects of the
organization suggested by early planning, so as to break out
of the original cocoon as a *new* business. If the new business
involves too much new organization—an amount better left
for later growth—the company may unfold its new wings,
take one trial flap and fold. If the company stays efficient
and elegant in design—making only the necessary formalizations, setting a precedent and looking ahead to future
formalization in an incremental fashion—it might fly. And
if the company refuses to break out of the cocoon at all, it
withers and dies.

It's said that one reason "entrepreneurial" owner-founders tend not to hire experienced managers soon enough is
that they worry about losing control. Well, losing control
is something to worry about. If it's overly feared, so that you
fight any smidgen of formality, refuse to share equity or
attempt internally to finance the greater part of the business's growth, fear begets the feared reality. On the other
hand—sorry, but there usually is one—an overly fearless
approach to such matters can be just as decisive in its un-
happy outcome. In this day of venture-capital firms holding
onto majority interest in some start-ups, an owner-founder
has to be very careful indeed that he, in fact, hasn't been
hired on to run just the first leg, then to be dumped. Moderate fear of losing control can be a healthy approach for any
entrepreneur with partners or investors holding a significant share. In the case of some of the more successful owner-
founders it very well may have been such a moderated dose
of caution that led to a rational approach to hiring on experienced managers.

Entrepreneurs, in general, *do* appear to hire acquaint-
ances, friends, classmates or individuals within their indus-

try with whom they are comfortable. On the surface they don't generally follow a professional or so-called objective approach to searching out personnel. However, in spite of what appears to be a somewhat subjective approach to the selection of experienced top managers, *successful* entrepreneurs are distinguished by the objectivity they employ in selecting among those with whom they are, indeed, comfortable. You can't call the end-result of the selections I cite below good luck.

Here comes the phone commercial: *Stay in touch.* Jim Collins didn't bring an experienced top manager into his organization until 1967, over a decade after starting the company. Jim didn't call on his classmate when he opened his first stand, though he occasionally talked to him and kept him informed on progress, as friends or classmates tend to do. Jim didn't offer him a job when he reorganized his company to handle the franchising and supplying of a chain of multiplying Kentucky Fried Chicken stands. Jim called on his classmate, a proven top manager, *when he needed* a top manager. But because Jim had his classmate in mind, and they had talked, he had consciously faced up to the need in a way that allowed him to get ready for change. Jim knew he would need additional managerial support. There was the plan to go public, and all *that* would involve, just over the horizon. Jim's calls to his friend became more regular. Jim hired an experienced top manager *before* he went public. More important, Jim was *thinking* about hiring a top manager even before this. He knew how he planned to deal with his needs and he had someone in mind who he had established a relationship with and who might make the switch even smoother. This top manager was brought on board as an executive vice-president. Ten years later he became the chief operating officer for Collins Foods International, and, Jim says, he probably will be filling his own shoes some day not too far down the pike.

Such an approach to managerial "courtship" can mean the difference between "one annual report stands," a divorce from a subordinate and a more lasting, mutually profitable and cooperative relationship. It takes a special sort of owner-founder, indeed, to make the transition from owner-founder to owner-manager. It also takes a very special sort of top manager to come on board and assist the owner-founder—to help the owner-founder and the organization make this transition. Such an individual, perhaps with experience in a more mature organization, has to be as flexible as the owner-founder.

A fellow top manager's expertise *and* loyalty are invaluable to the owner-founder who wants to grow (to go public or give up equity in order to grow). Sharing the top management bases with a trusted *and* competent manager can allow the owner-founder to *relax* about some of the anxieties that might prevent him from growing to his and his business's full potential. Had Jim Collins so feared losing control that he hadn't risked seeking out a classmate who had already proved himself as an exceptionally competent manager with another company, the personal relationship could have dragged the organization down, as it too often does in entrepreneurships. On the other hand Jim could have brought an equally competent but otherwise unknown quantity on board for this top position and the two men might have spent months and years trying to figure each other out at a time when there were no months and years to spend. Jim was fortunate to have chosen someone more than just competent—someone who was not only competent but who had come to share many of Jim's views before he was brought on board.

We are talking a bit on the edge of the razor here: It's fine to take on a known quantity—known through some sort of prior relationship—but only if you assess honestly not just who you know but *how* and *how well* you know who you know. So the "knows" have it, but be selective.

Stanton Avery did not invite his classmate Russell Smith to stand on top of the flower refrigerator he had rented from another classmate to help build his self-adhesive sticker machine, though he did borrow some money from Russell's brother at a bank. Stanton Avery was not out to start a tree house or club; he was out to start a business. But eleven years later, after the Second World War, when it was clear he had a viable business in the making, knowing Russell Smith's organized approach to financial and management matters was needed to complement his concentration on product innovations, Stanton Avery formed a corporation in which Russell Smith was brought on board as a vice-president and director to help build Avery International into a public multinational corporation. Stanton Avery gave Russell Smith an option to purchase a one-third interest in the company to be paid out of profits realized by the corporation over the next ten years. Ask Stanton Avery how he built his company and he will answer how "Russ and I" built the company. He considers his bringing a classmate on board one of the wisest choices he ever made. The two men knew, respected and *liked* each other. One doesn't grow to like or respect another person overnight—although in young entrepreneurships such bonding under duress and the close contact and long hours of battle can be dramatically accelerated.

Perhaps even more important, Stanton Avery and Russell Smith knew how they were *different,* as well as how these differences *complemented* each other—they'd already had a chance to learn to respect and complement these differences in the course of a friendship. The two weren't forced to deal with their differences as strangers, feeling each other out. They could immediately allow the other fellow to make full use of his strengths without the obligation to compromise and tiptoe in order to get along.

As mentioned, when Leonard Weil put together the start-up team at Mitsui Manufacturers Bank he recruited a number of experienced banking professionals, the majority of whom were already known to him. Of two vice-presidents in the loan area—one involved with personnel, one with commercial clients—and an operations manager supervising tellers and clerks, only one person failed to work out and grow with the company.

Nick Javaras, president of the brokerage division of the

Terranomics Group, was a broker who ten years previously worked closely with Merritt Sher. Merritt couldn't pay his tab at the start. Nick was working for a large company. But they stayed in touch, did deals together when they could, and they kept talking. They got to know each other over a period of years. When the opportunity came for Merritt to reorganize and build a brokerage division as an independent venture, all it took was a phone call. Merritt has followed the same tack with others. He knows where he wants the company to be, say, two years from now, and he has thought through what the personnel needs are going to be then. He keeps his industry contacts up and doesn't hesitate to pursue "what if" conversations when they seem appropriate—when prior dealings lead him to believe an individual might fit.

"The trick is to stay in touch, to keep your eyes and ears open, both to what you might need down the road and to who is or might be available. You don't want to get caught grabbing for anyone available at that last minute, because the last minute is not when you want to bring an unknown quantity on board."

Necessity may be the mother of invention, but a little foresight is often the groundwork for survival and success. Thinking through future personnel needs assures a better chance of meeting those needs head-on *before* a need becomes a crisis. And when this prescient thinking-through of personnel needs is combined with a habit of exploring applicants, as with Bill Kaufman's firm—making it a habit annually to screen top grads from a local college—or in the case of others through the habit of keeping doors open with industry and acquaintance contacts, then the owner-founder is even better prepared to deal with the demands of healthy growth.

Which, of course, isn't to say that some internal candidates won't appear for upper management positions. Indeed, most entrepreneurs tended to prefer to try to grow their own top managers wherever possible. Gordon Moore, for example, believes raising his own to be one of the cornerstones to Intel's success. He is extremely pleased about the way Andrew Grove, among others, moved up through the Intel ranks to head the company's operations.

The entrepreneur is a person with an open mind, with more than one string to his or her bow, and a willingness and ability to use whatever whenever to make things work and grow. In the case of employees, the smart entrepreneur who like Gordon Moore wants to have people move up from inside will also realize the need to start to stretch those already in place so they'll fit the larger shoes down the road. Foresight, openness and anticipation are the keynotes.

Mr. John E. Anderson.

Ray B. Anderson, Jr. *(Ceromet, Inc.)*.

Roy L. Ash *(formerly of Litton Industries).*

R. Stanton Avery *(Avery International).*

Michael L. Bobrow and Julia Thomas (*Bobrow/Thomas and Associates*).
Credit: Los Angeles Herald Examiner.

Dan McF. Chandler *(Chandler-Pacifica)*.

Wilfred P. Charette *(Systonetics, Inc.)*.

James A. Collins *(Collins Foods International).*
Credit: Norm Schindler ASUCLA.

Ralph E. Crump *(Frigitronics, Inc.).*

Warren Dennis *(Casablanca Fans).*

Paul E. Griffin, Jr. *(Griffin Homes)*.

Harold A. Haytin *(Telecor/sold to Panasonic).*

Leo Imperiali *(Tile World).*
Credit: Rick Cline Photography Unlimited.

L. Bill Kaufman *(formerly of Calmark).*

Gordon E. Moore *(Intel Corporation).*

Howard B. Morrow, Jr. *(Betty Zane Corporation)*.

Dr. Simon Ramo *(TRW Inc.; Aetna, Peterson, Jacobs and Ramo).*

Stanley R. Rawn, Jr. *(Pan Ocean Oil/sold to Marathon).*

Baldemar V. (Rod) Rodriguez *(Rodriguez, Jones & Company).*
Credit: Tony Kawashima.

Tim Sevison *(Nighthawk Productions)*.

Merritt I. Sher *(Terranomics).*
Credit: Images West.

Joseph Solomon *(formerly of Vidal Sassoon Hair Products).*

Edwin J. Stevens *(formerly of Compunet Inc.).*

Leonard Weil (*Mitsui Manufacturers Bank*).
Credit: Roger Marshutz Photography.

Chapter EIGHT

Doer—Delegator

Delegation, delegation, delegation. The importance of the chant is no less important than the restaurateur's well-known refrain: location, location, location.

Small new entrepreneurships are said to sink or swim depending on the abilities and tenacity of their owner-founders. Beyond the innovation and risk-taking that may be involved in an initiation, it is the entrepreneur's ability to see things through, his ability to cover all the important bases, if need be personally, that allows a company to survive and thrive.

Our old friend (nemesis) the typical entrepreneur, by now a bruised, battered and, I hope, retreating chimera, is criticized for not adequately formalizing his organization to meet the demands of an established professional business, for continuing to believe that his personal input will be enough to carry his business through. The blame for failure to formalize is most often put at the feet of the "entrepreneurial" personality—the set of traits that make up the myth I've tried to debunk. The daring, innovative, quick-draw artist entrepreneur is just not considered to have it within his power to sit back and let others independently perform and achieve. There's too much at risk, and besides, the typical entrepreneur presumably has intervention encoded in his genes. He is an autocratic megalomaniac who not only likes but is passionately attached to doing things his way. Which is why he struck out on his own, after all. So he faces great difficulty, big emotional trauma giving up

213

any authority, decision-making or control. Add on his pathological aversion to bureaucracy and the mediocrity he feels it nurtures in its formalizations, and you have good reason to suspect that the entrepreneur is not going to be your best delegator.

It's not a myth, of course, that even some very successful entrepreneurs do suffer in letting go of their creations. Among those I spoke with who sold their companies or stepped down from active involvement, several acknowledged this transition was the most stressful of their lives. Even those who stay with their companies and go on to manage them beyond survival and initial success do often become very personally involved in many if not all facets of their businesses at the start and so can have their problems delegating.

But placing the blame of poor delegation, or any other management malpractice, at the foot of a typical personality ends up with a grim, and inaccurate, view of the possibility of any entrepreneur *ever* making the transition to being a top managing generalist. It not only dismisses the model of successful entrepreneurs but fails to pinpoint just what the average entrepreneur might attempt to do to escape such a fate. Besides, by a little exercise in logic, if the "typical" entrepreneur is a myth, then so too is the fatal flaw that brings him down. Or at least the degree of the problem and its susceptibility to being handled ineffectively are overplayed.

Before I had conducted my first interview I knew that much of the writing on owner-founder management fails to stress sufficiently the examples of successful owner-founders who make the grade, basically, by doing business better than their competition, by covering some key fundamentals of management practice in a sounder manner. And this is just as true in the area of delegation as in any other area of management practice. Successful entrepreneurs, though rarely, it's true, skilled delegators from the start, do appear to be considerably more professional than myth and legend suggest.

Delegation is a very personal aspect of management. As the thoughts of a number of successful entrepreneurs suggest in this chapter, delegation hinges on trust, faith, rapport, relationship. It's the stuff that brings to life the structural lines of an organization.

After hearing a couple dozen successful entrepreneurs describe their own experiences making the transition from doers to delegators, I became convinced that there are some matter-of-fact steps as well as general approaches that distinguish the successful entrepreneur from the compulsive interventionist.

THE ABC'S OF THE BIG D

Delegation consists of more than simply identifying something that needs to be done and telling (or asking) someone to do it. There's also a difference between delegating and asking for assistance. I'll use myself as an example here. I learned the difference on the job as a manager.

I was still in my midtwenties and a long way from the day when I would become comfortable assigning a project or position and saying "keep me informed," fairly certain that this might not even be needed. As a management trainee in a large corporation I'd had subordinates—clerks and administrative people—who at times were called on to give *assistance.* But I had no experience with line authority over a subordinate. For the first few years purchasing, maintaining and managing apartment complexes, it was not uncommon for me to take three changes of clothing to work each day. In the morning, I would be cutting lawns, fixing sinks and painting apartments. At lunch I would change into a suit and tie, sometimes in my car, to meet with a banker or mortgage broker about financing of the property I had made an offer on the previous afternoon. After lunch I might have changed into the togs of a rental manager, pointing out the benefits of the location and facilities of a complex I was managing. When it came to hiring my first employee I was mostly thinking about how someone might help me, make it possible for *me* to perform these tasks in a more efficient fashion. I wasn't thinking about how I might turn any of my responsibilities over to someone else so I'd be freed up to concentrate on more important areas.

One afternoon while I was doing some maintenance and my employee was off buying some parts the light began to dawn. My "assistant" was probably driving down the freeway, drinking a Coke, thinking about the upcoming weekend while I was hustling to get everything done. Not surprisingly, he didn't share my degree of incentive. I had no illusions that he would do a better job than I was doing, was pretty sure he would not perform the task as quickly or as carefully. But it at last began to be obvious that I was just going to have to put up with someone else's lesser performance in some areas of the business so my growth-oriented responsibilities could be better met . . . for me to be the one driving down the freeway thinking—thinking about the business and how to continue to make it grow.

I realized I had to delegate. I made an employee responsible for a list of duties . . . a list eventually to be inspected by a foreman who had a list of his own to be reviewed by a property manager with a list to be reviewed by a general manager with a list who then reported to me with the help of legal, training, accounting and data-processing staff. And there came the day when I found myself turning over matters to others I felt were *better* qualified to carry them out than I was. That can be not only a revelation but a relief.

There are a few lessons most successful entrepreneurs have to learn along the way. To repeat: Defining a task and sending someone to perform it amounts to asking someone to *assist* you. Delegation does not take place until sufficient authority is at the same time assigned to an employee so he might independently accomplish the task. And delegation isn't complete until full responsibility is assigned for the accomplishment of a task for which authority has been given. If the job isn't done, the goal met, swift and appropriate correction is in order.

The flip side of correction is equally important. Sound delegation doesn't take place until there's defined incentive accompanying a delegation. No meaningful carrot, no inspired performance. And no justifiable correction. I wonder whether there would be so much talk about the need of the Big E (entrepreneurial management) in large corporations if managers addressed the absence of defined, future-oriented incentive, the most entrepreneurial fundamental of the Big D (sound delegating.)

So, principles for sound delegation:

the clearer the authority delegated . . .
the more fitting the authority delegated . . .
the more clearly defined the task and purpose . . .
the clearer the line of authority from top manager down . . .
the closer the responsibility to the authority delegated . . .
the more the decisions associated with a task and authority level are allowed to be made at that level;
the more singular *the reporting relationships within an organization . . .*
the more successful the delegation will be.

WHAT SUCCESSFUL ENTREPRENEURS DO AND DO NOT DO

I can say right off that many successful entrepreneurs *do not* call on the above formalizations associated with professional delegation *during the early days of their firms.* They *do* tend to retain decision-making authority over tasks performed by subordinates during initiation, particularly when untrained employees are being brought up to speed. But those who go on to success learn to shed this heavy hands-on approach as the company grows.

In a small firm, unity of command is preeminent and fairly easy. Who needs formally defined reporting relationships when you can hear the boss on the phone through the wall? And objectives are not always stated in a small firm. As I've said, entrepreneurs like Gordon Moore, Fred Charette, Ed Stevens, Leonard Weil and others did call on formal project, program or product-development schedules with formal milestones and markers early on if not at the outset of their entrepreneurships, but it's true that for a good many successful entrepreneurs the objectives stay informal, communicated orally and by example rather than in structured pronouncements.

It seems clear, though, that what the successful owner-founder may lack in detailed, documented, numberized objectives is made up for by the clarity and *enthusiasm* with which the entrepreneurship's mission and purpose permeate a young company.

To risk generalizing some previous observations as they relate to delegation: In small entrepreneurial companies destined for survival and success, morale and motivation, consequences of clear purpose and opportunity, are high enough to guide and in some sense control performance; in too many large organizations numberized goals and objectives become requisite in view of the difficulty of adequately recreating, communicating and inspiring a sense of group purpose throughout the organization.

Perhaps some *unsuccessful* entrepreneurs also managed to communicate a clear sense of purpose and sense of command within their organizations during the early days, but they failed early on to make conscious efforts to improve delegation, thereby paving the way for future growth. The ones who make it have the entrepreneurial bug, but they also seem adept at skirting the symptoms of the clinging commander and understanding that it is only through delegation that they can hope to stay at the wheel.

SOMETIMES THE STRETCH MARKS SHOULD PRECEDE GROWTH

As Gordon Moore tells it, Intel started out as a collegium of specialists who knew each other. Many had worked together in a similar capacity at Fairchild Semiconductor. When Gordon and Robert Noyce started the company they sat down with a team of five employees, all of whom had very attractive incentives to make the company work, and divided up the tasks in front of them into specialties. Gordon took charge of all equipment purchasing, evaluation of vendors and related financial matters. Gordon and Robert Noyce functioned more like team leaders who also were responsible for a specialty, then as general managers. The team concept continues at the heart of Intel's success. The first of this initial group to be let go was fired because, in Gordon's words, "not enough of a team player."

Nevertheless, there comes a day when all the team can't sit on one bench anymore, when the team might fill a small stadium and when captains are needed, particularly if you are going to survive going from a scratch start to several thousand employees in a few years.

In the case of Intel, by the end of the first year the company had grown to fifty employees, and most of the specialty areas were set. Growth was mostly a matter of hiring on subordinates under each specialty or project leader.

It was not until Intel was forced to split off a second production facility to handle the company's constant acceleration that steps were taken to insure that there would be a formal general manager overseeing operations. At that same time Intel also put in coordinating councils within its formal set-up to deal with the drop-off in efficiency that came with geographical diffusion (though at that point it was only across the street).

"It may have only been across the street," Gordon Moore points out, "but the fact was you stopped seeing people every day. That was when we hired Andy Grove, an engineer and manager who took over operations and has since grown and moved up to become president. Andy introduced more formal tools as a means of monitoring and controlling activities that could be handled less formally when we were all together. We set up an intense legal staff and hired some financial analysts. 'Personnel' became 'Human Resources,' and there was elaboration in that area too.

"Delegating was not terrifically difficult because from the start, even though we had all at one time worked in the labs ourselves, we knew we had to have state-of-the-art technical people. Growth was the order of the day. We set ourselves up to grow rapidly into a deep management structure from the first day by breaking off specialties that were and would continue to be at the heart of the business. As far as I am concerned, the biggest mistake a high-growth, high-tech company can make is to start off hiring helpers and one day call them managers, hoping they might work out. You have to bring in the best people you can at the start and from the first moment begin to develop them as managers. You have to thrust responsibility on them from the start and see who can stand up to the growth and who can't. When you are dealing with dramatic growth it's the best strategy. When you delegate something and someone comes back for help, you offer any relevant expertise you may have. (At Intel this is increasingly not the case, with graduates coming out of school knowing what we should be doing next.) But after you offer your input you make sure that you *don't* make a decision for them. You have to attempt to grow your own. You won't be able to afford to hire people who call themselves managers later on and wait for them to fit in and come up to speed. You should be delegating and testing your people from the start, or you will find yourselves unable to deal with the growth when it hits you.

"We were a little different than some you [the author] have been talking to, in that we *expected* to grow to $100 million in sales in the first five years. We were all a little surprised to see how fast we made it and how far we surpassed it, but we knew we had to gear up as soon as we entered our first warehouse. We are looking to be a

$4-billion or $5-billion company. There are only a few bigger ones now, and to my mind many of them have made mistakes that we won't repeat. Companies can grow and get big, and top management levels can multiply, but not necessarily keep up with the growth demands of the company. It is one thing to have the formal mechanisms in place to assist delegating, but it is another to have the capable and competent managers in place who can do the delegating and make the decisions. You have to have the management knowledge grow with the company, and the only way to do this is to stretch early team members, to find out what they can and cannot do *before* the demands of growth drown you."

Stretching employees, using the organizational rack—in their fashion all successful entrepreneurs use it. So do some *un*successful entrepreneurs. The difference, as I've suggested, comes when an entrepreneur learns to step back and let go. The following are some accounts of a wide variety of approaches to delegation, all of which pinpoint some prevailing hurdles and lessons no matter the differences in approach.

THE MYTH OF IMMACULATE DELEGATION

For entrepreneurs like Roy Ash, experienced professional managers accustomed to operating as top manager from day one, making the transition from doer to delegator was not as difficult as for most other entrepreneurs.

Roy Ash had functioned as a manager at Hughes. Roy knew the success of Litton Industries depended on the work of individuals expert in areas that did not fall within his own personal expertise. As I will touch on here and discuss more in the next chapter, an entrepreneur who sees himself as a generalist or top manager from the outset specializing in facilitating the efforts of experts and specialists beneath him has much of the problem licked. Such an entrepreneur will tend to pay his operational dues with great fervor at the start, like any brother entrepreneur, but also will be goal-driven to do everything in his power to work toward the day when he will no longer be in the slot.

I was surprised to hear from a great many entrepreneurs, particularly those who went on to manage firms through the quickest greatest growth, that they'd *sought out* the position of top manager or generalist from the outset. So successful entrepreneurs seem early on to perceive the business as more than a product or service. They have a vision of an organization. They may not set out to create that organization through formalization, but they have begun to think about just what the business could become. And they've begun to realize just how much they are going to have to delegate if they want their vision to take form.

As Roy puts it:

"We didn't break down and design an organization chart until near the end of our 120-company purchase binge, when it became necessary to establish division leaders and coordinate the activities of all the different companies, but at the start, even though we didn't have a formal chart, everyone knew the organization and authority relationships very well. Don't misunderstand, they were communicated, even if they were not set down in writing. We didn't just leave things like that for people to figure out on their own. But on the other hand, if you give someone incentive, show him or her the general way of your strategy, tell who they're to report to and make sure they understand how the control system works, what more do they need to know?"

How did Roy personally keep track of delegations?

"I managed entirely by exception. If there was nothing in our reporting systems to indicate that someone was off the track, I let them continue to run on their own. The trick is in selecting the right people. I've had a great deal of luck with this, which isn't to say we didn't have to keep an eye on how people were doing as we grew. We did not hesitate to bring in experienced professionals at higher levels the minute it became clear our growth had surpassed someone's organizational abilities."

Roy Ash's version may sound like the sort of delegation you would get if you combined textbook prescriptions and entrepreneurial savvy. Yet as I have mentioned, Roy insisted on hiring one level below his direct subordinates as a means of reducing politics, which by some by-the-book types might be considered encroachment on decision-making or authority.

Roy also felt that there were some things he could never delegate out of headquarters:

"I could not and would never delegate relations with investors or investment bankers out of headquarters. To a great extent I continued to deal with these duties personally. I could not and would never delegate strategic decisions out of headquarters, nor would I delegate financial control, legal licensing and patent matters out of headquarters. These duties were handled by others but they were under my direct control. In other areas, after the strategic-decision level, I would simply say 'everything else is up to you' in handing a project over to a manager."

Mostly those aspects of business Roy Ash refused to delegate are in areas of management often described as the domain of top management and its staff. But in any business, especially in start-from-scratch entrepreneurships, there are going to be other key areas that need the special attention of the top manager to ensure survival and continuing growth. Roy Ash's practice of hiring one level beneath the subordinates reporting directly to him is only the tip of the iceberg when it comes to the variations in methods of delegation practiced by the entrepreneurs I spoke with—very successful methods that might not sit squarely on the page of a book outlining formal prescriptions for sound and complete delegation.

Delegation is never immaculate. Delegation, as you will see, is a human-to-human process. Delegation is made successful as much by the spirit or attitude of the owner-manager as by the letter of prescribed rules. In the end I was convinced that the entrepreneurs I spoke with, especially those who went on to manage the largest and fastest-growing companies, understood the spirit of delegation very well indeed—though, as you will also discover, many practiced anything but immaculate delegation during the early days of their ventures.

ONE STEP AT A TIME: INCREMENTAL DELEGATION

In earlier chapters I described a strong contingent of entrepreneurs who call on inexperienced, inexpensive, ambitious and often young entrants into the job market as a means of covering the bases and still being able to afford a bat and a ball if not uniforms at the start. (Sorry about that extended metaphor.)

Eugene Rosenfeld had grown accustomed to deep delegation as the chief executive of a NYSE builder before he set out on his own. Delegating to proven professionals was not new, but he could not afford to hire proven professionals when he started the Anden Group. And he found himself spending much time training and working closely with some of the young people he had hired and offered incentives to to build his fledgling organization.

Eugene Rosenfeld wanted to delegate as much as he could as soon as he could, but at the start he often found himself having to step back in to keep things on track. But Rosenfeld only got back in if there was a noticeable drop-off in the quantity or quality of the work, a drop-off that was beginning to impact other aspects of the business. When it came time to delegate the planning and buying of land to the regional offices, when standards and progress goals were not being met, he did need to step in, for example. But it didn't become a pernicious habit.

"From the start I had the life-style goals I mentioned. I wanted to make more money with less stress. I wanted to be independent. To me this meant building an organization so that I could turn matters over to others. *And this meant delegating as much as I could as soon as I could.* But there are variables. You can't afford to delegate too much to unproven professionals until they have their feet wet. You have to pitch in until the newcomers are trained. Still, even when a few of these delegations don't work out, if you are driven to be free of the operations, you stick with it; you do everything you can to bring on board people who you think can handle it. You give them financial incentive and training and you step back as soon as you can so that you are free to pursue more expansion that will lead to further delegations."

Bill Kaufman experienced some of the same growing pains and has a similar view on the incremental nature of delegation in a young entrepreneurship.

"You never delegate everything all at once, even with a proven professional. Even in a larger company there is always a period of more intensive cooperative involvement and joint decision-making in an area before you are sure expectations and communications are straight. This gets magnified in a small company because of the number of new delegations taking place every day. You tend to retain for a while decision-making power on some points. Delegation isn't static. You need constantly to pick and choose what you will and won't become involved in at the start. You need to think this through and set priorities. Early on, the lines surrounding areas of responsibility are not set hard and fast, so you have some flexibility to work with. And if you have given a subordinate financial incentive and communicated your desire to see him grow into a job, you aren't going to find too many noses out of joint if you do share responsibility to some degree for a limited time.

"I personally had a harder time than some others delegating, letting go of the strings. As a subordinate I had established a reputation as the type of guy you could give the ball to and let run, and who would assume responsibility and take charge. That's how I put myself in the position of being asked to be a founding partner in an entrepreneurial firm at the age of thirty. You would have thought I would have understood delegating. But at first I tended to expect way too much of others. I had to learn to moderate my expectations. Also, I am a naturally curious and impatient person. Maybe other entrepreneurs are too, I don't know. I am the type of guy who wants to know what is going on and the type of guy who wants to have things done now—today. If you have that streak, you are going to have to be very disciplined with yourself. You have to sit down and discuss a responsibility or task with a subordinate and let the subordinate tell you what a reasonable goal and time frame are. If you agree, you are going to have to wait it out. If necessary you are going to have to sit on your hands, but you are going to have to give him a chance to do the job.

"On the other hand, if you do this you have to expect that the goals are going to be met. You can't accept a person coming back to you to say that the goals and time frame weren't reasonable. You have to stick to those goals and reward and correct accordingly. You have to be disciplined and consistent. The people working for you have to know what to expect.

"An ideal manager would be totally unselfish and capable of sitting back and watching and reaping the benefits. But this is a hard thing to do. It is something you almost have to force yourself to do. I wouldn't say it was natural for me. Everyone enjoys putting his mark on one area or another. There is always going to be one area you feel you do best."

Dan Chandler strongly believes delegating to inexperienced employees in a small firm has to be a gradual process.

"In a young company, you never suddenly delegate 100 percent. People should first be asked to assist you in an area, until they become familiar with it. For a lot of young employees it will be the first time they have encountered a particular aspect of business. Even if they were born with a briefcase crease in their hand they are going to have some things to learn. What it really comes down to is a matter of confidence. You have to prod them on but give them time to become confident. You *do* make a point of letting them know that you hope they will take the entire area off your hands. That is an expressed goal, and if there is incentive and you have a go-getter on your hands, he or she will take it from you, begin to assume responsibility. At the start, you reserve the *right* for a final decision, even if by practice it is no more than a nod and a rubber stamp. You reserve the right, just so things are out on the table in case there is a need to step back in. You have to have a series of checks and balances in any size organization. You may eventually delegate your personal check over a decision but responsibility runs up and down the line. When you delegate you don't delegate your responsibility for a subordinate's decisions. And you have to do everything you can at the start, including staying involved for a time, to make sure those decisions are the best for the organization when you are fighting to survive.

"Delegation is always a process of taking one step forward to introduce a task and responsibility area to a subordinate, then taking two steps back, to allow for growth. At some point you have to step all the way back and give up that final personal check on decision-making. This is always a hard thing for me to do. It is something I am having to learn to force myself to do for the sake of the growth of subordinates. I try to get in a position of being kept informed, after we have set strategy and goals together, so that decisions are all but unspoken. I have been an entrepreneur in one shape or another as a broker or developer for too long a time not to want to be involved. There is also the issue of personal risk. When you are personally signing on the line you tend to want to be a little better informed in some areas, to say the least.

"One way I force myself to keep my hands off things is by taking vacations. Leaving town is one of the best ways of testing delegations. When you leave town you are forced to delegate things more completely. You are forced to leave some decision-making behind. At the same time you force a subordinate to step up and assume more responsibility. You both build confidence in the delegation. Skiing works pretty good, but if you really want to test one, I highly recommend fly-fishing in a remote area where there are no phones. That's like going cold turkey."

"A big thing necessarily comes about in a big situation, and a big situation necessarily comes about with a big thing . . . Why be so anxious about it?"
—Chuang Tzu 399–295 B.C.

Maybe the above date should read B.E. (before entrepreneurs). Quite a few of those I spoke with characterized their delegating during the early years as an "act of faith." The greater the confidence one gains with delegations, the easier holding to the faith.

But if delegation is an entrepreneur's ultimate business-related faith, then worry has to be an entrepreneur's ritual of prayer. Ask successful entrepreneurs how they really held their companies together during the early days and a good many, if they are honest, will probably say it was through vigilance that bordered on constant anxiety. Most I spoke with said if they had it to do over again they would have delegated far more at the outset, knowing now that much of their worry resulted from their inexperience and lack of faith in delegation. Most also conceded that a good deal of their early worry was unfounded. If someone could learn to separate the emotions of worry and apprehension from the desire for challenge and excellence, as well as the fear from the concern that often accompanies risk, the entrepreneurial world would be a lot more comfortable.

I remember how it felt at the start, and I don't consider myself a big worrier. In fact I tend to be an optimist, to think that things will work out one way or another. In my case let's just say there was a great deal of persistent concern. And it's not that you ever lose the worry, it's just that at some point you begin to realize that things tend to work out more often than not.

"You become more Pollyannaish with the years," says Ray Anderson. "At the start, if you're like me, you find yourself learning that most employees don't match the intensity of your commitment and enthusiasm and standards for performance. I'm talking about a basic though innovative manufacturing and engineering firm, mind you, with a great number of unskilled workers. At the start I found myself having a hard time swallowing the drop-off in quality that came with turning tasks over to others. Every drop-off when you're struggling as I was at the start appears as a personal threat. You're fighting, after all, for your independence. This is something you are totally committed to. And you're fighting for the survival of your company.

"With time, you begin to realize that things will work out, even if, for instance, you will never again match the low percentage of scrap you were maintaining the first few years. In my case, by bringing in a more people-oriented, professional manager-type adept at seeing through the short-term drop-offs to the long-term gains, I insulated myself from some of the difficulty that I faced delegating early on. But then I only insulated myself from those smaller delegations by making a larger one. You can't get away from delegating. In the end, it solves most of your problems or, in its absence, it becomes your final problem."

LEARNING TO ACCEPT YOUR EMPLOYEES' WORLD VIEWS

Warren Dennis had a somewhat related problem with delegating. In started-from-scratch manufacturing firms there is a good deal to be learned about differing perspectives on work and motivation. At the start Warren tended to delegate in his own image.

"It took me a while to understand and appreciate the world views of my employees. As charged up as I was in my twenties I tended to take it for granted that everyone met their career as a personal challenge. I enjoyed diversity and challenge so I expected that others either did or should too. It was really a shock to learn that some people just treated their work as a job, as something they did to make other parts of their lives possible. At the start there just weren't any other parts of my life. There's a conflict built into the situation between an entrepreneur and his employees. No matter how much you try to use compensation to fire up the others, they are never going to be as into their jobs as you are.

"When I redesigned the production line for a larger facility in 1980 I created an entirely new set-up with eight production stations. The idea was to train the production employees to be skilled at each station so that they could be interchangeable and, I thought, more interested in their work. But they didn't like it at all. They weren't comfortable. They wanted a sense of confidence and of having both of their feet on the ground at one station. I learned to understand others' world views and to cater to them. It was probably the most important lesson I ever learned about managing. Now if I design another production line I will be designing it around the sensibilities of the people who will be working it, not around what I think they should be. And the nice thing is, once you learn this, once you accept that most other people treat work as a job, you are every so often really surprised to run into the odd employee who *does* demonstrate inspired commitment. That is extremely gratifying, something like a reward for learning the lesson."

GETTING COMFORTABLE DELEGATING

Leonard Weil operated in an entirely different context from Ray Anderson and Warren Dennis. As top manager of a privately chartered bank he had no choice but to delegate extensively from the first day. His hands were full meeting with regulators, community leaders and large customers, as well as managing growth strategy. Weil has recommendations that deal with some of the intangible aspects of delegation that make it more difficult for some people.

"An entrepreneurial bank may be a little different than what people consider a typical entrepreneurial company to be. At the start, as well as now, we have been successful because we were organized to do some things *better* than large banks. A small entrepreneurial bank works closely with its customers. It plain and simple gives better service, in our case to a good many entrepreneurs running small- to medium-sized companies. An entrepreneurial bank is flexible within its guidelines and is willing to go the extra mile to satisfy the customer.

"To do this we had to have the specialties covered from opening day. We had to have them covered just to get past the regulators. I had to bring on board proven professionals from the start just to get the bank chartered. My number-one recommendation to anyone starting a business, once they reach the point of needing intervening management levels, is to hire competent people to whom you can fully delegate with confidence. If you don't have the confidence you just aren't going to delegate in an adequate manner.

"If you don't hire people with whom you are comfortable delegating, people you feel you trust, people with whom you have an easy time communicating from early on, you are not going to be able to delegate smoothly no matter *how* competent they are."

Fred Charette comes to the point when it comes to prescribing means of dealing with some of the less tangible aspects of sound delegation.

"Never hire anyone who is going to report directly to you who you do not intuitively just plain like from first impressions. If you don't have that sort of comfortable chemistry going you are going to end up wasting hours deciding which side of a stamp to lick. You may think you can work things through for the good of the company with someone with whom you don't have good rapport but at the start of the company you can't afford to waste time working things through. If your instincts tell you you're going to have a hard time working with someone, pass."

DELEGATION: THE ONE AREA IN WHICH A GROSS LOSS CAN LEAD TO A NET GAIN

When Leonard Weil hired specialists, loan officers, controllers and the rest he often felt very confident that these people would be doing a better job than he could hope to do.

Many of Leonard's subordinates were professionals in specialized areas in which Leonard had not concentrated. Roy Ash, as mentioned above, felt much the same way. He didn't pretend to understand the science that was being practiced by the project managers to whom he was turning over checkbooks.

On the other hand most entrepreneurs start out with much smaller businesses and numbers of employees than Roy and in a much less structured and regulated environment than Leonard Weil. A good many, as I've related, begin firms on the basis of personal expertise in one or another specialized area of a business. Many quickly learn just how much *more* than one specialty area they have to cover for their businesses to survive. Once the business is beginning to get on its feet many are also faced with turning over operating or other activities at which they have become not only good but even expert to subordinates whose efforts may or may not be quite as inspired or productive.

To my mind one of the most important signs of a good delegator is not so much whether he can turn over authority and responsibility and keep an arm's length while managing subordinates with greater expertise in one area or another. The true test is whether an owner-founder can turn over something he knows as well as or *better* than a subordinate. This ability distinguished many of the successful entrepreneurs I spoke with from their more "typical" cousins.

A lesson learned by Ray Anderson is that sometimes short-term drop-offs in the quality or quantity or both of individual performance in one or another area of the business have only to be tolerated for the good of the growth of the company.

Fred Charette *wanted* to delegate as much as possible as soon as possible—as a policy. He knew that if he was going to meet his goal of going public within the first five years of business life he would need to be free to dedicate a good deal of time and energy to Systonetics' nonoperational growth demands.

"I didn't ask anybody to do anything I wouldn't do. I made

the coffee, swept the floor . . . I handled whatever the bot-
tleneck was, as well as about thirty phone calls a day and
the marketing and finance activities.

"It was fairly easy for me to delegate product development to my tech partner. He was, plain and simple, better
at it than I was. Why should I make decisions about something someone else knows better? But otherwise delegation
was extremely difficult for me. There were so many things
others were doing that I was better qualified to do. I would
try to delegate a whole area. But there was always an initial
drop-off in an individual's performance. Sometimes that
drop-off, as a person came up to speed and put their own
stamp on a department, would begin to sop up too much of
the company's resources. If product development was running behind schedule there was no point in my being out
flying across the country marketing. When things began to
bog down there was a tendency for everyone to pitch in,
which included me stepping back in to become a force in an
area I had tried to delegate. But by the third year, with the
product developed and with greater demands on other areas
of the business, I just had to bite the bullet and put up with
the drop-off. I promoted or hired people to be top managers
to oversee our separate departments.

"Everything took longer than I thought it should, but I
just had to learn to accept it. It isn't easy. You may accept
it but you don't stop worrying about it or feeling the urge
to step in and do something about the drop-off while people
are coming up to speed. You just have to learn that people
are probably going to learn faster if you don't. But the truth
is, you are going to be worrying even as you are doing the
right thing.

"With sales, for instance, there seemed to be an inordi-
nate amount of time spent in training. But it was an entirely new field, you couldn't just go out and hire people
with experience selling software applications when you
were one of the first companies in the field. Sometimes it
seemed I should just dive back in and hit the road, that we
would actually be making more sales that way during the

training period. But I didn't. And eventually when the sales team did come up to speed the company was making more sales than I alone could personally dream of making. You have to accept that there may be a gross drop-off in performance compared to what you were doing but at the same time realize this is for the good of the company. Tolerating that gross drop-off is the only way to net continued growth.

"Many draw a triangle to describe an organization, but at the beginning it is an inverted triangle. You are carrying the organization on your back, which makes it that much more difficult to step back and delegate. You worry that the whole thing is going to topple when you step out from under it—after all, during the early days it's often the case that your actions do determine your company's survival.

"You also quickly find out that you sometimes run into problems from delegating *too* much. I delegated too much in the product development area to my tech partner. Some mistakes that were made took years to unravel.

"I may have learned to delegate, but it was never easy. I went through three controllers in a year and a half trying to find someone who would hit the mark I had set for the company as chief financial planner. If I had it to do over again, and if I could afford to, I would hire someone ten years older than myself to be chief operating officer from nearly the start. I would have hired someone to keep tabs on all the delegations, someone who *enjoyed* dealing with the people problems. I would have hired someone with greater patience than myself, and I would have focused in on problem areas and on the demands of going public."

Warren Dennis felt that quality control was of particular importance to Casablanca. At the start of the company the goal had been to produce the highest quality high-end product on the market. Warren had personally built the very first fans at Casablanca, knew in his sleep the difference between the best and the also-ran. Everything about Casablanca, including its ornately painted advertisements on the sides of its semi-rigs, bespoke Burton Burton's and Warren Dennis's joint commitment to craftsmanship and quality. In Warren's mind, if the products began to belie this commitment Casablanca was just another struggling entrant in the market. So even after a quality-control department was set up, there was a close eye and perhaps even intervention now and then by top management.

Ralph Crump also kept close tabs on quality control at Frigitronics. His core product, as mentioned, was a medical instrument used in eye and other surgeries—a microrefrigerant on the tip of a penlike device. Ralph didn't sever his ties with quality control until three years after the company went public—almost ten years after the company was founded. He had reason to be concerned. Prior to going public the company had been hit with a crisis that almost took it under. The introduction of microrefrigerants into the operating room was a highly regulated process. Before the medical instrument could be routinely used by doctors it had to be tested. A doctor who had not been authorized to use the product borrowed the equipment from another doctor. Though it of course had been designed to be foolproof, the doctor's nurse managed to do what the engineering staff believed to be impossible: She managed to reverse-mount the microrefrigerant tip, jamming the equivalent of round pegs into square holes, turning the instrument into a microsoldering iron that the unauthorized doctor, not testing or noticing that the tip of the instrument was burning hot, not cold, proceeded to use in an operation on a one-eyed patient in a veterans' hospital. The government, government hospital and government doctor couldn't be sued so Frigitronics was. Frigitronics was just barely able to settle and continue to do business. It was the kind of experience that would lead anyone to spend extra time checking on quality-control procedures, though the quality of the Frigitronics product continued high.

The secret of retaining the entrepreneurial enthusiasm associated with the early days of started-from-scratch firms hinges on a perception of top management's continuing concern for and involvement with customer satisfaction, which in turn depends on the quality of service and product. An entrepreneur doesn't want to intervene in areas he has been able successfully to delegate, but he wants to stay involved as a leader vitally concerned with the enthusiasm with which the needs of the customer are met.

Leo Imperiali has delegated responsibility for the presentation and order within his stores to store managers but still finds himself making the rounds with a scrutinizing eye, sometimes even stepping in and taking on a customer in an especially busy store. Merritt Sher has had the most difficult time delegating creative decisions on the mix of final design and tenant. Though he believes others might be able to duplicate one or another type of project he has undertaken he wants his firm to stay at the front of development—which to Merritt Sher means questioning the latest success, forever trying to do the next both differently and better. Merritt has not given up the final word in this area. Ray Anderson described his holding onto the purse strings, the "housekeeping" matters of accounting control for some time, as a result of his belief that "the bookkeeping area may not be able to make you money but it sure can lose you money in a hurry."

The success these entrepreneurs either had or will have in managing at some point to delegate these last frontiers within their businesses affected or will affect their continuing success. It's clear that entrepreneurs like Roy Ash, Jim Collins and Gordon Moore could not have achieved such growth without considerable delegation, but there are stepping-stones and stopping places along the way. Managing a growing entrepreneurship is a little like leading a choir in a series of coordinated "rounds"—as each new group is brought into the song the entrepreneur's leading voice may be needed until their contribution is firm and strong and he or she is free to hand the baton to the next one.

DELEGATION WITHOUT CONTROL CAN BE THE EQUIVALENT OF ENTREPRENEURIAL ROULETTE

For Ed Stevens, moving up to tackle the responsibilities of top manager of a growing software firm servicing the broadcast industry meant giving up a specialty.

"For me, programming was like playing the piano. It was the art of the business. There were trade-offs, both for me personally and for the company, in my separating myself from product development and moving into other areas."

Ed had to learn a number of lessons.

"I had to accept that I had to stop creating at a certain level. I had a policy of never going back into an area once a lead person had been established because it would have been an infringement. I would stay involved in a not yet established department, such as documentation or advertising, where, say, only one person had been hired and my input was needed to set a level of quality as a standard that would be maintained as the department was built up. But otherwise I tended to treat people as I would have liked to be treated in the same situation. Even when I knew an idea was not the right idea or the best idea I tried to find good points in it because eventually that person would come up with a usable idea. Ideas are extremely important in any business, but especially in a creative business like software applications. I tried never to squelch subordinates' ideas, even when I was still retaining final decision-making in an area that had not been fully turned over. I have always had a blackboard and used it extensively with key, responsible managers to talk things over and stimulate discussion.

"There were a couple things I had to fight in delegating responsibility for product development. First, there is something of an unwritten rule in programming that the minute you get more than one individual involved in a program both the quantity and in a sense the quality goes down. Two people do about one and a half times the output of one person working alone. Three people do about two and a quarter times the work of one on his own. In general the programs become less creative because they are not one person's puzzle. The trade-off is that you get better documented, better organized, more understandable, more communicable and in the end more marketable programs. You get a more responsible, balanced, checked-out product.

"What you lose is the speed with which you creatively solve customers' problems, the speed with which you react to on-the-spot requests. Your product development department works as a unit with cooperative goals of turning out an overall compatible product. Programming becomes a lot more coordinated.

"So personally I had to give up the tremendous gratification that came with creating. I had to give up the enjoyment that came as a craftsman and artist. This wasn't as hard as it sounds. There were plenty of new gratifications. I would say that for every gratification lost there was at least one to replace it. I was beginning to deal with top executives in computer companies. My contact at Control Data, the only person in the entire organization that I could get to admit that we were having a problem with computer down-time, the only person who would admit it was a problem that was not good for me or my customers, went on to become a chief executive with that company and it was a pleasure doing business with him.

"I did run into problems delegating too much before we had adequate control systems in place, and had to learn a few lessons there. After you have delegated, as I mentioned, you can't impose your ideas and decisions. So during the early days in some areas you tend to partially delegate, you turn things over but attempt to guide people in the right direction. You find yourself involved in a great number of new meetings as new people are brought on board, concerned with communicating basic philosophies that were taken for granted during the early days. As an organization we lost that sense of total oneness that was there during the early days.

"Unfortunately there were a couple of areas I delegated to subordinates who I didn't think needed as much direction. I put my trust in people before the control systems were in place. If you don't have adequate control systems in place you have no way of tracking progress. And it is a little difficult to deal resolutely with deviations when you don't learn about them until it is almost too late. You have to delegate, control *and* correct. It's not just a question of delegating per se. Delegation is a fluid process, depending on the responsibilities, risk, the people involved and the level of development of your company."

Merritt Sher experienced problems when he both delegated the management of a brokerage division to a new partner and geographically split the division off from headquarters.

"I didn't have the systems in place to monitor an off-premises operation, and the company began to pursue a strategy I didn't agree with. We lost a lot of synergy. The brokerage division stopped complementing our development activities. I finally had to buy the partner out and bring the company back in-house and set up adequate controls."

Paul Griffin, as mentioned in an earlier chapter, also suffered problems from not adequately addressing control systems at the very start of his business that impacted his ability to delegate, though unlike Ed Stevens, Paul believes he tended not to delegate enough at the start.

Like many others, Paul tended to hire inexperienced people during the early days to help the overhead.

"My mistake was in only filling in the base of the pyramid at the start. I hired a bunch of people who were all very good employees but who primarily assisted me. It's sort of a chicken-and-egg problem. You don't think you can afford to hire proven professionals, so instead you pay the personal price of continuing involvement, which impacts far more than your business. I wasn't aware of any drop-off in quality at the start when I delegated because we were thriving during a boom time. But when a recession hit and things slowed down I found out how much more efficient we would have to be to survive. If I had hired professionals during the first boom and delegated to them, both my life as a manager and a family man would have been much easier. But it took me two cycles to figure it out.

"Before you can delegate you not only must have confidence in the people, you must have confidence in your organization and control systems. If you don't have adequate control systems in place, no matter how much you try to delegate, you will end up personally involved. It wasn't until I put my mind to organizing and controlling my company that I was really able to delegate and step back. And it was only then that we were really able to grow as a company—growth that coincided with my delegation. The organization is not completely mine anymore, but it is a lot larger and stronger organization, so that the part that is mine is greater than it was before."

Though a far rarer circumstance, some entrepreneurs actually begin to suffer delegation-related problems as a result of an excess of control within their companies. Bill Kaufman, for example, had to educate a subordinate to become a less enthusiastic "reporter" so that he would more efficiently get on with his work and so Bill could do his job as a manager.

"I had this one employee who was so detail-oriented that he wanted to give me a twenty-five-page report on his progress and the status of his responsibility area each month. But I have always been too lazy a manager for telephone book reports. I don't want to wade into the detail that isn't going to help me do my job. I had to explain to him that I didn't need to know every time he took a breath. I asked him to figure out a way to shrink down his report to a page with visuals. Not to mention the waste of one's own time, one doesn't want subordinates *over*-reporting or wasting their time past a necessary level."

FOLLOWING THROUGH, ONCE YOU KNOW THE SCORE

From the start John Anderson understood the important relationship of control to delegation. Because his beer distributorship was struggling he had to do law work to feed it. But in order to hold down two jobs he had no choice except to delegate. Within six months he hired a supervisor to manage the loading docks and drivers, and after three months of training he turned over the distributorship's operations to him. John was only able to do this through a series of reports and control tools and mechanisms, which he personally monitored during a portion of his day, otherwise devoted to the practice of law. Because this worked, John was able to continue to work two jobs and use the proceeds from his law work to continue to buy distribution routes and rights, which allowed the business eventually to take off.

One thing John learned early on was never to be tentative.

"I was only a tentative delegator, meaning having a tentative reaction to the progress of delegations, until I understood what was going on. A ship can't be led without a captain. You absolutely owe it to everyone in your organization to be decisive. You should be honest and up-front about it, but you should be decisive. Early on, through my control systems, I became aware of a problem of a driver who was stealing petty cash and apparently encouraging others to do it as well. Times were thin for us and attitudes weren't what they became when we managed to gain a second product and began to grow, but still, there was no question about dealing with the incident. The employee had to be fired, and it had to be made clear that that sort of behavior wouldn't be tolerated, however dire our straits might have been at the time."

USE, DON'T BOW TO, CONTROLS

Dr. Si Ramo believes a secret to strong delegation is sound control and regular meetings, which allow a manager to stay less formally abreast of a subordinate's progress. On the other hand, Si also believes one of the true secrets to successful delegation is the quality and "entrepreneurial" nature of a subordinate.

"The difference between a bureaucrat and an aggressive, ambitious employee makes all the difference in the world when it comes to your being a successful delegator. What you want are subordinates who don't dwell on the negatives or the limitations in a situation. You want an employee who sees limitations as obstacles, not as laws. If you want to be a successful delegator make sure you aren't about to turn something over to someone who can't see past the letter of the law to get something done.

"I had a manager under me once who wasn't making the sort of progress we wanted in his division. I called him in for a chat, and he gave me a number of reasons why things weren't going the way we wanted them to go. But they were basically excuses, just a summary of existing limitations. It became clear to me as we talked that the real problem wasn't the list of limitations, it was a lack of a list of new areas we should be tackling. What this manager needed to do was drop existing projects that were limited and enter more productive areas. I told him as much. 'But what about our budget?' he said, again looking toward a negative. 'What budget?' I asked. 'That was the budget for what we used to know. We need a new budget based on what we know now.' A good manager thinks of what he should be doing and sees a budget as a means of getting there, not as some rigid deterrent."

DOING WHAT COMES NATURALLY . . .
AND MAKING SURE OTHERS DO IT TOO

Ed Stevens was honest enough to admit that his own inability to correct or fire employees who failed at delegations caused him problems. In an earlier chapter Warren Dennis related problems he faced when he had to move from being one of the boys, a fellow production worker, to being a manager—detached, objective, matter-of-fact and unwilling to accept the shenanigans of former production mates. Most owner-founders suffer the consequences of not being firm enough the first time out. If they are lucky it is before they start their own businesses. Very few start out with the confidence, experience and talent for managing of Ralph Crump, who took to delegation like a duck to water. From the start, he says, he liked to make waves.

"As a child I was always bossy. I was always managing the kids in the neighborhood before I knew what it was to be a manager. While I captained a ship in the navy I learned there is absolutely nothing to be gained as a manager from being tentative. Things were fairly black and white. I didn't expect that everyone would necessarily do things the way I might do them. In fact in most areas I went out of my way to be sure I hired people who would do things better than me. If I had to teach someone how to do something or explain their job to them and then only hold them to myself as a standard, what the heck was I doing hiring them as a specialist? But I knew enough about each of the specialties to know when performance was helping or hurting the company. If it was hurting there wasn't much of a decision to make. If a person didn't come around when you brought things to their attention you fired them. If they were doing the job, as I said, I tended to put up with a lot at the start.

"As soon as I could I set up engineering and production departments and promoted two guys to run them. I don't think I was really tested as a manager until I had to deal with subordinates who were having a hard time delegating.

To my mind, delegating activities doesn't really become a problem until you are delegating *through* people."

Once an entrepreneur sets up three or more levels of organization, employees accustomed to experiencing directly the owner-founder's authority have to be educated to deal with the authority of an entirely new position and person. In production-intensive firms, with the very first promotions of supervisors, managers or directors, the problems encountered by owner-founders seem to fall into two camps: Either a supervisor or manager steps back and doesn't pitch in enough, or he stays too involved in production activities and does not devote the proper amount of time and activities to supervising the work of others. Warren Dennis reported that he experienced both of these kinds of supervisors while trying to hire a production manager—indeed, one after the other.

Sometimes the owner-founder must teach, even *force,* his employees to delegate. Ralph Crump had a problem with his first production manager. He tended to stay too involved in production and not to delegate enough to his supervisors and lead workers. Ralph wanted him to spend more time planning for production schedules and personnel and less time fighting fires. Ralph's effort to help facilitate the transition was straightforward, and in a manner befitting a self-possessed benevolent despot—he "collared" the guy.

"I had tried explaining the problem without much success so I finally just sat down with him and insisted that he wear a white shirt to work. I knew how careful and conscientious he was and that he would be afraid to get it dirty and would have to get his hands out of the gears. . . . I'll tell you what, that was about all I needed to do. He got the message. He kept his shirt clean and he learned to delegate."

A white shirt was, of course, symbolic in this instance, but it bespoke what Ralph was trying to get across.

LEARNING TO KEEP YOUR DELEGATIONS DOWN: ANTACIDS ALONE WON'T WORK

Elaborating on early delegation within Frigitronics, Ralph highlights another key lesson entrepreneurs must learn if they are going to weather the storm.

"What does become a problem during the early days is trying to keep delegations *down* in a small company. There are still a small enough number of people to keep up personal contact and interaction with everyone. The company is still personal and like a family and you want it to stay that way. You want to keep morale high. You want people to feel wanted. You don't want to hide in your office. But there are too many things to do to remain personally involved with everything each of those employees is doing. I stayed in touch with all our employees on a *personal* level. I would try to get to know them, but I refused to talk about authority or production matters with them. It's a temptation but you just have to be cut and dried. 'That sounds like something you ought to talk to Andy about. . . .' or something to that effect, even if it's something you know that Andy is going to have to turn right around and bring to you. What you lose by undermining your subordinate is not made up for by your grandstanding or sense of personal control. Employees even tend to respect your authority more, through Andy, than they would if it was scattered all over the place. You have to cut off the end-runs or you'll undermine your own act of delegation.

"Employees learn pretty quickly if *you* are willing to learn pretty quickly. I tried to reinforce my delegations by having my production manager place the ads and hire all of those who would be working under him. I didn't routinely interview applicants and in no case did I intervene within my manager's decisions. At first we did have disagreements about the strategy of hiring. For instance, we both agreed that we wanted to attract and end up with a higher caliber of production worker than we were getting. My production manager favored hiring at a higher wage to begin with. My attitude was that all that guaranteed was that you would be starting out with a bunch of high-paid unknowns, some of whom were statistically bound to be mediocre. I preferred to hire at the existing wage, make it known what we were after and what would be rewarded, then weed out the mediocre and reward the excellent. But once we hammered out the overall approach, I left the rest up to him.

"Generally it was fairly easy for me to delegate. I had the experience of the navy and a number of years with a mom-and-pop company. I always knew if I didn't make it as an entrepreneur that I could make it as a manager in a market-driven company. The real secret does boil down to hiring the smartest people you can, people that you honestly feel are smarter than you in a given area. If you find yourself tending to hire deadwood you're going to end up a deadwood company. I wanted to be a generalist and a manager. I wanted to run my own company, not work for it. I had already worked for a company. I could have done that without setting out on my own."

Fred Charette did not have such prior management or military experience, but he learned to take a similar tack.

"I made a point of staying on a name basis with everyone in the company as long as I could, but I conducted all my business through my controller and vice-president of operations. I would say our biggest problem concerning delegations came more from interaction *between* departments and managers than it came from the top down. We were all fairly inexperienced, maybe even immature as managers. For some of the founding team it was a first-time business experience. We tended to have problems, say, with interaction between marketing and development because we were small enough and familiar enough with each other so that line authority was not always called on or respected. This became less of a problem as the company grew and interaction started to follow the lines. My own respect for the line, my own delegations and detachment from squabbles helped reduce some of these problems. Which wasn't really very hard for me. Despite my own struggle with knowing that there were some areas I might have improved on with personal involvement I expressly wanted to step away from operations and people problems and get on with tackling the process of going public. I would rather sit across a table and have to negotiate with a gaggle of lawyers than be bogged down dealing with the personal problems of employees who happen that day to be getting in the way of operations. That was something I had no problem delegating."

Michael Bobrow, of the Bobrow-Thomas Associates architecture firm, also experienced problems with end-runners.

"Very early on I turned over the technical areas of architecture, within which I had less expertise than others. I concentrated on design, dealing with the clients and minding the books, something that came to me naturally. I was very control-and-budget-oriented. I loved to worry about cash flow. My wife, partner and now the chairman of our company, Julia Thomas, has taught me to loosen up in this area.

"At the same time I was very much people-oriented at the outset. I understood that you have to be a little tentative with strong-minded, creative subordinates. I had an open-door policy. We operated like a collegium. But as we grew this turned out to create a lot of problems with delegating because people were always coming to me to intervene on levels I thought I had already pushed down. To compound matters, when I delegated office management to a managing architect the first time, it was to an individual who was an extremely capable planner and tracker but not good at following up with people on matters caught by his tracking systems. The result was that we ended up realizing just how much more objective and formal and less people-oriented an organization we had to become. At first Julia took over the management of the office, and then we eventually hired a professional manager, an executive vice-president to formalize and standardize our operations. I think we let things get so human-oriented at the beginning—understandable considering the business—that some of the humans started to become very *me*-oriented human beings. Loyalty faltered because we had grown dependent on my personal interaction and motivation, and this was no longer possible as we grew. So in order to delegate and keep things down we had to move toward a more professional environment. We also had to get back that sense of common purpose that we had when we were just starting out through personal interaction, *but* communicate it in more formal ways now that we were larger."

When Big Just Doesn't Fit: Grin and Bear It

For some entrepreneurs, the change that comes as the company grows is just too much to bear. They simply don't accept it and they simply don't grow. Entrepreneurs like Ed Stevens and Joseph Solomon may not have liked the change but they learned to live with it.

Joseph Solomon considers himself in the first instance a marketer. If he could go back and do it over again he would subcontract production at Vidal Sassoon Hair Products to an outside firm and stay a small marketing concern with his continuing involvement as top marketing manager. Joseph is one of those entrepreneurs who definitely and consciously *prefers* to stay small in spite of his success in founding and managing a company that went from scratch to almost half a billion dollars in worldwide sales in little over a decade. After selling Vidal Sassoon Hair Products to a larger firm Joseph returned to his small marketing company concept, putting together a small staff and selectively and profitably taking on products and projects at their discretion. He enjoys working with a bustling team. His advice to a budding entrepreneur is to quickly build such a team, paying particular attention to your own weaknesses.

"Know your weaknesses," he says. "Acknowledge them. But don't worry about them. As long as you understand your shortcomings you will go out of your way to hire people with strengths to offset them."

At the start Solomon had three employees in a warehouse in Canoga Park, California. "Those first days I did everything. I would get to work at the warehouse at 7:30 A.M. after stopping at a local Hughes market to pick up the cardboard boxes I would use to deliver the previous day's orders. I would pack the boxes and personally deliver the products to salons. Then I would return to make phone calls and take orders for the next day. As soon as I could I got into marketing, flying to other cities like San Francisco or Tucson to visit salons and spread the word. To do this I had to delegate the phone sales and paperwork to others. Generally it was no problem. These were all doable tasks and I had given a little stock to each of the initial employees to see that they stayed motivated. The pace alone, the rate at which we were growing, was enough to keep everybody happy and working full speed. With growth I was able to increase the compensation of key employees. Everybody wanted the company to keep growing.

"The real problem was that *I* could not get over the feeling that the organization as a whole was not as lean as it could have been. We went from three employees to five hundred employees, from three thousand to 250 million in domestic and 150 million in international sales in about ten years, but I still believe to this day we could have done it with one hundred employees. It really comes down to the fact that I just don't like a large organization as much as a small one. I like the action, and when the company reached a stage when it seemed we were having to do as much to organize and expand to meet the expectations of Wall Street-types, bankers and government agencies as we were to meet the market, it just wasn't as much fun for me. Almost all my delegations worked out with a qualified yes. The company was running as smoothly and efficiently as it had been before them, but it was not running as efficiently as *I* wanted it to run. I wanted it to run as smoothly as it was running but I wanted the same level of productivity to result from fewer people and greater spirit. I preferred that atmosphere. There was no drop-off in the quality of product or marketing, but there *was* a drop-off in the enthusiasm and spirit of the organization. It was no longer possible to keep everyone motivated with stock. There were too many employees and we had to departmentalize personnel and everything that goes with that. Once we had grown to a couple of hundred employees things were never quite the same. I did the things the company had to do to grow that fast but I didn't necessarily enjoy doing them. I prefer to stay hands-on. If I did it all over again I would delegate even more of certain aspects of the business but less of others. Doing our own production at the start dictated the size of the organization. If I have someone else doing production I don't have to face the same problems and demands of a larger organization. As an entrepreneur, I am able to be in the end just as productive. And beyond that, I am able to stay happier as a person, being more hands-on in marketing, which I enjoy.

"I didn't enjoy the spirit of the business after I had delegated. I did what I had to do because I was resigned to satisfying the outsiders. I knew enough to know there was no other way for things to work, but I never got over the feeling that without outsiders we could have done things differently. I know we could have stayed leaner. In a way, I don't think entrepreneurs ever really get a chance to show what they might be able to do in terms of productivity and efficiency. In some ways I think they are forced by outside investors and regulatory agencies to organize in ways that reduce their productivity and efficiency in order to do business on a certain financial scale."

Not everyone I spoke with was as open or blunt about dissatisfaction with a larger or so-called "more professional" organization. A few even found a larger organization in some ways more to their liking.

By now it should be clear that not all successful entrepreneurs delegate, let alone think, alike. With this in mind it is both interesting and worthwhile to take a look at the variety of more personal experiences, attitudes and general approaches to running a business encountered while talking to this diverse group of successful owner-founders, especially those approaches and attitudes that appeared to meet with the least resistance down the long, winding entrepreneurial trail.

Chapter NINE

Independence: The Costs and Returns

LIFERS, IN AND OUTERS AND CONTINUING SAGAS

Not meaning to counter my point about the myths surrounding entrepreneurs and entrepreneurship, I don't want to imply that entrepreneurs are not individualists with a strong attraction for independence. The successful ones, though much more professional in their fundamental approaches to management than myth suggests, are very much their own men and women, and don't continue along one commonly tread path to start or grow.

Some, those I refer to as "Lifers," entrepreneurs like Stanton Avery, Leonard Weil, Ralph Crump, Gordon Moore, John Anderson, Jim Collins, choose to stay with entrepreneurships as they grow into very large corporations over the course of decades and sometimes for the duration of their careers. Learning to delegate and isolate themselves from the sort of demands one might not forbear over the long haul, Lifers manage to continue as fountains of leadership and strategy, at the helms of the businesses they personally founded and built.

Others I call "In and Outers," people like Joseph Solomon, Warren Dennis, Ed Stevens and Harold Haytin, manage a firm's dramatic growth for a decade or more, then sell their ownership position in the company and move on with the proceeds. A good many of these go on to start new firms, and some of them, like Joseph Solomon, who has established a smaller marketing firm after selling his position in Vidal

Sassoon Hair Products, take a different approach the second time around. They may do so because they have grown to realize that they find more enjoyment in a smaller firm, or have reached an age at which they wish to continue running a business but at the same time want to *enjoy* some of the fruits of their initial success.

Still others, among whom I count myself, the "Continuing Sagas," haven't yet fully faced up to a clear-cut choice between a continuing involvement in a dramatically larger corporation or disengagement from their entrepreneurship in spite of financial success and asset-building. People like Merritt Sher, Leo Imperiali and Ray Anderson, by personal choice or as a result of the current state of their industries, find themselves involved with financial and organizational structures that seem to have dictated, to date, a continuing full- or part-time hands-on personal involvement in the management of their firms.

JUDGE NOT—THE CHOICE MAY ONE DAY BE YOURS

It would be a hustle to suggest that one can develop an "attitude" or "approach" conducive to success as an entrepreneur without some of the underpinning experiences. But it would be just as bad to assume that there are not a few things with which one might have an easier time with a little prior knowledge of some of the alligators lying in wait.

Of course it is a lot easier to look back with the perspective and humor and confidence that come with having survived, when one knows he has paid his dues and earned the reward. It's much easier to be detached and philosophical about some of the lessons that had to be learned *after* the fact of learning.

It's also true that some entrepreneurs actually *do* have an easier time of it than others in spite of the common pitfalls and life-preservers I've talked about. Some start out with larger teams and deeper delegation as a foundation; some with better-educated and more self-motivated em-

ployees than others; some with more prior management or
life experience than others. Still, I'll make some observations about general attitudes and approaches that make for
less trouble in the face of the demands of building a business.

GUARANTEED COSTS: BUSTING YOUR CLOCK

Ask the family of the chief executive of a Fortune 500 corporation if owner-founder entrepreneurs have a copyright on
long hours and you will learn that there are many in America who curse the fact that the sun chooses to set so frequently. A good case might be made, however, for the claim
that the entrepreneurial path is the least democratic when
it comes to long days and weeks. In a large corporation an
individual has some degree of choice over the length of his
day. If you want to get to the top and into the till you work
long and hard wherever you might be. Still, if you don't
work your longest or hardest, presuming you are reasonably competent *and* cooperative, you are probably not going
to be sent packing. Some entrepreneurs might say that this
is exactly what is wrong with many large organizations and
institutions: They have not only lost any sense of direct
positive incentive for performance, they have also lost any
meaningful sense of *negative* incentive as well.

If an entrepreneur doesn't work long and hard there will
be no question of there being a top, bottom or middle seat
for him in an organization. Rather there's a good chance he
will no longer have an organization—will no longer be an
entrepreneur.

The cost of independence during the early days for Lifers,
In and Outers and Continuing Sagas alike is enslavement
to the "independent" entrepreneurship. The freedom
demonstrated by opting to go into business for oneself most
often turns out to be the freedom to have no choice but to
give it one's all, all day and all week. Obviously many aren't
cut out to handle the demands of this sort of "freedom."

Some three-quarters of the successful entrepreneurs I interviewed worked sixty to ninety hours a week during the initiation and survival periods of their firms. Very few worked less than six days a week the first years. Fred Charette worked fourteen hours a day, seven days a week, for the first two years of the life of Systonetics. Roy Ash had become accustomed to working eighty-hour, six- to seven-day weeks at Hughes, so it was not a shock to him to do the same during the earliest days at Litton. Joseph Solomon was putting in ten- to twelve-hour days every day of the week with Vidal Sassoon Hair Products the first year. Si Ramo worked seventy-hour weeks before, during and after the founding of TRW.

If you can't see yourself pulling a couple of years of such hours and you still find yourself with a burning desire to be in business for yourself, the only thing I can suggest is real estate development. The real estate developers I talked to tended to put in fewer hours than some routinely ambitious middle-managers within large companies.

"There is only so far you can push things yourself in development," offers Merritt Sher. "Some stages of development are more up to you than others. During project and site planning and as you hustle to sign up tenants you can personally push. But even as you attempt to secure tenants you are at the mercy of the inner workings of financial institutions and local governments. Very few tenants are willing to sign leases until they see just what the final project is going to look like, which might depend on the desires of one key tenant who is holding his commitment off as long as he can. Both the key and other tenants generally don't want to sign a lease until they get a nod from the bank that the project is going to go ahead. It's a process of courting and bringing everyone together. Some tenants want to wait until you've broken ground, including a few key ones who could make or break the center. You can only push lenders, governments and key tenants so far and hard when you're starting out. There is a lot of waiting in the development business."

Which is not to say one can't be working while waiting out the stages of development. As Merritt puts it: "I used to just drive around when there was nothing else I could do and try to scout out locations and tenants unknown to me, trying to look ahead and keep my mind off the personal risk I was facing at the moment."

Stanley Rawn, an entrepreneur in the highly risky business of oil exploration, has a similar attitude about the relationship between risk and the extent to which personal effort alone might contribute to success: "In the oil business almost everyone from the rig operator up is sharing in the risk and the potential rewards. You hire the most competent people you can and you do push them but you can only push them so far. If a well doesn't pan out, it doesn't pan out. You can become efficient to a point, but after that it doesn't matter how many hours you're working if there is nothing under your platform. You can't pump rock. You put in long hours evaluating properties and planning when it comes to choosing drilling sites and dealing with governments and oil ministers, and you sink that well as efficiently as you can, but there is no direct relationship between total hours spent drilling and barrels pumped, as there might be in a manufacturing concern facing ready demand. If you come up empty you've failed. If you hit a field, even if it took you a number of attempts and hours, you are suddenly efficient."

Stanley Rawn and Merritt Sher highlight a truth that pretty well holds for all fledgling businesses struggling for survival. Even in supposedly less risky manufacturing industries, if the product and market aren't there and don't stimulate each other they just aren't there, no matter how long and hard you work. Again, the importance of the sort of concentration strategy that makes up the better part of entrepreneurial planning covered earlier can go a long way in determining whether the long hours turn out to be a futile exercise.

When it comes to long hours, the longest do seem to come for entrepreneurs heading either manufacturing firms or firms with an initial objective of developing and bringing a new product to market. If there is a definite goal that is dependent more on brute human exertion within the firm or within a market than on timing or third parties, the difference between success and failure in a competitive environment might very well hinge on one entrepreneur's willingness to go the extra hours. If the challenge ahead is mostly a matter of slugging it out in a relatively static market until a niche is secured, you are going to *perceive* the challenge before you, rightly or wrongly, as a simple challenge of measuring your willingness to work long hours.

"If you ask me why I have been successful, I would have to say it has been my willingness to work Saturdays," Ralph Crump says. "During the early days if I wasn't working on the weekends I was traveling. I expected a marketing representative working for me to do the same. It boils down to a matter of mathematics. There are fifty-two Saturdays in a year. That adds up to about ten weeks. If there are sixty working weeks in my year and fifty-two in somebody else's, or say fifty if he takes a vacation, who do you think is going to get ahead over a ten-year period?"

Be prepared and forewarned . . . if you are attached to weekends and relaxed evenings, stay where you are.

ALTERED STATES

Describing the importance of a willingness to work long hours is a bit misleading. Most spoke of the *passion* with which they enjoyed working long hours at the start. Entrepreneurs like Fred Charette, who from the outset had the goal of disengaging from a successful public corporation, give new meaning to a "labor of love." Fred did not take his first *day* off until two years after the initiation of Systonetics.

"I was in a euphoric psychological orbit the first three years, before we went public, loving every minute of it, being in business for myself after all those years of planning and dreaming of being in business for myself. The sense of achievement was tremendous, and it grew each day. The sense of becoming someone you felt very good about, of realizing a dream that was becoming more real and making your reality that much more exciting—all of this was wonderful, in spite of the exertion."

Warren Dennis also experienced some of the heightened state that came with personal exertion and achievement, but he also says it wasn't always good for him or the company.

"I carried Casablanca with me twenty-four hours at the start. I didn't take a vacation during the first four years. But building that company was a very satisfying experience. It was my entire life at the time. I was not just building a company, I was learning new things about myself, about my capabilities and potential.

"But there were also times when I worked beyond my limits. We were in a continuous situation of back orders from the moment we formed Casablanca until the moment we sold the company. If I hadn't been partners with an older, more experienced entrepreneur I'm not sure I would have fared as well. Burton had run a machine shop and he helped keep the early pace at Casablanca within reason. We didn't work around the clock as an organization. We didn't routinely run the line on Sundays. Even so, there were definitely times when I personally worked to the point of losing perspective. You just can't be productive working every day of the week or over ten hours a day as much as you feel both the desire and the need to grab on and not let go. Burton was a tremendous help in steering me away from taking on too much. My tendency was to try to do everything myself. When I took my first vacation after four years I was amazed not to think about the business for the first few weeks. It began to dawn on me that I had been developing one part of myself but that I had lost touch with a good deal else that I didn't want to eliminate from my life—both for my own and the company's good."

THE LONG HAUL:
THE IMPORTANCE OF PACE

It is well known that most people perform better under stress—to a point. After a blowout no one is going to go anywhere in a hurry. With a shorted fuse it's a little hard to see the light at the end of the tunnel. It is not enough to prescribe long hours to the prospective entrepreneur, as much a part of the territory as he or she may be. At a certain point, a business becomes much like the family: Quality time becomes as important as quantity time. There comes a moment when the entrepreneur either does or does not learn the importance of Peter Drucker's differentiation between doing the right things and merely doing things right—between concentrating on formulating and meeting the needs of growth strategies, and incessantly applying oneself against the squeakiest operational wheel.

In order to think long and well, a good number of the Lifers I spoke with early on learned to establish limits around their involvement with their businesses. . . . "Despite my having become accustomed to the long hours, both at Hughes and during the early days at Litton, as soon as I had our control systems set up I established a personal policy I have kept the rest of my life: long and hard, Monday through Friday, but weekends with the family," says Roy Ash. "You owe it to yourself as much as to your family. Even if work took me to another country I would fly home for the weekend to be with the family.

"The most important thing to remember is that you can't give *all* of yourself to anything. You have to keep some part of yourself detached in order to remain competent and fresh and objective in your work. There are going to be lots of worries no matter how professional you are. The first five years at Litton we worried a good deal of time about whether we were going to make it or not. And as soon as we were able to overcome those worries we right away turned to worrying about the monster we had created. The only way you stay detached enough to face up to the pressures and deal in a controlled and positive manner with the sources of your worries is to make sure you have a life away from your work, and for me that has always been my family."

The importance of Roy Ash's lessons about a disciplined approach to personal work habits was reinforced by many others. As a matter of fact, more than a few of the longest and hardest-working In and Outers went on to be the most adamant about determining that their organizations would not make the mistake of overworking once initial survival had been managed.

Fred Charette, too, learned to downshift a gear or two, after his initial binge. . . . "You have to remember that I wasn't the only person putting in those hours. We were all working that hard the first few years. After we went public I began taking Sundays off. Though in some ways we were more solid after we went public, the pressures for both me and the organization in many ways increased. At the start there was only the venture capitalist and our own goals to satisfy. After going public there were shareholders, the SEC and all the other agencies. We had to satisfy the same agencies that GM has to satisfy. I took my first week off after our fourth year, a year after we went public, and by the fifth year I had begun to advocate a formal policy of a mandatory vacation for everyone in the organization. I realized that I was getting stale and I didn't want our company to become stale. I began to better appreciate the importance of pacing. My original plan had called for me taking the company public and disengaging after five years. I ended up staying thirteen. When I started the company our monthly expenses were $5,000. When I left they were $800,000. The value of my decisions had equally escalated. I was making bad decisions that cost us a couple of million dollars, and I was making good decisions that made us a couple of million dollars. You try, of course, to make more good ones than bad ones. When you're president of a surviving and growing firm you can't afford to have a bad day. The ramifications of your having a bad day become too great at that point. You realize you have to take time off and pursue other activities as a simple matter of rest and restoring your equilibrium."

Leo Imperiali established a formal policy of mandatory vacation with his first salesmen in his Tile World stores. . . . "You have to stay fresh. I had learned this myself working a stretch of almost ten years, seven days a week, running the first store myself. You have to get out of the store every few months just so you'll want to come back, just so you'll want to be there and will be able to communicate that to the customers. Now I try to make it a rule that all salesmen take a week off every six months and that my general manager takes a week off every four months, though I sometimes have a hard time getting my manager to take all of his."

Bill Kaufman feels the same: "I learned early on as a consultant that you just can't work seven days a week. At first you seem tremendously strong and productive, pushing yourself that hard, but after a point you can actually become less efficient and counterproductive and not just during your extra hours. Working too much can begin to affect the overall quality of your work. We always tried to keep our organization from overworking, but it was hard. Though I personally knew enough to take weekends off, after a while I had to establish a four-and-a-half-day work week just to keep everybody else down to six days."

STILL FISHING AFTER ALL THESE YEARS— AND TALES OF OTHERS THOROUGHLY HOOKED

Very few entrepreneurs demonstrate the discipline and consistency of Gordon Moore, especially amid the heat of the battle in Silicon Valley, where the reckless bravado of shooting stars has been well chronicled.

Gordon took the same amount of vacation the first year at Intel that he takes now—two weeks. He keeps the same hours now that he kept the first year at Intel: "Ten to twelve hours a day, five to six days a week, mostly five now," he reports. "We've fixed up our house a little but we've lived in the same house for a number of years. And I'm married to the same woman who helped put me through Caltech."

And how does Gordon spend those two weeks' vacation?

"Still fishing. I go fishing two weeks every year. I'm able to forget the business when I'm fishing. I just block it out of my mind. . . . I don't think it made any difference whether I was gone or not the first year, and I don't think it makes any difference now. There is no change when I leave."

The shareholders of Intel should be happy to hear of Gordon Moore's stability and self-discipline, tailor-made for the long haul.

Even though most *successful* entrepreneurs do learn the lesson of stepping up to manage for the future, many entrepreneurs, including some successful Lifers, in one way or another continue to dedicate the lion's share of their lives to their businesses. In fact, most I talked to had an alien relationship with the notion of a formal annual vacation. Almost three-quarters of them took no formal vacation of a week or more prior to the time of their first major expansion, which generally meant within the first five years of their companies' lives. Only a quarter took a regular vacation of a week or more from initiation on. And almost half asserted that they *still* do not take a regular annual vacation years after having achieved both material success and success in organizing and delegating within their organizations. In other words, they *choose* to continue to dedicate their lives to their businesses even after they have managed to delegate direct involvement in operations. Many of the Lifers and Continuing Sagas I spoke to, as well as they might understand the concept of pace, stay committed to business. Si Ramo says he's never altered his six-days-a-week, twelve-hours-a-day work habits since World War II. Roy Ash puts it this way: "Business is and always has been my only hobby. . . ." "I travel with my business," was repeated again and again to describe the notion of going places away from home.

In the end it seems that while In and Outers may not take as much time off the first decade or so, a good many Lifers, though learning to pace themselves, *never* come to take vacations as such. In and Outers who sell a successful company and semiretire or start a smaller firm, as well as some Continuing Sagas who consciously limit their personal engagements in smaller but successful entrepreneurships tend to experience considerably more recreation in their lives.

It's almost like the tortoise and the hare, perhaps even a form of poetic justice. In and Outers may experience the early days in a more intense fashion, but in the end the commitment and sacrifice seem to balance themselves out. For some Lifers and Continuing Sagas, entrepreneurial survival and success seem akin to a performing artist's coming of age. Once a performer has succeeded in being recognized, he or she is "free" to stay on stage until no longer able to perform.

STAYING FRESH IN THE MIDST OF A MARATHON: SOMETIMES YOU HAVE TO FORGET TO REMEMBER

You have to forget to remember; you have to look away to really see. In my own business, my partner and I learned to force ourselves to take days off at the start. And whether I was attending a ball game or riding a motorcycle across the desert it was uncanny how often a solution would come to mind for some problem that in the day-to-day snowblind blur of operations seemed hopelessly complicated. The importance of maintaining an objective perspective and mental freshness can't be overemphasized.

All this may seem self-evident, but it is very easy to deny the value of rest and recuperation as you become increasingly enthralled with your seemingly superhuman abilities. You will be working harder than you ever worked before, and it will seem as though you are blessed with a limitless store of second and third winds. Like any other compulsive behavior, as important as the long and hard hours will be to your success, you will one day have to learn to moderate at least the extreme edge of your excess. No one can work forever without paying the price.

"We all leak oil." The quote is not mine. It is Lee Trevino's, meant, of course, to point out that even a pro has a heart and a nervous system.

It's also true that as a group successful entrepreneurs appear to have rather deeper oil pans than most, to be capable of a great deal of effort and exertion without encountering as much of the stress-related physical side effects that many others encounter after much less battle. And this depends on the nature of entrepreneurial stress as it was described by a group of successful owner-founders.

"I was having too much fun to be stressed."
That's a lot easier to say with money in the bank.

There is a difference between sacrificing for a positive goal perceived as reachable by personal effort and sacrificing in the face of what seem to be insurmountable odds or a stacked deck. The negative side effects of entrepreneurial stress generally seem related to a lack of control. Frustrations such as chronic under-funding or negative cash flow don't make for "enjoyed exertion." Most successful entrepreneurs perceive the stress of the early years as a condition they can personally influence by continued personal effort. For many there's an almost giddy relief that comes with finally having one's fortunes rising and falling on one's own will rather than on the will or folly of others. Stress then seems to be more a challenge than a problem.

Says Ed Stevens: "When I started my first business, owning the radio stations, there was a good deal of stress because we were undercapitalized. We just didn't have the money to buy stations in the markets that would allow us to make a go of it. But with Compunet I cannot remember experiencing the same kind of stress. We had adequate financing, we had a bank behind us and a relatively open field, however uphill the battle. When the financial side is relatively under control making your business survive

seems more a matter of hard work to overcome surmounta-
ble obstacles, and you just don't feel the stress in the same
way. I might have become exhausted now and then, *but
never once did I feel like not going to work."*

How many people can say *that?* And Ed's opinion was
backed up by most of the others. Only two suffered stress-
related physical ailments that required medical treatment.
For one of these the ailment occurred during the process of
selling his firm, perhaps a sort of separation anxiety. For
another it happened in the midst of fighting a period of
sliding operational control that happened as a result of a
failed delegation to an operations manager. Only about a
quarter, a figure below the national average, experienced
a divorce during the course of managing an entrepreneurship. Of those who headed the larger firms for the longer
period of time, the divorce rate was next to *zero*.

True, such statistics are qualified by the fact that divorce
rates are generally higher among younger people, but
within my limited sample I think the figures are valid and
apply to a wider group as well. Indeed, for the majority of
the successful owner-founders I spoke with, building a business did not appear to be a road well-traveled alone. Especially for the Lifers, a consistent and stable home life
seemed an anchor, a balance permitting a long-term entrepreneurial journey.

FAMILIES: A MATTER OF PRINCIPLE AND INTEREST

It would be a distortion to paint *too* rosy a picture of entrepreneurial family life. Even with the realization of the importance of pace and the limits that some successful entrepreneurs learn to put on their hours, an entrepreneur's
family can sacrifice nearly as much as the entrepreneur.
Almost half of those I spoke with said that their families did
at one point or another, usually during the early years,
suffer stress that could be related to their being in business
for themselves. It would seem, to be frank, that the only way

to insulate a family from feeling the overflow of some of the demands that confront the entrepreneur is to postpone having a family until the business has at least one foot firmly planted.

Most often stress experienced by an entrepreneurial family was related to an owner-founder not having had enough time for the family during the earliest years or to an owner-founder having often been preoccupied and having had difficulty devoting the sort of energy he might have liked to his family. Again, though this is a problem every working spouse or parent faces to some degree, the problem is certainly compounded for an owner-founder entrepreneur.

"No, no, no. Emphatically no. There was never enough time for the family. There was a constant, overriding feeling," says Ed Stevens.

Ray Anderson echoed his words.

"I did the best that I could, but it was extremely difficult to take time off from the business at the start. I couldn't take off a week at a time for the first five years. But I did make a point of taking off a day here and there to take the family on an outdoor outing to keep our sense of family strong. This is something you have to do if you all are going to stay healthy in the long run."

Much like the nature of the stress experienced personally by the entrepreneur, the sort of sacrifice a family makes as a unit can be a much more positive experience if goals are shared. Seeing a parent or spouse enthralled with purpose, even if one would like to see them more often, is better than watching a spouse or parent suffering away under the press of a job they find intolerable.

Says Ralph Crump: "My family had to pick up and move from an extremely comfortable home and situation in California to Connecticut. But it was not as if I came home and issued packing orders. We talked the thing through. Everyone had their say. There was no question that it would lead to good things for all of us if we met with success. There's no question we've materially benefited beyond the initial expectations we were willing to accept as worth the sacrifice. More important, I have now been able to put some of my children into business for themselves. Every family has its ups and downs, but I think I know what my entrepreneurial children might say if you asked whether it was worth the move."

FRIENDS AND OTHER FADING MARKS ON THE HORIZON

Entrepreneurs have been portrayed as loners fixed on their businesses with personalities not easily suffering casual friendships. David McClelland's seminal studies assert that entrepreneurial types don't have a very high need for affiliation compared to individuals working for large companies.

Not too surprising. The entrepreneurial life can be a solitary one during the early years. Starting out on one's own means giving up (or escaping) a number of peer relationships in another work setting. Still, as I reported elsewhere in this book, there is also some intense affiliation with employees during these early years of entrepreneurial life, but it's not the circumscribed, stratified affiliation that takes place in other organizational settings. Anyone who has ever worked in a big corporation and has also been in the military has seen the similarities. Generals don't fraternize with privates; CEOs don't invite junior execs to their clubs.

Friends do, though, tend to go by the wayside. As Warren Dennis says, "Being and succeeding as an entrepreneur made it difficult to keep up some of my friendships. Fairly soon it became clear to me that I was losing a sense of commonality with many of my friends. I was extremely excited about what I was doing. For me there was this huge challenge and a great deal of potential change and uncharted waters out ahead of me, while some of my friends were learning to settle in on tracks that weren't going to change that much for them and going about their lives in ways meant to compensate for this.

"Also, before too long I was making about five or six times as much as I had and as *they* still were making. I didn't personally think I had changed but others seemed to pre-judge that I had. It's difficult to overcome such changes and keep up preexisting friendships. On the other hand, the long hours and the fact that you aren't going to have a large peer group that meets in common places is going to reduce the opportunities for cementing new friendships, even though there are opportunities to meet other entrepreneurs. In the end, although you don't have to go it completely alone, you probably are going to have fewer friendships than before.

THE REWARDS

At this writing there exists a very popular television show advertising the life styles of a class of individuals who don't ever need to ask how much. I suggest, though, that most successful entrepreneurs, though often possessing the means, are not as flamboyant as our popularly fed imagina-tions suggest—chiefly via the wondrous fun and games of the fabulous Malcolm Forbes.

I could run down a list of castles in Ireland, ranches in Santa Barbara, homes, cars and similar creature comforts, but in a profound way this would be misleading. For many successful entrepreneurs, Scott Fitzgerald and Ernest Hem-ingway's telling exchange (Scott: "The rich are not like you and me." Ernest: "Yes. They have more money.") does not seem especially appropriate. The commonalities that sounded the loudest and clearest among the conceptions of rewards described to me were more concerned with self-determination and creation than currency and caviar.

Almost all the owner-founders described their greatest reward as being able to just sit and look at the business itself. The company is something in most cases they had started from scratch; something they had at times them-selves thought might not make it; something that was now *there, real, for anyone to see.* The greatest reward, then, is the business itself, the realization of what was once only a vision, a dream.

The rewards differed to some extent for Lifers, In and Outers and Continuing Sagas. In and Outers experienced the pace of a sprint for the duration with their firms. They tended to be most attached to the early days, since often they had only a year or two to experience the setting of a more established firm and so best remembered the intensity of their early involvement. On the other hand most of the Lifers said they found their work lives without exception to be more rewarding each step along the way as their companies grew and became more complex.

"There is always a tendency to feel nostalgic about the early days and struggle," says Leonard Weil. "But there is nothing I really miss from the start. Many of our founding employees are still with us. In a way we have brought our past along with us and don't need to look back at it. I have enjoyed the present of our business more than the past, excepting, of course, downturns. At bottom I am doing more things for more people, employees and customers, than ever before."

But I came away with another impression. I could not help feeling that in some way Lifers, whether they had had specific plans for growth or not, did not experience the same emotional release or charge that some In and Outers felt during initiation and the first year or so. For some In and Outers start-up and early survival seemed close to having been a reward or end in itself—a very tough act to follow indeed. The greater the drive to be an entrepreneur, the less the chances of that individual turning out to be a Lifer, the moderate of entrepreneurism. Lifer Jim Collins was candid about the balance between feelings for the early and present days.

"I went to give an employee a twenty-five year pin the other day, someone with whom I had once worked much more closely, and I realized just how much I had enjoyed the early days, working closely in my few hamburger stands with the part-timers. But for every enjoyment that is lost along the way, as you give up certain kinds of direct engagement, there is always an equal enjoyment that comes with a new involvement. The excitement and involvement that come with mapping out key strategy and seeing decisions come to bear fruit bring every bit of the same feeling of engagement within the company. As you delegate more and more and step up you travel in different circles within and without your business. All of this is tremendously rewarding."

SO WHICH ONE WILL IT BE FOR YOU?

To Warren Dennis's mind a good many entrepreneurs run into trouble, perhaps even bring needless struggle on themselves, as a result of taking themselves and their businesses so seriously that they have a hard time tolerating the people problems and changes that are the heart of doing business.

"The more you view your business as some personal crusade, the less flexible you become. And the less flexible you are, pure and simple, the less successful you are. If you begin to take your competition or anything else involving your business too personally you are bound to start making personal decisions that stand a good chance of not being the right decisions. If you take yourself too seriously, there is a tendency to start drawing a line and doing business from behind it. It's important to remember that it's just a business and not to keep in your mind that it is *your* business. The biggest lesson I learned, as I mentioned, was to concentrate on seeing things from others' viewpoints. If you try to make your company over in your own image you are going to run into nothing but headaches. Being intractable might seem like the way to survive the early struggle but it's also the best way to guarantee that you will continue to struggle.

"I have my own ideas about why some people stay with companies and others leave. From my experience there are just some people who like beginnings, middles and ends. People who go to work for someone else and stay there apparently just like middles and being stuck in them. People who start companies and stay with them seem to like beginnings and middles. Once they have started a company, they seem to lose the itch that got them there and they admirably manage to continue to build a company. But personally I have always by temperament been a person who liked the whole story, beginning, middle and end. Whether I was working on a machining project at the very start, crafting something with my hands, or whether I was building a company later, I was just that sort of person who wanted to see something through to a definite point. There is probably a certain amount of frustration that drives anyone on to achieve anything. Some people continue to carry this drive even after they have built a company and met with some success. Some people are always going to be looking for new beginnings, middles and ends. Right now I am more that type of person than a middle person. Though who knows, if we're lucky, life is a long enough proposition to give us a chance to change our minds now and then."

So an entrepreneur who has made it has the choice of staying and growing, or selling and going on his way to experience the freedom he's achieved. There are middle-ground choices, of course, which more often than not turn out to be the preferred choice. An owner-founder can disengage from operations management and step up to disengagement from all but the very top, strategic decision-making. He or she can sell a firm and work on a management contract for shorter or longer periods of time (my experience is that more often than not they turn out to be shorter).

For an entrepreneur like Eugene Rosenfeld, a Continuing Saga with plans for becoming an In and Outer, a conscious approach to the process of deciding just what the continuing involvement will be seems to have worked well.

"I knew from the start that I wanted to leave the company I was working for, build a company of my own to a certain point of success, then sell it in a manner that would allow me to live a certain way. I had a particular life style in mind

for the building of the company, which I have more or less
managed to stick to. And I have a particular life style in
mind for how I want to lead my life after I sell the company.
Those were goals, as I mentioned. I do have to make decisions about what I have to do to accomplish this. And your
goals change and you do come to enjoy running the company at times after you have built it. But I had thought at
least some of it through. I think you have to recognize it is
going to be a difficult choice and plan some for it."

The decision appears easiest for those with the broadest
management and life experience prior to the start of the
firm they might contemplate leaving. Such broad experience often creates a sense of continuing opportunity beyond
the business with which the owner-founder has become so
personally identified with.

Roy Ash, in retrospect, considers that what he was doing
at Litton—a company with sales of between $5 billion and
$6 billion and with 120,000 employees at the time he disen-
gaged and less than twenty years after the corporation was
founded—to have been dwarfed by his next personal challenge. Roy's government service as the nation's director of
the Office of Management and Budget was very special to
him. His career as an entrepreneur turned out to have prepared Roy for delegations, strategy and decisions that had
an impact on worldwide trends.

Few entrepreneurs, needless to say, manage to develop
the skills and opportunities that might readily avail them
of greater challenges than initiating and shepherding a
company through the early years. But a number I spoke
with, particularly the Lifers, have become more broadly
involved in business and their communities than the popular conceptions of the selfish loner would suggest. Through
directorships, investments in other firms and philanthropic
involvements they continue to be challenged in new if not
always as demanding ways.

As for the new entrepreneur, a number of them have
chosen to bypass established philanthropic channels and to
pursue aggressive philanthropic or social-minded works

ranging from campaigns to feed the hungry to technical expositions. We can expect to see a great deal of philanthropic entrepreneurship of this kind begin to chart new ground, as it once did in the days of, say, Andrew Carnegie, who broke with established patterns of social engagement to give birth to charitable giving as we now know it.

Still, there will always be a built-in contradiction facing entrepreneurs: Many of the skills and leadership qualities that allow an owner-founder to feel confident in stepping away from the firm to tackle new challenges are the same ones needed *within* the firm if growth is not to be thwarted by an owner-founder management. The lesson, it would seem, is: Whether you plan to stay or go, you would do well from the outset to explore some of the practices and approaches imparted by those who have been there. If an owner-founder does not take a fairly conscious approach to the transition in leadership required within a growing firm, he or she may risk the reward of having a choice about continuing involvement at all—he or she may be sentenced to stay or be thrown overboard.

PATTON, MACARTHUR, EISENHOWER— WHICH GENERAL SHOULD YOU CHOOSE TO BE?

What we are talking about here are questions of leadership: How is it that successful entrepreneurs differ from mythical or "typical" entrepreneurs as leaders? In theory at least the personal goals you may set about a continuing involvement with your entrepreneurship should not affect the manner in which you attack the fundamentals that will build an enterprise you might either profitably sell or personally continue to manage. As a leader your approach to management should be the same if you want to go down either of the avenues after survival. Warren Dennis noted that it was through a conscious decision to lead Casablanca Fans through a bout of professionalization that he and Burton were able to maximize the proceeds of a sale. Joseph Solomon had to bite his tongue and pinch his nose while he was professionalizing Vidal Sassoon Hair Products, but he did it. In practice my observation is that overall those owner-founders who do go on as Lifers tend to demonstrate some crucial leadership characteristics early on in the development of their entrepreneurships.

It is clear the early days of many entrepreneurships are set up for a particular sort of leader. As the management writer Harold Koontz points out, people tend to follow those whom they see as providing a means of satisfying their own personal needs and goals. I might go one step farther, treading dangerously close to bromidic stuff like charisma and inspiration, in saying that at least in the short-term people have always seemed to demonstrate a marked propensity for being swayed by leaders they perceive as acting out or on their own most personal frustrations and dreams—particularly during times of struggle or crisis.

The owner-founder entrepreneur acts on a dream we have all held or continue to hold: the dream of being more in charge of our own affairs, more independent of the direct authority of others. Throughout this book I've spoken about the sense entrepreneurial employees often feel of being caught up together in a positive assault on the settled state of affairs they have encountered. All of which suggests the owner-founder entrepreneur ought to exert a strong, in-the-trenches sort of leadership during the early days—like a Patton perched atop the lead tank, signaling the troops on.

Though my observation is that subordinates tend to follow well during the early days of most entrepreneurships, the conventional wisdom of management "experts" is they do so *in spite* of the relatively weak leadership of the "typical" entrepreneur.

The typical one is widely described as a soloist who commands not through referent power, not through influencing subordinates on the basis of affection and respect but rather on the basis of having the loudest voice and the highest pedestal.

This is an exaggeration. A leader is a symbol of an organization. Management writers tend to focus more on the mechanics of leadership and to find the owner-founder wanting in terms of the mechanics needed to run a large, established organization. Mechanics can fix a car—someone still has to be seen driving it.

Professional leadership, in my view, is the ability to inspire, motivate and lead subordinates when the bombs aren't whistling, when the horizon is clear but when the heat of your competition might just as easily leave your organization dried up and shriveled. Professional leadership allows a general to walk, not march, quietly into the White House after a round of golf, like Ike, to ask how the staff is doing and be confident that they'll be doing damn well or else.

Men are made for moments and stations. The sight of Patton driving a golf cart over his caddy in a mad dash for the louse who dared to score well in the foursome ahead of him would have undoubtedly inspired our electoral fear had we ever been presented with that prospect. The usual end of, say, a MacArthur, a man who attempts to employ battlefield methods and manners at political tables, provides a ready means of assessing the chances of the owner-founder ever making the transition to leading in a more established setting.

You can pick up a copy of most any magazine devoted to entrepreneurs and find an article about some guy in cowboy boots who likes to kick up his heels at the front line and shoot off the expletives as he continues to rely on the motivation he can muster through personal interaction with the troops—only to in the end find frustration and personal suffering as the company grows beyond his maverick ways and means. The image has become part of the lexicon of business and entrepreneurship. Young people are being taught that it makes no more sense to consider continuing to manage an entrepreneurship past a certain point than it does to dream of doing your own taxes once you have a salaried job. This is the age of specialization, and the position of entrepreneur has been given a title and all but a job rating. From now on, if you want to be an entrepreneur you are going to have to prove yourself to a venture-capital or financing committee and sign up for a prescribed number of years. In truth, this is not too far from the state of entrepreneurship in some corners right now.

On the other hand, the overwhelming morbidity associated with the transition in management style or practices that must take place as the young entrepreneurship grows is a little like the obituary Samuel Clemens read reporting his death while he was traveling in Europe: greatly exaggerated.

There *are* specific things an owner-founder can do to smooth both his and his organization's transition to a more formal and established manner of doing business. Many of these actions have been discussed: The use of incentive, incremental formalization, an early reliance on sound control and a good hard thinking-through of the future needs of the business, formal or informal.

As Peter Drucker points out, there is a paradox to growth:

" 'If you want to be a big company tomorrow you have to start acting like one today,' is said to have been Thomas Watson's [the founder of IBM] favorite aphorism. The company that wants to be able to grow has to support the key activities on the level on which they will be needed *after* the growth has taken place."

Some of the men I spoke with said they originally had no grand schemes about the growth their companies went on to accomplish. Some had ideas from the get-go about the scope of the growth they wanted. But both of these sorts, and in particular the Lifers among them, were set off and apart from the mythical or typical entrepreneur by approaches to leadership and management that turned out to stand up to the tests of growth.

Most tended to consider themselves generalists. Though Gordon Moore had worked in the lab, he knew that for Intel to be state of the art they needed students right out of the prestige research institutes to step in. Ralph Crump was an engineer, had studied engineering, had worked as an engineer and had learned how to run a business, then returned to engineering in his own garage to develop a technology he might use to set off on his own. When it came to starting the business the first employee he hired was an engineer. Ralph could have continued to specialize as an engineer at the start, or later as a marketing manager. He could have hired others to cover other specialties. But the point is, the successful entrepreneur early on understands that his job is that of top manager—his job is that of being the generalist who *oversees* all specialties, including his own. And the sooner he steps into this role, the sooner will his company be poised for growth beyond survival.

Like Warren Dennis, initially a craftsman who built precision, antique-replica ceiling fans, the smart ones tend to see the whole picture—they *want* to see the whole picture—early on. They understand that the early days of operational involvement are a stage through which they must pass to realize their true skill. Sometimes they might even feel they were forced to step up to guarantee the survival of the firm, but they are more committed to growth than they are to a stranglehold on a state of personal involvement.

Each entrepreneur I talked to tended to have a special strength—engineering, marketing or control—that got him into the business and insured that he would stay in business. But successful entrepreneurs learn that even this must go. If you want to succeed as an owner-founder, the thought of stepping up either will have to appeal to you from the start, or at some point, like Paul Griffin, you are going to have to learn to appreciate it.

"At the start, in some ways I just didn't understand what it took to run an established, growing, thriving entrepreneurship," Griffin said. "I knew how to build homes and take advantage of a favorable sellers' market. My guess is that a lot of entrepreneurs start off with little more and probably much less. I was extremely lucky to stay in business long enough, gritting it out, to learn the importance of stepping up to be a generalist and professionalizing aspects of the company. Hiring a consultant who in effect tutored me in professional management practices and organizational design was a tremendous help. Before that, I had a company. Afterward I had an organization. I can now look at that organization and know it will survive without me. I can continue to separate myself from it and be free to do as I like, which I am doing. I can get the same satisfaction looking at the organization that I used to get from looking at a home or tract we had just put up. It is just as much a product of our efforts as anything else we have built."

As long as an owner-founder, often out of a lack of confidence or fear of losing control, hesitates at adopting the selective professional practices necessary for continued growth, he will be driving a wagon rolling on square wheels.

So say successful entrepreneurs. Now it is your turn. And to you, however much I have discounted it along the way, I say "good luck."

Stalking the New Entrepreneur

As I have suggested, the "new entrepreneur," meaning the entrepreneur who breaks away from our tarnished portrait of the mythical or typical to practice what it takes to succeed, has actually been around for quite a while.

Still, having talked with a good many successful entrepreneurs whose careers span the last five decades, I was left wondering about the future. The rate of new business start-ups has more than tripled over the last decade. Who *are* all these new owner-founders? Is there any way of estimating whether they are destined for greater or lesser chances of success? Is there any way of judging just what the future of entrepreneurship might be, beyond raw numbers?

So far the record would seem to indicate owner-founder entrepreneurship is still as tough a row to hoe as ever. The majority of new businesses are still failing at an alarming rate. Some cite statistics suggesting that venture capitalist–funded start-ups have a better chance of succeeding; such businesses are more likely to have a higher degree of planning and a greater emphasis on a complete management team from the outset. Most important, venture capital–funded businesses are purely and simply more likely to be screened; they are more likely to have been thought through by a greater number of critical minds, as well as to have employed extensive market research and analysis before start-up. Yet many of these fail too. And they don't begin to comprise a full cut of the pie representing the ground swell of new businesses. So who are all these other entrepreneurs?

I thought it might be interesting to see how entrepreneurship was doing in the garage. I thought it might be interesting to see what it was like to start a business from scratch in the eighties.

I set a few arbitrary rules for myself in setting out to find a new entrepreneur.

Rule Number One: No High Tech. High tech will undoubtedly make up a significant number of the new entrepreneurships that will succeed in this country through the coming decades. We will continue to read about a stream of new ventures in the fields of electronic data processing, communications, bio- and chemical engineering, as well as a host of lab-to-leveraged sagas in areas of science still rattling around the craniums of toddlers destined to calculate their way through the halls of the world's most prestigious institutes and universities. But high tech is old hat. We have already learned the typical history of such a firm: Great idea spawns great return in investment; new technology sprouts up to slice through the market with the speed and heat of a laser. The stereotype, as I have suggested, maligns the realities of building a business, but in relief it does help explain one sort of much-covered entrepreneur I wanted to skirt. What I really felt like finding, just for auld lang syne, was a new entrepreneur who had come out of nowhere, without specific expertise or grooming, to carve out a business where none existed before. The future never lies entirely in the predictable. Ask Jim Collins. When Jim opened his first hamburger stand, fast food still came in a can. No one was predicting that an industry consisting of an alphabet soup of fast-food chains would one day be serving up one out of three meals consumed in this country.

Rule Number Two: No Gourmet Ice Cream, Taoist Back-Scratcher or New-Wave Exercise Machine. What I was after was a new entrepreneur, not the next trend or product. We have read much about the entrepreneurs who have taken advantage of our burgeoning tastes and appetites during the last decade. At the same time an entire industry of no pain, no gain, as well as "painless loss," has grown up to assuage our lust for pleasure, assuring that our waist sizes continue to hover just one notch below the Baby Boom's age. No doubt we will continue to see a proliferation of both ends of the pleasure-sacrifice personal consumption market, with a growing senior citizenry with time on its hands as it enters twilight adolescence, with a shrinking birth rate and with the growing affluence of the two-income family. Even if, God forbid, our tastes, appetites and concerns might mature, we already have it on good word that a lion's share of new ventures will be concerned with the entertainment, housing, recreation and care of an aging populace. Many large corporations are already reaching for the bedpans, buying into health-care organizations and sunset real estate developments. Undoubtedly future entrepreneurship will continue to be closely related to demographics. It is inevitable, considering current birth rates, that at some point early in the next century there will be a lurch toward the conversion of existing housing and land use. The new entrepreneur, for instance, might right now be establishing a cooperative housing environment, senior hostel, limited health-care or even licensed hospice facility in the first of a chain of Old Victorian houses.

But again, I wanted to stay away from the predictable. What I wanted to find was an individual, come of age as a Baby Boomer, who had simply struck out on his or her own, not necessarily in a business that promised immediate mega-returns. Moreover, I was particularly interested in finding an individual who had become an entrepreneur more or less *in spite of* him or herself. I didn't want to talk to a business school grad. I wanted a mainstream person who had not started out with bonuses, mortgages and the federal reserve on the mind. I wanted to take a partial reading of the current state of grass-roots entrepreneurship. What had become of that part of the Boomers' experience, at one time seemingly so much a part of the mainstream, that search for consciousness and alternatives, that general sense of rebellion and independence that in some ways seems so akin to the entrepreneurial spirit? Could this, after all, have been as responsible for this latest upsurge in the popularity of entrepreneurship as Accounting 101? Never mind the boys and girls of the last few years streaming out of business schools with six figures on the brain. It is quite clear that the entrepreneurial spirit and need to achieve has never had much to do with making money.

The postwar generation now entering their prime business-starting decade, the ages thirty to forty, having come of age in the 1960s and 1970s, has been in many ways prepared almost en masse for the entrepreneurial way. With a distrust for large organizations, a growing up under conditions of mild social and later economic chaos (a state much akin, as suggested, to the early days of an entrepreneurship) and a strong streak of individualism, however much it was at times experienced in alarming conformity, we might only have begun to see the effects. What might be waiting? Will the Boomers be more likely, if not compelled by demographics, to work independently? Will they be more likely to want to build companies or just initiate them? What will their past and present have to say about the way business might be conducted through the next thirty years?

We are in the midst of an entrepreneurship boom throughout society, from the popular media, to business schools, to the realities of the thousands of new owner-founders. In this regard there is no doubt entrepreneurship is becoming both more accepted and studied. Graduate students at all the top business schools are clamoring for courses that might help prepare them to go into business for themselves. This, I believe, is a healthy trend, however much it may just be a trend. There is nothing more important this society might do than somehow manage to preserve the heart of entrepreneurship by making it into a collective *value*.

If we are to learn anything from the so-called British Disease, it is the harm that comes when a society begins to value tradition, established occupations and the professions over roll-up-the-sleeves commerce. When the upper segments of society begin to view bootstrap business as beneath their refined reaches, that society is in for a decline and maybe a fall.

Much of the psychology and sociology of business was once focused on a negative portrait of the entrepreneur. It is plain and simple a good thing that for this period entrepreneurship is being examined as a positive social value, and is being studied and taught. But the success of the generations of entrepreneurs I have related did not come about under conditions of academic support. Entrepreneurs and the entrepreneurial way may be in vogue for the nonce, but the drive needed to succeed in business may well be a lesson beyond the bounds of an academic environment.

I think it is safe to say the preservation of entrepreneurial values and the entrepreneurial spirit will not take place primarily in the media and schools. In spite of recent social and educational trends, there continues to be a dangerous preference for the cleanliness and order of the professions and professional management among a good many of our brightest young people. In fact it may be too much, both to hope for and for society to bear, to have a majority ethic of entrepreneurship.

All right then, so who are the new entrepreneurs and who are they likely to be? I thought it might be interesting to have a look beneath the Baby Boom's surface to see if I could find any clues.

When the media dust has settled, the vibrancy of entrepreneurship will continue to be carried forward by entrepreneurs themselves. Wall Street and M.B.A. start-ups notwithstanding, what I wanted to find was an entrepreneur who had come out of nowhere, from an *anti* business generation, to see how the entrepreneurial torch was being and might be carried forward.

When I came on Tim Sevison and Nighthawk Productions, I thought I might have stumbled on my subject: an entrepreneur who had struck out on his own in a manner and business that might have much to say about the continuing vigor of entrepreneurship as this century comes to a close.

Nighthawk describes Tim's company well: in flight at

hours the rest of us spend sleeping; on the prowl; striking
with efficiency and swiftness; a winged muscle that goes
about its business with a fixed and focused discipline. In the
end I had no doubt that this once antiwar organizer and
antibusiness activist was, in fact, a good old-fashioned true-
blue entrepreneur.

To illustrate, allow me to tell you something about how
Tim Sevison came to be in business for himself. Tim graduated from Northern Arizona University in 1970, having at-
tended school during the height of the Vietnam protest. Tim
had studied political science and actively organized demon-
strations on campus. He not only enjoyed arguing politics,
he enjoyed living politics while at school. When he left
school, in spite of a love for the ocean that took him back
to his old stomping grounds of southern California, Tim was
still looking for a political connection in his work.

After traveling and working at odd jobs, all but a desig-
nated occupation at the time for many of the best and
brightest but less ambitious Boomers, Tim found himself
living with a wife in Newport Beach, California, wondering
what in the world he was doing.

"I got this idea in my head that I might like to go into the
newspaper business. It never struck me that my peers who
were making it in the news business had gone to the right
schools, had always known what they wanted to do, had
followed a well-tread traditional path and were already
working for large dailies. My mom had once had a small
community paper for a while, and although I never worked
for her or learned much about the business, I had this idea
that it would be fun. So I started looking up the addresses
of some local newspapers. That's what brought me to the
door of the Tustin *News.*"

Tustin, California, was not a bastion of antiwar protest.
It was about a three iron away from Richard Nixon's Western White House. Tustin, Tim knew, was in the heart of
Orange County, U.S.A., as conservative a geographic locale
as one might find on our map. But one of the saving graces
of the Boomers right along, it seems to me, has been the

refreshing naiveté that has always seemed to accompany their more concerned and serious side.

"I just showed up one afternoon at the newspaper's door and asked to see the publisher. I was led into this room where this gruff old guy was sitting behind a desk looking mean. 'What do you want?' I told him I thought it might be interesting to learn the newspaper business. All he managed at first was a snort of sorts. Then he asked me what I had studied in school. I told him political science. 'Good,' he said, 'anything but journalism. Journalism majors aren't worth the powder it takes to blow them up.' I was encouraged.

"I told him I was willing to work for free, anything, just to hang around and learn the business. I've always taken this approach. It's pretty old-fashioned and probably sounds ridiculous, but it has worked for me. This guy didn't seem to be buying it. 'That's what they all say. . . . Well, I don't have anything. See you later.' He didn't say good luck.

"I felt let down. I turned and started out. But before I could open the door he shot back at me, 'Can you cover a city council meeting tonight?'

"I went and bought a notebook and a pen and went to the meeting and filled it with notes. Then my wife and I canvased the neighborhood and bought every newspaper we could lay our hands on. I read every article that seemed like what I was supposed to be doing. I wrote out this incredibly long story in longhand, then typed it up in the only form I knew, a term paper. I took it to the guy the next morning, not knowing that he had assigned me to a story another reporter was already covering. He and the reporter, a woman, told me to wait, took it in his office and closed the door behind them. I could hear them laughing and saying stuff like, 'This is just awful' and so forth."

If Tim had walked into a major daily and seen the video displays and the Ivy League crew he might not have got the news bug, which eventually turned him into an entrepreneur. If he had been overly sensitive, he might not have stuck around to see the publisher's door reopen. But his very first experience in the business turned out to be with an old-timer, a character right out of a copyboy's nightmare who left Tim wide open to be seduced by the reporting business.

"When he finally called me in he just threw this dirty old United Press stylebook at me and told me I had a lot to learn before I could write for a newspaper. I turned around and started for the door a second time and he called out, 'When do you want to start?' I said, 'But you said you didn't need anybody.' 'That was yesterday. Sit down. Come on, sit down.'

"He made me sit at a desk across the room from him and handed me a bunch of notices to rewrite. For six months I sat there, hunting and pecking, not knowing what I was doing and being constantly reminded I didn't know what I was doing. He would just walk up and rip a piece of paper out of the typewriter every now and then, read it, grunt, say, 'This is really lousy,' then ball it up and bounce it off my forehead. Just like in the old movies.

"Every Friday he would growl 'quittin' time' across the room and pull my chair over to his desk, then open a drawer and pull out this bottle of rye. Have you ever tasted rye? He had these two dirty tumblers he didn't wash and he would pull them out and fill them and hand me one. We would then proceed to shout at each other in the guise of political discussion. I was right up on that stuff then and gave him a run for his money. I think he got off on the fact that he could go up against this young cutting-edge liberal and keep his mind sharp. We would shout from opposite ends of the spectrum for a couple hours, then in the middle of things he would say 'discussion ended,' and we would go home and then back to work on Monday.

"One day he handed me a camera. 'Take some pictures.' I asked how, and he just scrunched up his face and said, 'Come on, get out of here, what do you mean *how?* Just take the camera. Take some pictures.' So I took the camera and I took some pictures. I got some mild criticism from the guy in the lab about my technique. But even he said I had a pretty good eye and knack for framing things. Before long

I was taking most of the paper's pictures as well as doing general-assignment reporting."

Tim went back to school, for, of all things, graduate journalism classes at the University of Nevada in Reno. He got a job doing sports rewrites at night for the Reno *Evening Gazette*. We are not talking about doing a stint at the New York *Times* or the Washington *Post* instead of law school. We are talking about learning the business—as you might recall, something entrepreneurs are advised to do. Tim didn't stay around long enough to get a degree. He poked around for a job and found one in Albany, Oregon, working for the Albany *Democrat Herald,* an award-winning progressive daily journal owned by Senator "Scoop" Jackson's brother. . . . "They were very demanding," Tim says, "and I was getting more and more into the life of a reporter. . . ." After a stint there Tim moved back to his stomping grounds in the suburbs of Los Angeles and went to work as a night crime reporter for the Pasadena *Star News*. After a matter of months, though he was advised against it, Tim accepted an offer to co-publish a small community newspaper, the Sierra Madre *News,* covering a town perhaps best known as the location of the filming of the original *Invasion of the Body Snatchers* and the much more chilling postnuclear explosion, *Testament.* Tim was promised half of the newspaper in turn for revitalizing it, which he proceeded to do, but the incorporation and stock never materialized.

"I had to fight for every change. I was too young to realize I had a problem working for other people. I still thought it was just this one experience. I hadn't developed a pattern. I have always had a real problem with authority, going back to when I was young. Looking back, I think it really was a certifiable personal problem when I was young. I've mellowed, but it's still a big part of me and probably has a lot to do with my having eventually gone into business for myself."

Tim had hired a guy at the Sierra Madre *News* named Dave Rust. They both quit at the same time. Dave went to work heading up the public relations department at a local

university. Tim hooked on with another local paper as a
general-assignment reporter, doing political analysis. The
paper was subcontracting all of its photographic lab work to
a small company. Tim took a look at the set-up. They
charged per photograph and print and seemed to be doing
well. He talked to his father-in-law, a past president of the
Photographic Society of America, a man nationally known
for some of his technical innovations. Within two weeks Tim
had arranged to take on the paper's photographic work.
Every night from seven until one in the morning Tim set up
a darkroom in a hall closet, strung clothesline across the
kitchen and spread out materials across the dining room
table. It drove his young wife nuts. It was Tim's first business, and lasted for almost two years.

On the side Tim and his friend Dave Rust were also trying
to break into the television news business. They called all
the stations in Los Angeles and pled to be given a break.
They were told they were too old to be interns. They offered
to work for free, just to hang around to learn the business.
They were told the union contracts did not allow anyone to
work for free. They called trade colleges that advertised an
"in" to the industry. But they were smart enough to see the
schools didn't offer anything they couldn't learn on their
own.

Tim finally managed to make a contact at the only nonunion station in town, KCOP, Channel 13, with a fellow named
Gary Brainard. Gary let Tim ride around with him in his
car and learn the basics of a television film crew. Tim
soaked up all he could and eventually did manage to land
an intern position for a few months. But when it came down
to it, Tim and Dave had to make their own break. Los Angeles had a tradition of stringers. Tim had had a glimpse of
the life as a night crime reporter. One day he made his
move. He gave up his photo lab business, bought an old
CP-16 camera, a used Bearcat police scanner and joined the
"Gore Squad." He had heard of a guy in New York City,
Sheldon Levy and his Action Movie News, who was making
money shooting freelance footage of accidents, crime calls

and the seedier side of life people seem either to love or hate
but nevertheless to watch on the late news before lying
down to their more personal nightmares.

"In Los Angeles, there was a whole subculture built
around the life of a stringer. It made Raymond Chandler
novels seem like sanitized outtakes. These guys were pretty
seedy. They hung around with cops a lot, chased ambu-
lances all night and generally did not have that great a
reputation with the local news media. But they made a
living. It took us about two weeks, shooting circles around
them, after we had taught ourselves how to work the camera, to establish our reputation and be able to make a go of
it. Dave worked some nights and mostly weekends. I finally
dropped my daytime reporting and went at it full-time,
night and day. There was this lab called the Film House
that processed all the film for the independent stations in
town. Stringers would drop their film in the night drop-box
with some notes describing the footage, and the Film House
would call around to the independent stations in the morning and see if there were any takers. They functioned like
an agent but didn't take any money since we were all paying
for the processing. The stations would send us a check direct, but only if they played the footage. They could have a
look at it for free.

"That was real heartbreak time. My wife and I would be
sitting up, frantically changing channels on this little television, trying to catch some of my footage to see if I could
expect a check or not."

Tim believes it was partly talent, partly hard work and
partly not having the abrasive personality of the typical
stringer that allowed him to stand out. He made a point of
checking in with all the stations that used his film, keeping
in touch and selling himself. He continued to do anything
he could to try to edge himself into the business, at that
point still believing that all he really wanted out of life was
to get a job as a news cameraman with a station.

About midway through the seventies it became clear to
Tim that the future was in video. Most of the stations had

either switched or were in the process of switching over from film. But none of the stations would buy tape from stringers. They claimed their contracts with the unions forbade it. Tim and Dave Rust spent months on the phone with the networks in New York, eventually getting lawyers at two networks to issue an interpretation that said that it was okay to treat videotape from stringers just as they had treated film: If it was a story that a union crew had not gotten to, if it was not a regular assignment, it was okay to use a stringer.

Tim knew where his niche was. His first story with the video camera he bought and taught himself to use involved a car over the side of the Angeles Crest Highway, up in the mountains above the San Gabriel Valley, a distance from the territory the regular union crews staked out. By staying about thirty to forty miles away from Hollywood and downtown Los Angeles and being willing to shoot any time, any day, anywhere, Tim was able to make a living.

As a result of his success stringing, Tim landed a job at a nonunion station in Eugene, Oregon. But he was hired chiefly on the basis of his editing skill, something he professed but had actually never even tried. He had a week to learn. He rented an editor, got hold of some old footage, invited some contacts over to offer lessons and criticism and went at it until he felt competent. Tim's news director at the station was a legendary refugee from the San Francisco media scene, a fellow named Pete Spear, who once threw a typewriter out of a third-story window to make a point. He was an aggressive no-frills reporter for whom Tim still has great respect.

The learning and experience continued, but the money was scarcer than when he had been on his own as a stringer. Within a year Tim was back in Los Angeles with TeleCam News. He went back to stringing, and made a go of it. But whenever he had time he would go through the Yellow Pages and make calls to small companies, trying to drum up business. He managed to get a few industrial clients, like Knotts Berry Farm, businesses for whom he would shoot news hand-outs the stations would play for free during slow newscasts. He also went to a store, bought a ledger and set up his first formal control system, logging in every shooting twice, once the day it was done and billed and a second time a month later when payment would be past due. If he came to that second entry and found himself with some money, he made a mark. If he hadn't received a check, he made a call. It was simple, but it was enough. The future looked good. If he could just build up enough industrial clients to stabilize the business so that he wasn't out chasing the misfortunes of others at all hours, life would be rosy.

Out of the legendary blue Tim got a call from Pete Spear. Ted Turner was setting up his Cable News Network and had hired Pete Spear to head up the Los Angeles bureau. There was a budget and opportunity, something Tim had been used to *making*, not having handed to him. Twenty-four hours a day of news! The chance to do national stories. People who were newsworthy for reasons other than the rate at which they were losing blood. Tim didn't hesitate. He closed down TeleCam News and accepted a job as head of the ENG (electric news-gathering) department. In retrospect Tim figures the entrepreneurial bug must have still been subliminal in him. He still thought the greatest thing in the world would be to have a regular job with a network as a cameraman. He thought he had been running a business because that was temporarily the only way he could do what he loved and still eat.

"With TeleCam News, if at the end of the week we looked in the checkbook and saw that we had $19.60, we thought it was just great and went out and had a meal."

Ted Turner quickly reorganized CNN so that almost all of the news operations were "subbed" out. The Los Angeles operation was turned over to Wold Productions, the largest satellite broker at the time. Tim got his check from Wold as CNN's chief photographer. He hired his old friend Dave Rust as a sound man. It was during his experience at CNN that Tim learned he would never again work for anybody else. It was during this time that self-employment became an unamendable law of Tim's personal constitution.

"A guy was brought in to take over for Pete Spear, because, it was said, Pete stepped on some toes running an aggressive operation. Unfortunately, we became organized and were managed to the point of being unable to do our jobs. Everything became *assigned* and no decisions were left for the field. It got so that one day we found ourselves doing a piece at the Bowser Doggie Boutique in Beverly Hills while half the mountain ranges surrounding Los Angeles were on fire. We had gotten in the habit of listening to the local all-news radio station because we didn't feel we wanted to rely on our own office to keep up with things. We called in and told them we thought we ought to doggie dooly the poodles and head for the hills, that there were multiple major fires under way. We were told there weren't any fires. We told them to read the wire, and they said oh, maybe there were.

"Under Pete we had been news commandos, making up for our lack of resources with our aggressive dedication. All of a sudden we were, we felt, being managed to the point of always being a day late and a dollar short. The straw that broke me had to be when we were assigned to cover the landing of the first space shuttle. One day we were just told to mosey on up and cover it. Dave and I and a reporter piled in our Dodge Aspen and drove over the mountains to Edwards Air Force Base. When we pulled up, we were speechless.

"The other networks had been there for two months doing advance work. Each network had two forty-foot trucks full of equipment. The coverage had been researched. NBC was doing the *Today* show from Edwards. There were these huge stages that had been built and camera towers. A couple of the networks were basing their nightly anchors there. We finally turned to each other, realizing what we were up against. All we could do was do the best job we could under the circumstances. We got some briefing material and by asking around learned that NASA was doing a trunk feed that we could use. How could we expect to do better than nose cameras in fighter jets anyway? So we concentrated purely on sidebars, on the off-beat stories about the landing. We did a pretty good job, considering our lack of preparation and equipment. We went right back to junkyard journalism and came through pretty well in spite of our overlords.

"But that's no way to work. I knew my days were numbered. I still had my contacts with the local stations. One night I just went home and told myself, Time to start another business. I fired up TeleCam News again and set off down the same road. I had no problem getting work with all the local stations. While I was at CNN I organized a union shop and as a result the unions finally let me in. First I joined NABET (the National Association of Broadcast Engineers and Technicians), then the International Brotherhood of Electrical Workers. I was able to sell to union stations on a regular basis that way, but I needed more clients and I had got hooked on the bigger national and international stories while with CNN. One day I called up the BBC and told them I was in Los Angeles and ready and willing. They asked me what kind of equipment I used. I answered with a question: What kind do you use? They said all of their crews used Sony 300s. I said that was just great, because that was exactly what I used. I ran out and rented one; I was using an old JVC at the time. It was a while before I heard from them, but eventually I did. The BBC always sends out a reporter and hires my company to provide the crew. I didn't make any money because I had to rent the equipment, but it got me in with them and eventually I was able to buy the equipment.

"About this same time, I couldn't get it out of my head that there was no reason why an independent production company couldn't do turnkey news production. It was being done in radio and in all areas of the print media. A freelancer or production company could put together the entire package, with preproduction story development, planning and research, shooting, furnishing the reporter, editing and transmitting or delivering the final news and feature product. I started contacting news agencies and offering our services. I hired local reporters to do voice-overs and stand-ups. Pretty soon we were providing the service for INN (Independent Network News), Visnews (perhaps the largest broadcast news agency in the world), ITN (the second network in Great Britain, the commercial network that competes with the BBC) and Newsweek Video, which later folded.

"I took on a partner, Chip Walter, who I had met while with Cable Network News. Dave Rust and I had been in Las Vegas covering the Sinatra hearings and were driving down the Strip and just about saw the Hilton Hotel fire break out, right on the heels of that first MGM Grand Hotel fire. Chip was sent in to help. He was the Atlanta bureau chief at the time. We ended up working together for two weeks on the fire and subsequent hearings. Chip was a reporter of our stripe and we hit it off right away. When he left CNN I asked him to join me. That's when we surfaced as Nighthawk Productions. Chip handled all the nuts and bolts, the writing of scripts, researching, editing and the logistics of delivering product. I coordinated the story ideas and shooting and selling of stories.

"Soon we were keeping three crews busy. We picked up a regular syndicated news magazine-type television show. Our spots on it were some of our best work. One crew was kept busy doing features for the show, one crew was kept busy doing daily stringer work for local stations, and another crew focused on news and multinight feature pieces we produced ourselves and sold to networks. I hired my mom, who had worked for a bank in the publications department, to handle our bookkeeping and office management.

"We were doing some really good work and having fun doing it too. I got the idea to cover the French atomic nuclear tests in the South Pacific. . . . I was always trying to come up with story ideas that would take me to some exotic location. I still surf and sail and love the water and island life. We spent a lot of time in Tahiti on that one, being followed nearly every step by the French secret service, and we sold thousands of dollars of tape based on that story to a number of agencies and networks.

"We were up to an average gross of about $35,000 a month. We didn't know what to do with all the money. Then, within a few weeks, the show was canceled and a few of the news agencies we had been supplying folded. We went from $35,000 to three thousand a month and had to retrench.

"This is a very fragile business. Production companies typically come into being because of an idea. Someone runs out to PIP and has some business cards made, rents an office month to month, hires a temporary secretary and an answering service and they're in business. If and when they do a project, the company often folds up just as fast as it came into being. Such is the nature of the business. On the other hand there are production companies that stay alive for quite a long time doing productions that are never seen by anybody. I just can't see doing that. I want to be a surviving viable business, and even though nobody else in this area is doing exactly what we are doing, it is still a constant fight to establish the sort of foundation or stability that a company needs to survive.

"What I really need to do is build that foundation. I have tried to do it through industrial accounts, but there are companies who do nothing but industrial accounts and even though we can supply national-network-quality work, work you can see on the *MacNeil/Lehrer Newshour,* the *Nightly Business Report,* on the BBC, people in business are wondering if you can do something that looks just like what the competition is doing. On the other hand, every time I start to branch out to try to stabilize the business it seems we get hit with the demands of a news story that pulls me back in.

"I have hired a full-time producer and delegated a good deal of our work to her, but it is hard for me. The only reason we are alive today is because of the personal touch I have employed. I still call the networks and agencies after every story to ask how things went, to talk about future work. If I haven't heard from someone for a while I call them up and ask them how things are going—just about anything to keep them thinking of us. But every time I stray away for a few days to concentrate on trying to sell some industrial accounts I begin to sense that the other part of the business is hurting and I have a hard time keeping myself from diving back in. This business has become a real human to me. It's spooky. I can't stand to see it hurting.

"Right now I'm waiting to hear on a contract that could guarantee our growth for the next year or so. We've already completed a few celebrity feature shots for a show put together by an international syndicator that is shown in the European market. I expect to hear any day now about a seventeen-week contract that could lead to a one-year contract that would guarantee our biggest gross to date. And that would mean hiring on one more full crew and surpassing our last boom time. (Tim got it.)

"At the same time, I also have an opportunity to open a division in northern California handling all the commercials for a station up there, which would allow me to live in a very nice area of the country. I hired a guy not long ago who I thought I could turn over industrial sales to, figuring it might allow me to head north. He didn't work out. His skin was just too thin. You can't be that way in this business. I need someone willing to work on commission, who knows sales and also knows our business. Then I can back him or her into the news sales and customer relations and turn it over so that I can head north and start up this new division. The more I can build the industrial accounts and diversify, the better off I will be. I would be happy with the money as it is right now if I could be sure we were stable.

"The fact is, it isn't completely a matter of finding the right person. It is going to take an entire conversion in my mind too. I love news. I may not be as caught up in the danger and adventure as I used to be, but I still love it and don't entirely want to give it up. Right now I've got a crew out with the BBC. It's a typical BBC shoot. They come to town to do a story in San Diego and then I get a call a week

later from Tucson saying they are on their way north for
another week. I get the itch and want to be along. When you
are doing national and international stories, maybe doing
presidential coverage, there is a built-in undeniable excitement. You are there, seeing things people never see, learning things before the rest of the world will learn them. You
can't help but get caught up. Last year I took a crew to
Orange County with the BBC and ended up at the end of the
day in Mexico City in the midst of the aftershocks of the
earthquake. We picked up a van and an interpreter at
the airport. Rescue operations had just begun. I mean, they
were still digging through the rubble with their bare hands.
You could hear the trapped people calling out from piles
they hadn't had a chance to get to. The electricity was out.
At night, it was really eerie. . . . You would be walking down
this darkened street with maybe the glow of a few emer-
gency lights off to the side, fires dotting the horizon and
sirens coming and going, and every now and then you would
hear the moaning of people that were just holding on. We
worked for two weeks, mostly twenty-four hours a day, and
I'll tell you, it took me quite a while to get that one off my
eyelids when I went to sleep.

"I've worked other disasters—the PSA plane crash in San
Diego, fires. I was shooting a barricaded suspect in a phar-
macy in Tujunga when I dove behind a car and found myself
crouching next to a deputy. I had no idea what a bullet could
do to a car. This guy was shooting at us and I could feel the
bullets moving the car with their impact. Some were going
right through.

"At one fire we got trapped behind a fire-line with a hot-
shot crew when the wind turned on us and we had to dive
into a ravine just before the fire burned right over us. I kept
poking my head up and trying to get some shots, and the
crew chief kept pulling me back down again. I do like the
thrill, it's part of the job, which means it's part of our company. During that same fire we were standing near a stand
of eucalyptus with a fireman and his truck. The guy mentioned that the trees looked like they were about ready to

go. He just wanted us to be prepared. He said they would probably explode once they caught fire. When he saw them starting to catch a few minutes later he dove under his truck and we dove into a drainage culvert nearby. He was right. The whole area blew up like a bomb in flame and smoke. There was a crew from a local station up on a rise watching. They said they were convinced they had just witnessed a few people being incinerated to charcoal dust before their eyes. They were going into shock when they saw us start to crawl, coughing, out of the pipe, and we had to listen to them showering their relieved profanity down on us before they got over it.

"I've slowed down a little, but I still enjoy the important shoots. I specialize in aerial shots. Other production companies will call us up just to do aerial work for them. I still enjoy standing out on the skids of a helicopter and doing shooting. Believe me, that is a real E ticket.

"So I know I've got some weaknesses as a manager. I don't have enough respect for the sort of future-oriented things I should be doing. I know, for instance, how important it is for me to read trade magazines to find new business. And sometimes I do find leads and run them down and sell a story. But at the end of the day, if I haven't sold a story, if I've spent time reading or doing something that hasn't panned out yet, I just don't feel satisfied. I find myself questioning what I am doing. It isn't easy for me to step away from the action, even if it's only the action of selling. I don't like the cold-call approach enough, and I tend to back away from it. That's why I need to get somebody who can handle that. It's not as if we don't have the product or service.

"There are a number of opportunities out there that might broaden our business and give us a foundation. It really shouldn't be such a hard sell to businesses and industrial clients. I read in a magazine that somebody has built a new crane, a crane capable of lifting a ship or something. Look what I have to offer them. They have a brochure, maybe they fly in their best clients from out of town. But I can shoot them a short feature that they can take anywhere in the world. It doesn't just tell them about their crane, it shows them, through a medium people are used to trusting. I can prepare a video for their other offices that shows someone how to repair that crane without them having to be flown from all over the country to a service center. With minor editing I can provide an in-house education, sales or motivational piece. With a little more editing I can prepare a video annual report for their board, investors and industry analysts. People talk about wanting to be efficient and save money. But they also think mightily about whether this will be a new expense, despite the advantages.

"So right now we have the experience and organization, but people are hesitant. They still view this as something back, as it were, from the future, not something we and they should be doing right now. Part of the problem is that our service has a high-ticket reputation, but video has been forced into being a high-ticket item by the stranglehold network television has on production. The price of advertising and the money involved in the narrow niche that television production is has led it to be priced out of the range of ready acceptance. As for cable, the local networks don't have an advertising base so they can't afford to produce. If they could figure out a way of building a local advertising base, we would be in a good position to take advantage of their success. There is just not enough work out there in any one market, so prices have to stay high. We are fighting this, and it really may only be a matter of time. . . .

"I like being small. I would like to be able to step back from Nighthawk, either through broadening our foundation or diversifying and turning things over to someone else, while staying an owner. My goal is not so much to build up one large company but to build three or four smaller ones. The exhilaration of shooting a dangerous story has also become the exhilaration of starting up a company. That's what I enjoy now. I don't have this one totally secure, and already I am thinking about how to start the next one. I would like to have several diverse enough to create more stability, allowing me to experience the start-ups. After I have them going I plan to bounce between them later on, to keep my interest up and to be able to live in different areas. That's how I want to live. As soon as I can stabilize Night-hawk, after I secure a contract on the features for a syndicated show or possibly head north to set up a commercial division, my plan is to move on to start a tourist bar in the Caribbean or Mexico. . . . No, I'm serious. I've checked it out. If you are willing to brave the social climate, you can get a liquor license and all the permits you need on St. Croix for two hundred dollars. I'm also interested in Cabo San Lucas in Baja because it's close. I've spent enough time on the other side of the bar to know, I think, what makes a tourist bar click. Travel is going to grow, not shrink, in the coming years. And I'd like to live in that sort of area for a while anyway. I am serious about this. Now that I have started a business and seen what a total experience it can be, I don't just want to start another business, I want to start another business that will allow me to live the way I want to.

"To me, that is the reward of being in business for myself. Even though I might have to work harder than someone else to keep Nighthawk going and at the same time open up another business in another part of the world, *it will be by my choice.* It's the same way I feel about time off. I might in the end work longer and harder than most, but when I can I carve out a few days and go off on my own. I am talking with you today after staying up until past midnight to finish a week-long project. But this Friday I will head up north for a few days. It's my time. I don't have to ask anyone when I want to take time off. I carve that time out myself. I don't care if I have to work harder, when I do take time off I know I feel more freedom than if I were working for someone else. There are aspects of running my own business I just wouldn't trade for the security or regular time off. Sure, there is more stress in running my own business. No two ways about it. I get tension headaches now and then. But I have never let the stress stop me from putting my head down and plowing right through. That's how I would describe running your own business. It's like running an obstacle course half-blindfolded. It can be exciting and it can be stressful. I am sure a lot of people with secure jobs wouldn't trade for my stress and lack of security. But a headache now and then can't compare to the terror that a nine-to-five strikes in me. I have had offers from the top networks. The money has been very good; more money than I need to be happy. The first one I had to think about. Now offers like that don't even figure with me. I started out with no profit-orientation, and money is still not that big a thing to me. I've done this work for nothing, and now that I make money it's even better. I started out with something of an antibusiness orientation, and the only way I can describe it now is that I've caught the entrepreneurial bug. There is nothing else in the world like starting and running your own business. I can't compare it to any other experience or sense of achievement I've ever had, in sports or anything else. You set a tall goal for yourself, surviving in business, and then you achieve it, or come close, and the sense of accomplishment is so very real and personal."

In another ten or twenty years will Tim Sevison be a successful entrepreneur of the order of some of the owner-founders I interviewed? No doubt Tim is doing some things right. He offers a percentage to employees who bring in new business, and that has paid dividends to the company. He has hired a top-notch outside accountant to keep the company's control up to snuff. He has life-style goals that keep his efforts directed. At the same time some of the life-style demands that Tim and many young entrepreneurs of his generation may be putting on themselves in the course of running their companies will certainly have implications for both the difficulty of their tasks and the organizational results of their entrepreneurial activities. Tim's generation was once billed as the "small is beautiful" generation. Will this have some effect on the nature of the businesses they build? Will they be less likely to want to build large companies or to stay with companies that threaten to burst at the seams? Will we see a new style of "commando" small businesses, staying small and lean and taking advantage of technologies and communications apparatus to go one-on-one with larger firms in selected niches? Or will the more recent emphasis on valuing material accomplishment, pure and simple, continue to rule? As I have suggested, the latter may be less conducive to entrepreneurial activity than some of the antibusiness sentiments of the Baby Boom's earlier years. Will we eventually or have we already begun to see some sort of synthesis of these two extremes, which would make for a very ripe field of entrepreneurial activity? For answers to some of these questions we will just have to wait and see.

Tim pointed out his managerial weaknesses that are keeping Nighthawk from growing in the ways it needs to grow. He is conscious of them, which is a first step. He continues to think his business through. He is aware of opportunities and finds himself questioning at times his personal desires and goals as he sits on the cusp of choices that could possibly affect his company's survival.

Like many of the entrepreneurs I spoke with, Tim doesn't put an overemphasis on short-term goals. He holds the goal of doing the absolute best he can each day, with an eye to the strategy he has thought through as a means of securing the future of his business. However, he is at the point at which he knows more long-range planning is probably needed. He still hasn't weaned himself from the binge mentality of the early years. He is sensing some of the problems of delegation, but has not yet fully learned all the lessons it seems entrepreneurs need to learn at some point in their careers if they are to go on to manage growing companies. He is undecided about whether he wants to give up his personal involvement in operations, an even harder choice in a very exciting and adventurous business. He hasn't quite yet accepted the reality described by most of the entrepreneurs I interviewed: A business needs to grow to survive. He is not sure he wants to grow. He isn't sure whether he is ready, and he isn't sure whether his people are ready, a sure sign, as Peter Drucker suggests, that an owner-founder

himself is not ready. The next few years will probably have
a good deal to say about whether Tim ends up an independent self-employed individual or whether he goes on to build
a larger company through one of the strategies he is now
considering. One thing seems certain: He is not about to go
to work for someone else.

Sometimes, as I suggested to Tim, one needs to take the
plunge, just as he had to take the plunge to set off on his
own. Sometimes one just has to go ahead and delegate and
bite off another chunk, fully knowing that one might have
to dive back in and patch things together. Sometimes one
has to take the big step and go for it, stretching both oneself
and one's organization, using incentive and control as a
means of limiting the cold sweats during the process. Without a doubt, opportunities played a big part in the success
of a good many of the entrepreneurs you have read about
in these pages. Tim has opportunities. He is weighing them.
Like most, he wants to consider and temper the risk. He
wants to make sure the opportunity is real.

Tim thinks he is about ready to make a move. He traveled
185 days last year and is now thirty-eight. Just a little bit
bigger, he tells me, just a few more clients; maybe if the
contract comes through for the syndicated show and lasts
beyond a year; just one more capable employe and he might
make his move, Tim says, with a gleam in his eye, with the
confidence of having made it through the significant first
five years, with the confidence of knowing just how motivated he is to realize his independently formulated goals
and dreams.

In setting out to find a new entrepreneur, I seem to have
come full circle. Like the successful entrepreneurs I spoke
with, Tim Sevison found he had to work for himself. His
sense of personal accomplishment made it difficult for him
to suffer the constraints and mediocrity brought on by others. More driven by personal desires to live and work a
certain way than by the goal of riches, Tim Sevison has

more in common with what I consider the true entrepreneur of the present and past than with others in his generation, said to hold the dollar above all.

The carriers of the entrepreneurial spirit are people who make very personal choices. We can teach entrepreneurship in our schools, in terms of the nuts and bolts of what it takes to run a business, but the level of entrepreneurship will probably continue to have a great deal to do with the number of individuals who find themselves driven to accomplish on their own terms. Without a doubt the level of competition and opportunity in a society greatly influences, if not dictates, the level of entrepreneurial activity. But the entrepreneurial ethic is not rooted in a society's need to achieve. The entrepreneurial ethic is rooted in the sanctity of the individual as a willful agent capable of making a difference. For all the supposed social ills and excesses we have experienced as an entrepreneurial nation, we must at the same time never forget the fundamental importance of continuing to celebrate—or at least welcome—the values of independence, self-determination and hard work. There will be a great need and demand for social cooperation in the coming years, as our cooperative problems defy a random approach. But such effort will be uniquely enhanced by a strong entrepreneurial contingent.

Of course independence is relatively meaningless out of the context of a continuing transaction with society. We must not, if I may be allowed to preach for a minute, just emphasize independence but also come to realize the value *and* pleasure of getting down and doing bootstrap business as self-motivated agents in a complicated, often chaotic, evolving world. The brave new entrepreneurial souls will not be people seeking established security in protected professions, in educational expertise or as cohabitants within large corporate cultures, no matter how broad their skunk stripes or however daring or innovative the organizations they might work within might be. The brave new entrepreneurial souls will continue to be pioneers who are willing to stand up and bend against the wind outside the confines of existing structures; willing to have their seeds tested so that they might plant and grow something new.

I believe that if we lose this drive within our society, we will be ripe for the picking. The battle of entrepreneurism will continue to determine whether or not we will progress and better ourselves as a global population. From all current signs, betrayal of our entrepreneurial endowment hardly seems on the horizon. We may not have even begun to tap our entrepreneurial resources. Let us hope as much. Achievement-oriented individuals with a knack for shepherding their drive and creation through the difficulties and compromises that face anyone wishing to bring something new to life cannot in my view be overvalued.

Here's to the entrepreneurs, who would not be able to live life any other way. May they continue to grace, and grate on, our present as they create our future.

Index